"There is nothing much funnier t
themselves too seriously and just 'tens it all. I know I've made a
pretty good living doing just that. As a Yard Bubba (you'll have to
read the book for an explanation), living in a house full of Southern Belles, I am here to tell you that Shellie Rushing Tomlinson is
laugh-out-loud funny. For anyone that has an ounce of Southern
blood flowing through their veins or those that wish they did, this
book is going to be a treasure."

—Jeff Foxorthy

"New research published in the *International Journal of Obesity* has
discovered that laughter really is the best medicine for a weight
problem. I know this to be true as I lost ten pounds reading Shellie's
latest book! It's the ultimate read, fully satisfying, highly entertaining, and burns calories to boot! Five diamonds in the Pulpwood Queen's Tiara of great reads!"

—Kathy L. Patrick, founder of The Pulpwood Queens
and Timber Guys Book Club, the largest "meeting
and discussing" book club in the world!

"Shellie Rushing Tomlinson is a bona fide treasure! Her Southern-
as-grits anecdotes and wisdom are delivered with wide-eyed clarity
and candor—and a lot of side-splitting humor. Shellie's goal (in her
words) is to "shine some Southern insight on the absurd," and she
succeeds with sparkling wit and a real love of her subject. So pull
up a rocking chair on Shellie's virtual porch, and be prepared to be
entertained—and you might just learn a few things, too."

—Karen White, national bestselling author of *On Folly Beach*

"Irresistible! Charming, witty, and real, it touched my heart and
tickled my funny bone. Makes me want to be a Southern girl!"

—Jane Porter, author of *She's Gone Country*

"As a lover of all things Sue Ellen, I was immediately taken by Shellie Rushing Tomlinson's new book. The Southern humorist has done it again with a book that is laugh-out-loud funny. Sit down and savor *Sue Ellen's Girl Ain't Fat, She Just Weighs Heavy* with a glass of sweet tea and an appetite to be entertained."

—Michael Morris, author of *A Place Called Wiregrass* and *Slow Way Home*

"Full of laughter, love, and common sense, not to mention great recipes, I loved this book. . . . Witty and insightful commentary on husbands, family, and life."

—Kathryn Casey, bestselling author of *The Killing Storm*

"*Sue Ellen's Girl Ain't Fat* is the funlovin'-est time I've had with a book in a good long while! I adore Shellie's cadence and authentic heart found on each and every page. Curl up with this feel-good book and giggle all you want, but don't forget to call your Southern Mama—apparently she's wiser than you ever knew."

—Nicole Seitz, author of *The Inheritance of Beauty, Saving Cicadas, Trouble the Water, A Hundred Years of Happiness*, and *The Spirit of Sweetgrass*

"Grab a bag of pork skins, an R.C. Cola and a copy of *Sue Ellen's Girl Ain't Fat, She Just Weighs Heavy*. Then get ready for a whole lot of belly laughter dished up by The Belle of All Things Southern herself. Shellie Rushing Tomlinson is slap-funny and this book is a hoot!"

—Karen Spears Zacharias, author of *Will Jesus Buy Me a Double-Wide? (Cause I Need More Room for My Plasma TV)*

Sue Ellen's Girl Ain't Fat, She Just Weighs Heavy

The Belle of All Things Southern Dishes on Men, Money, and Not Losing Your Midlife Mind

SHELLIE RUSHING TOMLINSON

Berkley Books, New York

THE BERKLEY PUBLISHING GROUP
Published by the Penguin Group
Penguin Group (USA) Inc.
375 Hudson Street, New York, New York 10014, USA

Penguin Group (Canada), 90 Eglinton Avenue East, Suite 700, Toronto, Ontario M4P 2Y3, Canada
(a division of Pearson Penguin Canada Inc.)
Penguin Books Ltd., 80 Strand, London WC2R 0RL, England
Penguin Group Ireland, 25 St. Stephen's Green, Dublin 2, Ireland (a division of Penguin Books Ltd.)
Penguin Group (Australia), 250 Camberwell Road, Camberwell, Victoria 3124, Australia
(a division of Pearson Australia Group Pty. Ltd.)
Penguin Books India Pvt. Ltd., 11 Community Centre, Panchsheel Park, New Delhi—110 017, India
Penguin Group (NZ), 67 Apollo Drive, Rosedale, Auckland 0632, New Zealand
(a division of Pearson New Zealand Ltd.)
Penguin Books (South Africa) (Pty.) Ltd., 24 Sturdee Avenue, Rosebank, Johannesburg 2196,
South Africa

Penguin Books Ltd., Registered Offices: 80 Strand, London WC2R 0RL, England

The recipes contained in this book are to be followed exactly as written. The publisher is not responsible for your specific health or allergy needs that may require medical supervision. The publisher is not responsible for any adverse reactions to the recipes contained in this book.

While the author has made every effort to provide accurate telephone numbers and Internet addresses at the time of publication, neither the publisher nor the author assumes any responsibility for errors, or for changes that occur after publication. Further, publisher does not have any control over and does not assume any responsibility for author or third-party websites or their content.

Copyright © 2011 by Shellie Rushing Tomlinson
Cover design by Rita Frangie
Cover photograph by Claudio Marinsesco
Book design by Tiffany Estreicher

PRINTING HISTORY
Berkley trade paperback edition / May 2011

Library of Congress Cataloging-in-Publication Data

Tomlinson, Shellie Rushing.
    Sue Ellen's girl ain't fat, she just weighs heavy : the belle of all things southern dishes on men, money, and not losing your midlife mind / Shellie Rushing Tomlinson.
    p. cm.
    ISBN 978-0-425-24085-4
    1. Women—Southern States.   2. Southern States—Social life and customs.   I. Title.
    HQ1438.S63.T665   2011
    305.40975—dc22   2010054135

PRINTED IN THE UNITED STATES OF AMERICA

10   9   8   7   6   5   4

To the memory of my cousin Lissa. From those long ago days when we hid under Grandma Stone's dining room table and pilfered Thanksgiving turkey before it was blessed until the end of a battle that may have drained your life but could not steal your spirit, you never stopped looking for the laughter. Yours is a legacy of grace and strength for three beautiful daughters. I hope you knew how much I looked up to you, how much you taught me. Today I look higher still and find comfort in knowing that you are whole.

CONTENTS

ACKNOWLEDGMENTS

To my steady-as–a-rock husband, who understands me, who knows the "why" behind the "what in the world," and treats my writing like I'm knee-deep in changing the world.

To my parents, my children, and the world's most beautiful grandchildren, indeed life with Keggie wouldn't be so crazy if I didn't have all of these words in my head that must come out, but never forget that normal is overrated.

To the Madness Czar of *All Things Southern*, crazy has a name. Thanks, Rhonda.

To my agent, Michael Psaltis, for teaching me the game, Penguin Group for letting me play, and my skilled editor, Denise Silvestro, for making me better than I would be.

To the best readers (shout out for the power of the Pulpwood Queens!) and radio audience out there, aka the porchers of *All Things Southern*, and to everyone who took *Suck Your Stomach In and Put Some Color On!* into your hearts and asked for more. You know who you are and I could never thank you enough.

Sue Ellen's Girl Ain't Fat, She Just Weighs Heavy

PROLOGUE

Lord knows I don't mean to brag, but it is what it is, and being as it does serve a larger point, I believe we'll just open with a fascinating little piece of personal bio. As an infant, yours truly had one of the earliest cases of appendicitis ever documented. I was nine months old when fifty-four doctors came to Natchez, Mississippi, to examine me and study my case. Mama has a faded yellow newspaper clipping to prove it. I don't remember this, mind you, but I do recall the first time I heard about their visit. I felt like quite the popular bellerina.*

In retrospect, however, it may have been better for all concerned had they studied my brain. In the interest of full disclosure, I hear voices. I realize they're all in my head and on some level I know they're all me, but it gets fuzzy after that. It's also quite busy up there.

For starters, all of the voices are storytellers, and they all think

Official Guide to Speaking All Things Southern

*bellerina (bell-er-een-a), noun: infant female of the Southern persuasion

the story they want to tell is more important/humorous/motivational or flat-out bizarre than that of whichever voice has the floor at any given moment. We—the voices and I—get along fairly well in private, but it does get difficult in the public arena, even more so lately, as they're becoming increasingly bold about wresting the floor from the speaker.

Yes, after two short and concurrent careers as a basketball coach and an interior decorator, I finally decided to pursue a writing and speaking career as the best way to let everyone be heard without the risk of my being committed and forcefully sedated. It's working out surprisingly well. By the time you read this, the little community I created called *All Things Southern* will be officially ten years old! That amazes me. I remember when I had no idea what I was doing. Course, that was just last week, but still.

You know, I can't explain this, but although I have a hard time remembering to stop and buy milk, my brain has duly recorded most all of our porch visits from that inaugural Web launch. That's why I knew what was up when that reporter called the other day looking for Shellie Rushing Tomlinson. He wanted to interview her about toe popping. "You've got her," I told him. I realized immediately that he had found one of our old chats floating around cyberspace. What I wanted to know was why it piqued his interest. He filled me in. Seems a principal down there had been suspended for popping kids' toes and it was all over the news.

I granted his interview and answered his many questions as graciously as possible. Yes, I like to pop toes. No, not just my own toes—I like to pop other people's toes, too, like those belonging to my husband and kids. No, I don't remember how old my children were when I started popping their toes, but I recall them being little bitty things. It was probably a game of "this little piggy goes to market" that got out of hand. Regardless, they grew to like it, and before long they began presenting their toes voluntarily.

Folks, on the outside chance that there are other toe-poppers on the porch, I should caution you. As that Florida principal discovered, toe popping can turn ugly. It's best to keep it in the family. I know this, for one day I was holding someone else's toddler on my hip, deep in conversation, when I inadvertently popped the child's baby toe. Have mercy! I reckon the poor thing thought I'd broken his toe in two. You've never heard such wailing! Fortunately for me, no one pressed charges. Toe popping is obviously an acquired taste.

That's an example of the sort of important work I do here at *All Things Southern*, where, true to my slogan, I endeavor to "bring you the charm and heritage of the South." It's been quite a ride, and it's introduced me to even more interesting people than those who live in my head, not to mention the many other unique opportunities it has offered me. To borrow a phrase from Bubba Dickens, it has been the best of times; it has been the worst of times. I'll elaborate on both before we're said and done, but right now I'm on a mission to get this book started.

I mentioned the voices earlier in part to explain my writing style, which you may as well know now is one prolonged state of digression, in order to confess up front that we, the voices and I, are at odds over what I'm about to say. There have been many oft-stated concerns among us regarding my intentions of commencing this work with a disclaimer. And that is perfectly understandable. I realize it's a most unusual way to open a how-to book. I told myself so many times. "Self," I said, "no self-respecting author opens a how-to book with a disclaimer of all things!" To which myself replied, "Where did you hide the

Official Guide to Speaking All Things Southern

*The Official Belle Doctrine, proper noun: a set of principles set forth from history's earliest known Southern Mamas, dictating proper behavior for both Southerners and Southern Wannabes. The Official Belle Doctrine is a compilation of the rules governing a Southern belle's life from cradle to grave. It remains such a highly classified document that whereabouts of the original continues to be a closely guarded secret. Throughout history only a small number of belles in each generation have been privileged to see it, but all know it exists. Contents of the doctrine are passed down predominately through the oral traditions of the Southern lineage.

Starburst Jelly Beans?" Sigh. That sort of thing happens more often than I care to admit.

All valid arguments and distracting voices aside, here's the controversial disclaimer: You've gone and got yourself a self-help book that's light on advice and heavy on the commiserating. Mea culpa. Storytelling runs in my veins. Building a story around whatever it is I'd like to say comes as natural as breathing to me and every bit as regular. Granted, there will be some advice here and there from **The Official Belle Doctrine,*** but it's gonna be woven in and around more stories than you can shake at stick at. That being said, it'd help if you'd be willing to adjust your expectations just a tad. If you could think of this as a "we're all in this together" type of book, we'll get along like a house on fire. Besides, it's like the old people say, "everyone's say-so is better than their do-so."

1

She Got Those Heavy Legs from Her Mama's Side

Thoughts on Fitness, Health, and
Self-Improvement with Sensational
Salads to Baby Your Curves

Nowhere will a relaxed perspective on advice be more helpful than it will be here in the fitness and self-improvement chapter. In all likelihood my thickening waistline will disqualify me from offering you expert fitness instruction. I don't have a miracle drink to present, either, although I feel sure I can whip one up for the amazingly low cost of $19.95 if the sucker in you insists. And I can't promise that you will be oh-so-skinny by the time you finish this book without making any changes in your diet or activity level. (Okay, confession: I wanted to, but it made the legal department nervous.) On the other hand, those itsy-bitsy teeny-weenie celebrity trainers you've been watching on TV do not have a clue where you're coming from, Sweet Cheeks. It takes a real woman to feel your pain, and for that, I am supremely qualified.

My husband, God love him, told me I've grown so much since we were married, that if I were a stock he'd be a millionaire. I chose to let him live.

~Brenda Agent Copeland
Bastrop, Louisiana

This is what I've learned here in the real world. The older you get the less you can eat without gaining weight. I shall now quote from **The Official Belle Doctrine:** "Thy caloric intake necessary to maintain thy current weight shalt be strictly calculated according to thy chronological years. For each year of thy life after the age of twelve thou shalt subtract one entrée per day lest thou pack on pounds like the great leviathan in the deep blue sea." (That would be a whale, for those of you raised outside the Bible Belt and anyone else not paying attention in Sunday School.) By the way, it is no accident that The Official Belle Doctrine sounds a lot like the Good Book. We belles are well versed in both. And I'm not jesting about the caloric intake. Being in my forties, I've now arrived at the point where my body weight can be sustained with three grapes and two peanuts, hence the aforementioned thickening waistline. Let me be clear. This doth stink. Not only is it requiring me to keep a vigilant watch over my diet, it is also making it hard to maintain my sunny disposition.

Of course, it is also true that these caloric challenges and resulting disposition issues are directly tied to other recent developments, too. For instance, a while back several of my readers wrote in expressing their concerns over the level of aggression evident in a recent suggestion I had made that we should look into feeding the politicians to the alligators. First off, I was joking. Kinda. But, I admit, it could be a little more than that.

I Fell Into a Burning Ring of Fire

Let it be known that out of all the things my Southern Mama taught, warned, and repeated over the years, I've entered a particular stage she somehow managed to gloss over. I am speaking of the stage that includes the female hot flash. Due to these Internal Infernos, I'm now experiencing mood swings—on a grand scale. I'm not talking about going from happy to sad. This is more like going from "I don't want to hurt you right now" to "I'd like to kill you more than once."

As I alluded to before, I was more than a bit ill-prepared for this season, which is why I'm willing to educate the females who aren't here yet—and the males who don't know how to treat the females who are. (Y'all know who you are; you can thank me later.) See, I had heard of hot flashes all my life, but I naively associated them with the heat one feels at the peak of a Southern summer. Let me shoot straight, ladies. Someone should tell you that you're going to burn from the inside out. This is the Ring of Fire Johnny Cash was singing about, okay?

To be sure, given the depth and range of volatile emotions my girlfriends and I have personally documented, I remain surprised that Raging Inferno Syndrome hasn't been used as a line of defense in our criminal court system. Well, think about it. We have syndromes for everything else under the sun. Myself, I'm generally a "lock 'em up and throw away the key" type of person, but girls, if you were to find yourself on trial for something you did in the "heat of the moment," so to speak, you would want me in the jury box. Trust me. I could have an open mind on this one.

Why, a couple of years ago, I personally took to the airwaves and went to bat for one of my fellow Americans who I thought was getting a bad shake in our criminal justice system.

Let's take a look back at that case, shall we? I'm talking about Samantha Jo Brown, the poor woman who broke into that fudge shop somewhere in Dixie. (I've changed the name and location to appease the not so innocent.)

I was cooking supper late one evening when this perky little news anchor came on and began dishing out the sordid details shown on a security video rolling in the corner of the screen. The footage depicted Ms. Brown carrying out her alleged crime. I'll be the first to admit that it wasn't pretty. Samantha Jo was clearly trashing the counters and pilfering large bars of fudge and a few of her other favorite treats. What she didn't want, she threw on the ground. What she did want, she stuck in her pockets and loot bag. Bless her heart, Samantha Jo even slipped and fell a few times in her excitement.

As sticky as Samantha's fingers were, I still felt it would be wise not to rush to judgment and risk a harsher penalty than was otherwise warranted. The way I saw it, this was a clear case of Fudge Frenzy. I've been there and done that. Okay, not exactly there and that, but I've been pretty close and I just wondered if there could be more to the story, like the possibility of entrapment. I noticed in the news clip that there was a hand-lettered sign in the window that clearly read "Free Samples." Perhaps someone should have clarified that advertisement for poor Samantha Jo.

All I'm saying is that there are times—hormonal times—in

Mama wasn't one to put a lot of pressure on her kids. When people asked how her kids were doing, she'd always say that she couldn't complain—none of them were in jail. Seeing as how that couldn't be said of all our kinfolk, it was a real point of pride for Mama. I like to think I've raised the bar a bit with my offspring, but I must say, the older they get the more I realize that it does bring a certain amount of satisfaction.

~Mike Blakeney
Monroe, Louisiana

every woman's life when she's just one bad decision away from a Fudge Frenzy. No doubt about it, Samantha Jo needed to pay for her crime and make reparations to the store owner. But in light of all the more serious crimes escalating in our nation today, I suggested we go easy on her. A chocoholic in crisis is a sad thing to behold, but we—I mean she—was really just hurting herself. I even tried to start a "Free the fudge woman!" campaign, but it never got out of the gates. (Go ahead and laugh. It worked for Willy.)

What Men Should Know About Raging Inferno Syndrome

No doubt, my sensitivity to Samantha Jo's situation can be attributed to the lengths I've been going to lately to control my middle-age midsection. Whereas chocolate used to have a star-ring role in my life, these days it barely has a supporting part. In the interest of my not blowing up (a term we'll elaborate on shortly), I've been forced to relegate the sweet stuff to a tragic cameo. I currently allow myself one minuscule piece of dark chocolate every evening after supper. I consume this tiny piece of heaven in oh-so-small bites in an effort to make it last. Let it be noted that my man, my dessert-loving beloved, thinks this is the funniest thing he has ever seen. He refuses to buy into this scale-back. I've tried to explain to him that we're supposed to consider this small unit of dark chocolate a "palate cleanser" and that a taste is all we really need. Beloved says his palate must be larger than mine because his doesn't come clean that easy. Apparently his palate can't be bothered by anything less than a substantial slice of cake or huge bowl of ice cream.

Speaking of my man, and since education is said to be the best form of prevention, I shall address this next section to the males among us in the hope of reducing the number of Raging Inferno Syndrome casualties.

Dear men people, the physical changes that occur as we belles mature may make us sorta testy, but with a little patience and understanding we can all get along. It is my pleasure to be able to offer you some guidelines to help you get through the most difficult stages. For instance, the temperature gauge in your home, office, or vehicle is now completely and totally irrelevant. If your Sweet Thang says it is hot, it is hot—and it is always hot.

> A woman always gets a little heavier in the winter, so don't worry if you gain a few pounds.
>
> ~Louise Searson Hull
> Savannah, Georgia

Now, hold that thought while we look at three handy dandy lines guaranteed to build a bridge across any number of communication gaps or relationship challenges. They are, in no particular order: "I love you," "I'm sorry," and "Have you lost weight?" You would do well to memorize these aids and keep them handy. You'll find them to be mostly interchangeable while at the same time extremely effective, especially when used together. By way of illustration, let's say your Sugar Plum were to say, "Honey, my bank account's overdrawn." You could choose, "I'm sorry. Have you lost weight?" and immediately set the stage for a more productive financial discussion.

Good advice, huh? Well, I've got more to say on the finances, but first, I'd like to jump a serious rabbit on this change-of-life thing and I hope y'all are sitting down for this one. I've just recently learned of something called male menopause. The experts say it's real and it's far more prevalent than you'd think.

They even have a few names for it. They're calling it andropause, viropause, and "we-were-tired-of-y'all-whining-so-we-have-it-too-pause." Okay, so I made that last one up, but really, this just smacks of one-upmanship! It was bad enough when some men started wearing eye makeup and carrying purses, now we can't even get a little sympathy for our menopausal moments cuz they're having those, too. Sorry, not buying it.

It's not like we girls enjoy having the market cornered on this one, but color me skeptical. From what I've read, these male changes range from decreased desire to fading energy levels. Tragic, isn't it? I'd play the violin for the poor fellows, but I'm too busy wringing my shirt out and wiping the sweat off the keyboard! Some experts even suggest that this misunderstood male passage is the root cause of what has previously been known as the male midlife crisis. Now, isn't that convenient?! We're supposed to believe that this is why some men trade in their wives and their cars for younger models. Again, no sale!

Despite that built-in excuse for losing your midlife mind, I suspect you'll be hard-pressed to get a Southern bubba to admit to having menopause, for which we can all be thankful. Double Menopause (which is what they're calling it when you and your Sweet Thang experience simultaneous symptoms) would most surely include ammunition where I come from, and it wouldn't turn out well. As for the rest of you guys, on behalf of my fellow belles who have to put up with the baby-making equipment, birth the wee ones, and suffer the subsequent effects this has on our girlish figures, we're gonna have to say, "No to male menopause." Sorry, guys, but your privileges are officially revoked . . .

And now back to the subject of finances. I think my man should give me some props for trying to make the best economic use of these seasonal moments I'm having. Case in point: I read where Holiday Inn is offering a human bed-warming service at some of their exclusive European hotels. As I pen these words, a person can, for a limited time, have a willing staffer dressed in an all-in-one fleece sleeper warm up those cold sheets for 'em. (And we thought Motel Six was doing everybody a big favor leaving the light on!)

A spokesperson for Holiday Inn said it'll be like having a giant hot water bottle in your bed, (which begs the question of why they didn't just do that, and the answer is 'cause people like me wouldn't give 'em free publicity, but I know they're using me, so it doesn't count). Rules are the thermometer-toting bed warmer will leave the room soon as the sheets reach sixty-eight degrees and before the guest arrives. No hanky-panky here, folks, just move along.

What really got my attention, however, was reading about Holiday Inn flaunting the approval of a sleep expert who confirmed that cold weather inhibits the body's ability to fall asleep. Well, no duh, so do hot flashes! So here's my creative idea. I'm thinking that before my next book tour perhaps yours truly should fill out one of those bed-warming job apps. It could be a great opportunity to offset our travel expenses, and Beloved Hubby says I can use him for a reference as to the intensity of my seasonal moments. It'd be a temporary thing, of course. I'm not seeing much job security here, which happens to remind me of a story.

I know a man, name withheld, who as a little kid, used to get out of his bed when nature called and "warm up" his brother's bunk in the middle of the night. When Older Brother discovered that he didn't actually have a *going problem*, so to speak, Younger Brother was slap out of business.

Look-a-here, it'd be a good idea for us belles to study some of the other problems associated with this delightful season of our lives, such as memory loss and . . . umm, give me a minute . . . oh, yeah—concentration, but right now I want to tie up something we touched on earlier before it gets away from me. The thing is: I'm still wondering why the older females in my Southern circle have been so uncharacteristically quiet where it concerns this particular aspect of my education. Seriously, it's like the women who have gone before us have decided to hide and watch the newcomers with a strange glee. I understand that in years past the subject was considered somewhat taboo in polite conversation, but really, I would've thought my own dear mother would've been more forthcoming about what to expect when the baby-making parts start wearing out. She has never, I repeat never, held back before.

Mama, Can You Spare an Opinion

It is uncommon to find a Southern Mama who can refrain from offering advice to her offspring on any number of subjects, but it is rarer still to meet one who can keep herself from weighing in (no pun intended) on her belle's physical appearance. My own mama is certainly no exception. And trust me when I say that the woman has shown exemplary dedication to the cause.

Let me tell you what my Southern Mama is much too gracious to admit. Yours truly remains a source of consternation to the lady my sisters and I long ago nicknamed Jackie O in a nod to her well-kept style. Mama will show polite interest in the where, when, and why of one of my upcoming speaking engagements only to get to the all-important question: *What do you plan to wear?*

Mama knows full well that I haven't given it a moment's thought, but you've got to hand it to her, the woman perseveres.

I'm convinced she'll take her last breath trying to instill me with some level of concern for my attire. Come to think of it, I wouldn't put it past her to have a few pertinent fashion notes for me and my sisters tucked in with her last will and testament. Mama's written funeral wishes may include something like "In closing, I do hope you girls won't have bare arms at the service. It's just not appropriate."

In my own defense, I'd like the record to show that I'd be a lot more prone to keeping up with the latest fashion if the shopping experience didn't include those horrible dressing room mirrors! I vividly remember one of the last times I sucked in my stomach and forced myself to venture into the nearest abyss (another excellent biblical term, used here for what is more commonly known as a mall). My first ever book tour had given me just enough impetus to ignore my usual misgivings. I was in the dressing room of a major store making myself totally miserable, when I overheard a lady in the stall beside me express exactly what I was thinking. "Ugh!" she said loudly and to no one in particular. I laughed out loud in spite of myself, and soon we were commiserating like old friends over the tops of the stalls.

One of our biggest complaints was with the dressing rooms themselves, and our points were valid. Are you listening,

Years ago when my mother-in-law was in between one of her infamous diets, she was lamenting the fact that she'd put on a couple of pounds and her clothes were a little snug. Ms. Claire, the lady who helped her at the house, wanted to make her feel better. I can see her now, big old smile and everything, saying, "Mrs. Boughton, you're not getting fat. Your clothes are just laying close on you." Both of those ladies have gone to be with the Lord now, but I can still hear "Ma" telling this story.

~Arilla Boughton
Lake Providence, Louisiana

retailers? Then tell us, for goodness' sakes, what's up with your dressing rooms? Do y'all intentionally set out to accentuate our every bump, bulge, and flaw under that harsh lighting, or are you just totally clueless? This may surprise your design team, but we didn't go in there to count our pores.

I've got two guesses on who's planning these dressing rooms and its either men or ninety-eight-pound teenage girls. News flash, oh great marketing minds, these poorly designed rooms are partly to blame for why you see everyone over the ancient age of twenty-two toting in armloads of clothes and leaving empty-handed. I'm just saying, you could make tons more money if you improved the mirrors and the lighting. It doesn't have to be candlelight, although that would be right nice, but those glaring fluorescents must be allowed to die a natural death. They make a girl want to give up and go with the flow, so to speak, although I haven't—at least, not yet anyway. Try as I might to befriend my mirror image, I can't seem to live and let live where my behind is concerned. Is it just me, or does going with the flow seem to be much easier for the male gender?

A couple weeks ago my parents were at my house having Sunday dinner. After our meal, I served caramel chocolate brownies and vanilla ice cream with our coffee. Papa promptly finished his and wanted seconds. Mama frowned. "Now, Ed," she scolded, "you don't need another helping. You know all that sugar is bad for you."

Papa just winked at her. "Aw, sweetheart," he said. "Something's gonna get me. It might as well be brownies. You know, it's like those people who used to fuss at Mama for dipping Levi Garrett."

Papa paused, looked around the dining room table at the rest of us the way the best storytellers do, and explained, "My mama started dipping snuff when she was five years old. They all said it would kill her—and when she was ninety-four it finally caught up to her!"

Sometimes, it's hard to argue with the logic of Papa's health plan, but Mama's always up to the task. By the way, that part about Grandma Rushing dipping snuff from the age of five, I've taken absolutely no creative license with that. It's the whole truth and nothing but the truth. My grandmother came from a long line of Kentucky hill people who did not consider that sort of thing one bit unusual. You have to appreciate family members that give you this sort of material.

Tell Me How You Really Feel

I thought about Mama's never ending figure and fashion advice the other day while on the cell phone with one of my dear writer friends. I'm sure everyone in Wal-Mart heard me laughing, but I couldn't help it. River Jordan was cracking me up! In a world of deadlines and very little "me" time, River, native beach girl, told me she had been pleased to discover a new tanning lotion that she thought was giving her a quick and healthy looking gleam. That is, until she took a trip home to Florida to see her mama. "Sweetie," her mama said with a note of concern and within a half hour of her arrival, "Have you had your liver checked lately?"

"My liver—" River repeated, to make sure she had heard correctly, "No. Why?" "Well," her mama said. "I don't wanna scare you, but you're looking sort of yellow."

To be fair, River's mama may have been sincerely concerned about her baby girl's health, but River and I doubt it. She and I both agree that Southern Mamas are known for being subtle, like a freight train.

The Southern Mama's subtlety is a clever art that can be seen in her penchant for delivering messages in story form. Consider the nuance of the following scenario. In our example, Mama and I are pulling up to Starbucks for my beloved caramel macchiato. Chances are Mama has declined to order because "it is ridiculous to spend that much money on a cup of coffee when you can buy a pound of coffee and brew your own for weeks. Besides, aren't those things *heavy*?" Several beats later, after watching me quietly with a frown between her eyes, Mama may, oh so casually, begin talking about Aunt Clarissa's daughter.

"You know, Shellie, Clarissa said Lindsey put on ten pounds last spring and she couldn't figure out why. Lindsey was watching what she ate and walking every afternoon. Come to find out, she was getting herself one of those fancy lattes every afternoon on her way home from work. You know, kind of like that one you're drinking." Message given, message received.

The Big Boned Theory* and Blowing Up

I should tell you that while Mama has always given my sisters and me this type of helpful advice on weight maintenance, she's never been unrealistic about it. She never once set standards that were unattainable. It was more about working with what the Good Lord gave you.

Mama knows full well that I haven't been petite since I was in preschool. I remember her consoling my high school self more

Official Guide to Speaking
All Things Southern

*Big Boned Theory, proper noun: the state of having larger than average bones that give one the appearance of extra girth

than once when I compared myself unfavorably to the tiny little girls on my cheerleading squad. "Shellie Charlene, you look as good as any of them. You're just big boned."

Growing up Southern, it never once occurred to me to question how Mama had managed to see right past my hide to note the size of my bones. I simply accepted her unusual X-ray vision, right along with my healthy skeletal system, and kicked up my heels with the best of 'em.

I don't know when and where the Big Boned Theory was first developed, but it is routinely subscribed to in Southern circles. By the way, I realize you wouldn't know this if I didn't tell you, but I've been lost in Google land since I typed that last sentence. Warning: Do not make the mistake of putting "Big Boned" in a search engine. Lord have mercy, I fell smack into a raging Internet debate between those who think it's an overused excuse and those who think it's hard science. (For the record, if the disagreement gets physical, my money is on the second group.) Apparently a Mr. Ian from Celebrity Fit Club disproved the Big Boned Theory right there on TV in front of God and everybody with an X-ray machine and a variety of body shapes. At least he did as far as the first group is concerned. The holdouts say he didn't prove squat.*

> **Official Guide to Speaking All Things Southern**
>
> *squat, direct object: nada, zilch, nothing

I decided to run the findings by my own expert. Mama was uncomfortable getting into the science of it all, but she did suggest that I remind everyone that the Big Boned Theory should be used with caution. As she so aptly put it, "Being big boned may give one a bit of leeway in the weight department, but it should never be taken as a license to blow up." Amen. Blowing up is akin to letting oneself go, as in "I saw Chrissie Gipson at the reunion. I still can't believe she has gone and blown up like that!"

Blowing up, it should be noted, is as unattractive and extreme as the pointy hips on those super gaunt fashion models. Well-disciplined belles frown on both. As a matter of fact, we'd like to force-feed those poor stick women some banana pudding. A little padding—why, we see that as healthy. We'll defend anyone's right to have some meat on her bones. I remember the day my friend Paulette called me in a twit about what she considered a horrible injustice in the media.

"I'm fit to be tied," Paulette said. "I feel so sorry for that poor girl."

"What girl are we talking about?" I asked.

"That poor Jessica Simpson, of course! First she gets blamed every time the Cowboys lose, like she's calling in secret plays from her little skybox, and now everybody and their mama is saying she's gotten fat—fat! Have you seen the child? I've seen more fat on a center-cut pork chop."

I told Paulette that no, I had not seen the singer in person, but I couldn't help seeing the pictures. They'd been all over the news.

"And that's another thing," Paulette said. "When in blue blazes did a girl's weight warrant a mention in the evening news? Folks ought to be ashamed, making fun of that poor girl. Maybe she just weighs heavy—reckon they ever thought of that?"

Weighing heavy*—there's another Southernism. It used to be one of my favorites, too, although the charm is currently lost on me. To be honest, I'm thinking that particular reasoning, coupled with this delightful stage of life and my buying into the Big Boned Theory are largely responsible for the extra pounds I've allowed to sneak up on my waistline. Either that or I've picked up the fat virus on one of my speaking trips. Don't tell me you haven't heard about the fat virus. Oh, please. This is too good. It fits our culture's no fault mentality perfectly.

Official Guide to Speaking All Things Southern

*weighing heavy, verb: an aberration of physics widely attributed to the presence of the Big Boned Theory

Researchers now claim they've discovered a virus that, if you catch it, will make you more at risk for obesity. I told Paulette about it, and just for fun, I asked if she thought Jessica Simpson might have caught it. Paulette took me seriously.

"Well, God love her, Shellie, I guess she could have."

"Don't be silly," I told Paulette. "That's ridiculous. It's just more of this everyone's-a-victim mentality. No one's responsible for their own actions anymore. They also said obesity runs in social circles. I guess you believe that, too."

"I might," Paulette said. "Skinny people do run in packs. Wait—I just had an idea! I wonder if I could go down to the gym and get some of those beanpoles to cough on me."

"That won't be necessary," I told Paulette. "Trust me on this. You're not well."

Delta Dawn, Paulette's Light Comes On

I was kidding of course. Paulette is as sane as the next person, which used to be saying a lot more than it does these days. Seriously, one of my early working titles for this book was *Crazy Is as Crazy Does and It Looks Like We Got Ourselves a Full-blown Epidemic*," but I was told it was too wordy. Whatever.

Nah, Paulette's not crazy, but the girl can be incredibly gullible. She's a sucker for every weight-loss fad that crosses her radar. Getting skinny people to cough on her is not outside the realm of possibility for someone who has an Abdominal Belt in her closet. Right now, the poor thing has her lip run out a mile long over the failure of her latest fad diet. Yesterday was the program's official weigh-in day. Paulette had been all excited at the get-go,* but, bless her heart, I think she lost about a pound and a half, tops. She dropped by the house on her way home, ranting and raving about how hard she had worked and how much she had sacrificed.

> Official Guide to Speaking
> All Things Southern
>
> *get-go, prepositional phrase: the onset, when something is begun

"And for what?" she grumbled. "I swanee! That dadblame Carol Lee, I should've known something was up when she said I could eat as much of anything I liked on this diet, and then she gave me a list of the things I was supposed to like. Isn't that convenient? And, if that's not all, I've been walking three miles a day in this heat and watching every bite I put in my mouth and for what I ask you—less than two pounds, two measly pounds!"

While she took a breath, I took the opportunity to mention that it had only been a week, after all. "What'd you expect?" I asked.

Paulette gave me one of her I-thought-you'd-be-on-my-side frowns. "Well, Shellie, a lot more than two pounds, that's for sure. Carol Lee has used the same program, and she said that she lost ten pounds her first week. She swore I'd do the same thing."

I reminded Paulette that it's a proven fact that if you take weight off slowly, you have the best chance of keeping it off in the long run. "Who is this cousin of yours, anyway?" I asked. "I don't think I know her, do I? Is Carol Lee a doctor?"

"No," Paulette said.

"Is she a nutritionist?"

"No, Shellie. She's not."

"Is she certified to help with the program as a group leader or something?" Paulette was steadily shaking her head.

"Well, then, what is she?" I asked.

Paulette took a minute before it hit her. "Now that I think about it," she said. "I think she's a bald-faced liar."

That's my buddy, y'all. With Paulette things are always darkest right before it dawns!

Designated Thinkers Are Underrated

Being as how we're knee-deep here in the health, fitness, and personal improvement chapter, and I have yet to offer any real counsel in this area other than those earlier caloric calculations from The Official Belle Doctrine, it occurs to me that I should stop here and take an *All Things Southern* look at some real health concerns. As is my custom, I'll begin with a story.

We've all seen the ads, "Drinking and driving don't mix" and "Smoking is dangerous for your health." Sadly, however, you just can't cover all the bases with some folks. I once read a newspaper account of a fellow in Arkansas who perfectly illustrates this truth. After a night of drinking, Jeff had headed home with his friend, Jerry Glenn, who was acting as the night's designated driver. And yet Jeff the passenger, still ended up in the ER. As Jerry Glenn explained to the police, "Jeff's cigarette fell out the window and he stepped out after it." Unfortunately, they were going 60 mph. See, what Jeff really needed was a designated thinker.

My sisters and I practiced this idea a good bit during our teenage years; we were designated to think of ways to outwit our parents. Unfortunately, the entire adult community was on their side. That's when folks weren't scared to tell someone what their kids were doing. Like the time we tried smoking and Papa said, "Mr. Joe said he passed y'all on your way to school this morning and he thought the car was on fire." Papa enjoyed our puzzled looks before adding, "You know, what with the smoke rolling out every window." Busted!

Smokers smoke everywhere. Believe me. I keep crossword puzzles, magazines, Sudoku puzzles, and books handy in the bathroom. And yes, an ashtray. I went in there one morning with a cigarette in my hand. There was a Sudoku puzzle that needed finishing, so ciggie and pencil in hand, I began concentrating on those numbers. After a minute or two I noticed an extraordinary amount of smoke wafting into my face only to discover the ashes from the stogie had knocked off and my Fruit of the Looms were on fire! Good thing I was near water! The question is, did that cure this queen from smoking on the throne? Nah, to be truthful, I didn't like doing those number puzzles anyway!

~Olivia King
Red Bay, Alabama

Cyndie and I covered our tracks better after that little heads-up, but our blond-headed middle sister Rhonda didn't fare as well. One day we came home to find Papa sitting at the table with a pack of filterless Marlboros.

"Whatcha doing, Papa?" we asked, nervously.

He smiled. "I bought me and Rhonda some cigarettes so we could take a smoke break, together." He lit up and slid the pack toward Rhonda, who had turned quite pale.

Papa never blinked. "Aw, come on, Rhonda. I'm tired of fighting. You know what they say, if you can't beat 'em, join 'em."

I read where the trooper who worked Arkansas Jeff's accident said, "If anything could make the victim stop smoking, this should be it." For the record, Papa's program worked, too, and it wasn't near as painful. I remember Rhonda deciding on the spot that she'd been meaning to quit for a while and she couldn't think of a better time.

Okay, that was both fun and informational, but all joking aside, here's my best health and fitness advice in a nutshell: I, Belle of All Things Southern, am all about personal improvement, and I consider weight maintenance to be a worthy goal, but after that—well, at some point, folks, you gotta work with what you've got, play the ball where it lies and all that.

I've learned that moderation really is the key in everything from chocolate and exercise to the latest fads and cosmetic procedures. You'll be better off mentally, emotionally, physically, and financially if you can learn the secret of moderation and how to take everything with a grain of salt, including advice (even mine), however well-meaning.

I speak from experience about the opinion thing. I get a ton of email at *All Things Southern*. Some people need advice and others want to offer it. Some of it I can learn from and some of it I can laugh at, and some of it stands out in my memory. I'd love to share one of those true stories with you, but first, some background.

Me, Reba, and Trisha—Together Again

In the event that you didn't read my first book in this series—
and if that's the case, I'm gonna have to ask you to rectify that
situation as soon as possible; the title was *Suck Your Stomach In
and Put Some Color On!*—it was chock-full of advice belles get
from their mamas from birth to the grave that I thought the
rest of the world should know.

One of my favorite things about that publishing experience
was the tour I got to take and the people I got to meet in book-
stores all over the South. But let's just lay all the cards on the
table, shall we? I have not been running all over the country
espousing the value of lip color and forgetting to apply my own.
I never, but never, leave home without my color. I have thin lips,
okay? No, to answer your question, I don't like it, but I've tried
to accept it, in a that's-just-the-way-the-Good-Lord-made-me
sort of way. It'd be easier if folks weren't always reminding me.

See, when I first started taping my video podcasts, I got a
few emails from folks telling me I look like Reba McEntire.
I couldn't see it. She's a little bitty blue-eyed redhead. I'm a
tall brown-eyed brunette. Then some folks wrote in and said I
looked like Trisha Yearwood. I didn't see that either, although
she was more of a blondish brunette *and* she's more of a big-
boned girl, no offense intended. Then it hit me. Do you see the
connection? We all have thin lips. And that brings me to my
favorite piece of reader advice.

That would be the note I got from the lady who said, "I love
watching you on TV, Shellie. You look just like family. None of
us have any lips." She went on to tell me about the lip surgery
she had to plump hers up and how she was happy with it, but it
faded away after a little while and she was gonna have to do it

again. She told me I should think hard before I did it, as it was painful and expensive. I didn't even know I was considering it. She meant well. That's another of Mama's lines.

There is something to be said for learning to appreciate ourselves. If y'all want to plump your lips up, by all means, get after it, but I'm gonna stick with what the Good Lord gave me on this one. Hear me, please. I'm not ruling out the possibility of ever having any work done, but I do hope I can remember my own "everything in moderation" rule. We've all seen the poor souls who become desperate about what they consider to be their defects, bless their hearts.

The Botox Bandit Strikes Again

I would like to think that, by the time you read this, the latest cosmetic crime spree will be a thing of the past, but here in the real world I won't be holding my breath. Authorities aren't calling it an official crime wave, but some are saying it's just a matter of time. Similar crimes have been reported in Reno, Houston, Phoenix, California, San Antonio, Tampa, and most recently, North Carolina. The capers have all been pulled off by females who are perfecting a scam known as the Botox and Bolt.

Apparently, cash-strapped women bent on Botox are getting the freeze-your-face treatments and making a run for it, past the receptionist and out the door without paying for the procedure, thus giving a whole new meaning to the idea of desperate criminals.

Most of the crimes have been solved quickly with the not-so-smart crooks apprehended in the immediate area. Perhaps they should've given more thought to posing for those before-and-after pictures in the doctor's office. I'm guessing it makes 'em fairly easy to spot. "This is Detective Brown. I'm holding a suspect in connection with that spiff-and-run on Fourth Street and she's demanding to see her lawyer. She's a real cool customer. Get this. She hasn't changed expressions during the whole questioning."

Still, this spree could be foreshadowing a bigger problem. Forgive the pun here, but with more women and men reportedly getting addicted to Botox all the time, if we have a Botox shortage, things could get ugly quick. I'm not kidding. Think about the possibilities. A Botox crime syndicate could spring up in your own hometown. Which reminds me: I'm worried about Paulette. She's been looking very, well, "perky" lately and she's been exceptionally interested in these Botox and Bolt cases. When I said I couldn't believe those women risked jail for a few wrinkles, she said, "Jail, smail, would you check out that smooth forehead!"

Heaven help us all, she also thought the name they gave that North Carolina girl was cute. "The Botox Bandit," she said, "you gotta admit that's kinda classy." But here's the clincher, y'all: Yesterday, I caught her doodling the words "Lipo Lady" on her shopping list!

"Paulette!" I said. "I hope you're not gonna do something stupid." All I got from her was a dirty look. I think.

Abs, Got to Keep 'Em Rolling

The truth is, a healthy amount of skepticism can also keep a belle from making serious mistakes in judgment. (Can you say *shoulder pads?*) I'm not saying you shouldn't take advantage of the latest medical procedures or that every new exercise program is a waste of time or money, I'm just cautioning us all to remember that the latest big thing is as temporary as Ashlee Simpson's hair color. I once read where the celebrity's publicist said, "Ashley changes her hair color the way the rest of us change underwear."

Well, now, I don't mean to pick on the Simpson girls. I realize they're in Hollywood now and there's the whole when-in-Rome-do-as-the-Romans-do thing, but perhaps someone has forgotten the oft-repeated clean underwear mantra of their Southern heritage. Besides, what exactly does Hollywood have against panties? I'm just curious.

I suppose we can hope that this "I'm Going Commando and I Want Everyone to Know It Thing" will come and go as quickly as every other health and fitness trend. Take the foods we eat for example. Coffee is good for you. Drink up! Sorry, our bad. Back away from the caffeine. Carbs are good—oops—make that bad. Ditto for the exercise crazes. Today's must have Ab-Roller becomes yesterday's Waist Away.

Actually, I don't know what they called it, but when I typed Waist Away just now I was picturing this little round orange contraption my mama had when I was a teenager. It was about the size and shape of a pair of bathroom scales, but it worked like a Lazy Susan, meaning it rotated on its base. One was supposed to stand on it and do the twist to

My friend Lisa and I would actually put on workout clothes (some ensembles may or may not have included leg warmers) and move the furniture in the living room. We would then sit and watch the video while commenting about how fit we would be if we could actually DO that stuff . . .

~Leslie Martin Young
Rayville, Louisiana

narrow one's waistline. I gave it my best shot but the only thing I noticed narrowing was Mama's eyes when my sisters and I would forget and leave it in front of the television.

The truth is, Sugar, when it comes to the hot new cosmetic and/or fashion trends, the best thing a belle can do is evaluate whether or not the latest greatest edict works for her. This is what personal style is all about! The great Dolly Parton is a beautiful example. The fashionistas have never swayed Dolly's style. Dolly proudly flaunted her big hair long after it was considered fashionable. I doubt she even noticed that her style was recently vindicated. Icons don't worry about that sort of thing, but yours truly here ate it up. Ate. It. Up. I'm talking payback, people.

Allow me to fill you in. For the second year in a row, the powers that be in the fashion industry made a startling announcement concerning the spring '09 look for our delicate tresses, or what our Southern Mamas call our crowning glory. Blindfold Al Gore and warn the ozone layer, those in the know declared that Big Hair was back!

Yep! I saw it in boldface print. I quote, "The beehive is reinterpreted for the season as either a smooth, more glamorous version or a more textured, sex kitten–ish look depending on the beehive's placement or balance on the head."

I believe some people owe other people an apology, and yet, in the spirit of hospitality, we in the second group are willing to offer those in the first group some

I was a teenager in the seventies when all the girls wore their hair long and straight and tucked behind their ears—everyone but me that is. My mom had convinced me it'd make my ears stick out permanently. "If you want to be a monkey, she'd say, I won't stand in your way, but I wouldn't do it."

~Susan
Atlanta, Georgia

Sweet Tea to wash down all those jokes about Southern women and their Big Hair. Yes, we heard 'em, and for the record, they didn't impact our grooming habits. Some of us gave up back-teasing, but most of us, like Ms. Parton, didn't. We may have embraced the flat-iron, but we have never renounced the power of big hair!

The truth is, we do live in serious times, and I'm thinking the rest of the world may just now be discovering something we Southern women have known all along: *Serious times deserve serious hair.* Why, just recently I was waiting to be introduced to a large audience and wondering if they were going to enjoy my prepared remarks. According to the Official Belle Doctrine, there was only one thing to do. I excused myself to the restroom, touched up my color, pulled out a trusty to-go can of hair spray from my purse, and gave myself a tad more volume. Like many a belle before me, I've learned from experience that Big Hair equals confidence, honey—and confidence never goes out of style!

On the flip side, a bad hair day can be more than a blow to your self-confidence. It can be dangerous to anyone in the vicinity. I once told my readers about a beauty shop meltdown I read about in Pennsylvania. It seemed a beautician shot her client because the woman was complaining about her hairdo!

Police say the beautician fired two shots, one into the ceiling and one into the client. I'm guessing the first shot was the "I've had

I remember growing up, I'd be leaving the house in blue jeans and a work shirt with pale lipstick (in keeping with the natural look of the day but not at all flattering to my brunette coloring), and my Southern Mama would say, "Are you *trying* to look ugly?" Later, I learned that I wasn't singled out for that comment. Both of my older sisters were given the same critique.

~Gayle Martin
Orange Park, Florida

enough" warning, but the customer wouldn't let it go. Bad call. A gunshot wound to the buttocks sounds like a tough end to a bad hair day.

My girlfriends and I understand the victim taking issue with a bad do, and yet, despite our trigger-happy reputation, four out of five of us agree the stylist went too far. That fifth respondent would be my aunt Marleta, a retired beautician. Aunt Marleta hasn't forgotten the run-in she once had with a client who always complained about her hairdos. That particular day the woman came in saying the beehive Aunt Marleta had given her was crooked. "Look at my ears," she whined, "and you'll see!" Now, Aunt Marleta had heard thru the grapevine that the night before Miss Beehive had been enjoying all the rides at the county fair. It was just like her to show up trying to get a free redo!

After Aunt Marleta stated emphatically that one of the woman's ears was simply lower than the other, the lady gave up and went willingly to the shampoo bowl, but she never stopped fussing! Suddenly Aunt Marleta announced she'd had enough. She ordered the surprised woman to get her large "posterior" up and out of her shop immediately. Aunt Marleta says Miss Beehive is lucky she left with a head full of shampoo instead of a bottom end of buckshot like that Yankee woman. Aunt Marleta even floated the idea of going up north to be a character witness for the defense, but the family managed to convince her it was a bad idea. There was simply too much that could come out at trial.

Health, Fitness, and Self-Improvement Tips

THUS SAITH THE BELLE DOCTRINE . . .

* Thy caloric intake should be constantly evaluated and downsized in direct proportion to thy chronological years.

* To refrain from blowing up, thy desserts should be considered palate cleansers and sized accordingly.

* Blood relatives may allow the use of The Big Boned Theory as a cover for weighing heavy, but the general public will be far less accepting.

* Moderation is not only the key to thy mental, emotional, and physical health, it should be considered vitally important as it relates to surgical improvements.

* Violence may be avoided by educating the men in thy life about the proper handling of thy summer moments (aka hot flashes).

* Serious times deserve serious hair and Big Hair equals confidence.

Sensational Salads to Baby the Curves

"When in the course of human events it becomes necessary for Southern belles to watch their curves, go easy on the home cooking, and consume smaller portions of the best food on earth, it behooves them out of a deep respect to their mutual heritage to declare the ingredients and recipes which they have chosen to employ." Perhaps you recognized the allusion to the opening of the Declaration of Independence. I mean no disrespect. I chose to model this section after that fine historical document because we belles feel strongly that our rather substantial salad recipes may separate them from the single lettuce leaf dishes of other areas of this wonderful country, but they are more than equal in flavor and satisfaction.

Mandarin Almond Salad

(SERVES 4)

This salad is perfect for a light supper with a load of French bread as is, but in the interest of full disclosure, I have been known to grill some chicken to toss in for my hardworking man. The dressing is sweet and the preparation is simple, just the kind of recipe to reach for when you're in a hurry.

Dressing:

1 cup salad oil

⅓ cup cider vinegar

½ cup sugar

1 teaspoon salt

1 teaspoon dry mustard

1½ tablespoons poppy seed

Salad:

2 heads Romaine lettuce, washed and chilled

½ bunch green onions, chopped

1 (5 oz.) package slivered almonds

2 cans mandarin oranges, drained and chilled

To prepare dressing, combine salad oil, cider vinegar, sugar, and salt. To wet mixture add dry mustard and poppy seed. Toss with lettuce, green onions, almonds, and oranges. Serve.

Delicious Dill Marinade

(SERVES 6)

This recipe pairs fresh vegetables with the tangy flavors of vinegar and dill to serve up a marinated salad that complements a bed of lettuce or a nice serving of your favorite pasta.

1 large head broccoli, separated into florets

1 large head cauliflower, separated into florets

1 red bell pepper, chopped into ½-inch pieces

4 carrots, sliced in rounds

½ pound fresh mushrooms, cut into bite-size pieces

8 ounces sliced black olives, drained

*optional for cucumber lovers: 1 cucumber, sliced in rounds

Marinade:

½ cup regular white vinegar

½ cup tarragon vinegar

1½ cups extra virgin olive oil

1 tablespoon sugar

1 tablespoon dill weed

1 tablespoon garlic salt

1 teaspoon each of salt and pepper

Combine broccoli and cauliflower in a large bowl with diced red bell pepper, carrots, mushrooms, black olives, and cucumbers if using.

To prepare the dressing, combine white vinegar, tarragon vinegar, and extra virgin olive oil. Shake well and season with sugar, dill weed, and garlic salt. Salt and pepper the dressing to taste and pour it over the veggies. Cover and refrigerate overnight. Drain marinade before serving over lettuce, or the pasta of your choice.

Bodacious Black Bean Salad

(SERVES 4)

My Bodacious Black Bean Salad is a meal in itself. It's also a strikingly pretty dish. This salad is perfectly at home served in your best china or your everyday Fiesta. Though, to be honest, it doesn't really matter which you choose, as it will promptly disappear.

1 (15 oz.) can black beans, rinsed and drained

2 (12 oz.) cans whole kernel corn, drained

½ cup chopped green onions

½ cup diced red onion

2 jalapeño peppers, finely chopped

1 (3 oz.) can sliced black olives

1 cup shredded cheddar cheese

Dash of garlic salt

Dash of sugar

½ cup store-bought Italian dressing

Combine beans, corn, green onions, red onions, jalapeño peppers, and black olives. Add shredded cheddar cheese. Season with garlic salt and sugar and stir in Italian dressing, being careful not to tear beans while stirring. Serve on a bed of lettuce or, if you're not counting calories, with a bag of Fritos! Either way, let it chill first to allow those flavors to blend.

Glazed Fruit Salad

(SERVES 6)

My Glazed Fruit Salad is the perfect little something sweet when you're trying to forgo a more sinful dessert. Whip it up with a sugar substitute and it's almost innocent.

- 1 quart fresh strawberries (you can substitute a big bag of frozen berries if you don't have fresh), halved
- 4 firm bananas, sliced
- 1 can pineapple chunks, drained

Glaze:
- 1 cup sugar or sugar substitute
- Couple teaspoons water
- ½ cup corn starch

Combine berries and bananas with pineapple chunks and set aside. Prepare glaze by dissolving sugar into water in a small sauce pot, before stirring in corn starch. Bring to boil. (It won't take but a minute.) Once it begins to roll, turn heat down and cook over medium flame until glaze begins to thicken. Cool, combine with fruit, and chill. Have mercy . . . that's gonna be good!

Mama's Wilted Lettuce

(SERVES 4)

I learned to cook from my mama, who taught my sisters and me that it was wrong to waste food. This is a salad we learned to serve when the lettuce no longer looked fresh, but it was still too good to toss out!

1 head lettuce
½ cup sliced green onions
¼ cup water
¼ cup vinegar
1 tablespoon sugar
Salt and pepper to taste
3 hard-cooked eggs, sliced
6 to 8 slices of cooked bacon, drained and crumbled (reserve pan drippings)

Wash and tear lettuce. Toss with green onions. Whisk together water, vinegar, and sugar. Add to reserved bacon drippings and season with salt and pepper. Bring to rolling boil and remove from heat to rest. Before serving, top salad with slices of hard-boiled eggs and pour hot dressing directly across the top. Finish by sprinkling with crumbled bacon.

Chicken Fettuccine Pasta Salad

(SERVES 6–8)

I once read a scathing review of a Southern cookbook. In it, the critic observed that nearly all of the salads had mayonnaise in them. I still don't know what point he was trying to make. My Chicken Fettuccine Pasta Salad uses mayonnaise and uses it well, I might add.

4 boneless skinless chicken breast halves

salt, pepper, and garlic powder, to taste

3 tablespoons olive oil

1 (12 oz.) package of fettuccine

2 cups mayonnaise (not low-fat, or low anything else)

½ cup chopped green onion tops, plus 1 tablespoon for garnish

¼ cup chopped fresh parsley

¼ cup chopped fresh basil

Cajun seasoning blend

Preheat oven to 350 degrees. Slice chicken breasts lengthwise into 1-inch strips. Place on shallow baking sheet and season well with salt, pepper, and garlic powder. Drizzle with olive oil and bake for about twenty minutes. Don't overcook. You want 'em good and juicy! Remove and set aside to rest. Cook fettuccine according to package directions, rinse in cold water, and allow to drain.

Prepare dressing by combining any chicken drippings with mayonnaise, ½ cup green onion tops, parsley, and basil. Season dressing to taste with your favorite seasoning blend, garlic, and pepper. Toss the fettuccine lightly with the dressing and put it in a pretty serving dish. Layer the chicken strips over the fettuccine and finish by sprinkling with remaining green onions.

Spinach and Strawberry Salad

(SERVES 6)

This is one of those tried-and-true recipes I reach for when our delicious Louisiana strawberries start coming in. (Combined with Louisiana pecans, it can't be beat.) My Spinach and Strawberry Salad is nutritious and delicious and packed with enough of the good stuff to meet Popeye's high standards. Your family will ask for it again and again.

Salad:

    2 bunches of spinach, torn in bite-size pieces

    4 cups fresh strawberries, cleaned and sliced

    1 cup pecan halves

Dressing:

    ½ cup olive oil

    ¼ cup white wine vinegar

    ½ cup white sugar

    ¼ cup paprika

    ¼ teaspoon Worcestershire sauce

    1 tablespoon minced onion

    2 tablespoons sesame seeds

    1 tablespoon poppy seeds

Combine washed and prepared spinach with strawberries and pecan halves. Prepare dressing by whisking together olive oil and white wine vinegar. Stir in sugar, paprika, Worcestershire sauce, minced onion, sesame seeds, and poppy seeds. Drizzle salad with dressing and chill before serving.

Shrimp and Black Olive Salad

(SERVES 6–8)

It's hard to beat the combined flavor of shrimp and black olives! This is not your everyday salad by anyone's definition. You'll enjoy its crunchy texture and taste bud–tickling surprises.

1 (16 oz.) box macaroni shells

1 cup mayonnaise

1 tablespoon prepared mustard

1 tablespoon olive oil

3 pounds medium shrimp, cooked, peeled, and chilled

1 (6 oz.) jar pimientos

1 (3 oz.) can chopped black olives

3–5 green onions, chopped

5 hard-boiled eggs, peeled and chopped

3 medium dill pickles, diced

1 teaspoon garlic salt

Salt and pepper to taste

Cook macaroni according to package directions, drain, and set aside to cool. Combine mayonnaise, mustard, and olive oil in a serving bowl. Fold in chilled shrimp and macaroni. Add pimientos, black olives, green onions, hard-boiled eggs, and dill pickles! Toss well and season with garlic salt, salt, and pepper. Refrigerate until time to serve. (You may even consider hiding a generous helping in the back of the fridge—it's that good!)

2

The Science of Bubba Whispering

~

How to Train a Bubba with Main Dish
Recipes He'll Sit Up and Beg For

Let me begin by saying that if you're expecting a male-bashing chapter here, you're in for a surprise! I hope to cover a number of helpful topics, not the least of which is the age-old dance between the sexes, but I do not have an ax to grind with the male gender. Au contraire, dear reader! I like men, in general, and my man in particular. There happen to be a lot of men in my trusted circle of family and friends, and I treasure them all, which is not only an enthusiasm I share with my fellow belles, but a most convenient way to get back on point.

The truth is we Southern women celebrate men. We enjoy the fact that women and men are different! As The Belle of All Things Southern, I have personally spent a great deal of time documenting these gender markers for the greater good of our relationships. In my previous book, *Suck Your Stomach In and*

Put Some Color On!, I presented an entire body of work I had done on MSS. In the event that you aren't familiar with my efforts, MSS stands for Male Speaker Syndrome, a condition I identified that causes our men to sweat while ordering at drive-in windows.

I'm not saying I've solved the problem, but I did open up some serious dialogue! For all those frustrated females struggling to reach over the console and holler into the sound system because Daddy is sweating over the burger order, just knowing they aren't alone seems to be promoting a certain level of healing and understanding.

This modest success has encouraged me to delve deeper into the mysteries of our beloved bubbas. For instance, why do our men enjoy falling asleep in their recliners when they know how hard it will be to wake up and go to bed?

I thought this was a family thing, a father-son tradition, but after thorough research (meaning I asked those same girlfriends), I realized the problem is much more widespread. (For the record, my beloved husband would like me to discuss my own sleeping sickness here—my inability to stay awake in a moving vehicle—but clearly we can only address one serious issue at a time, and it's so much more fun to study theirs, isn't it?)

I've spent several decades now trying to get Phil not to fall asleep in the living room. When we were younger, I'd get so irritated when I couldn't wake him up that I'd turn off the lights in a huff and leave him there. I don't do that anymore. We're older now and it takes too much energy to fight. Now we laugh at our differences—and I take notes for my work here at *All Things Southern*. Just the other evening I recorded one of his comments for inclusion in this new study of what I'm calling RMS, Reclining Male Syndrome.

He was busy taking his *CSI* nap when I nudged him in the side. "Phil," I said, shaking him awake. "Why are you going to sleep in the living room?"

"Because, Shellie," my husband replied, with a this-is-so-simple-I-don't-know-why-you-don't-get-it attitude, "it's too early to go to bed!"

We've Got Ourselves a Random Mutation Problem

Indeed, we belles don't always understand our men, and vice versa, but let it be known that we are very much interested in seeing the distinctions between the two sexes survive! That's why yours truly was ready to sound the alarm recently when I heard about a most distressing study released by some genetics expert who was contending that men, as a whole, are on the road to extinction. According to this so-called authority in the field, the Y chromosome is shrinking and slowly fading away. This news came to me via a phone call from my good friend Paulette.

"I read it on the Internet," Paulette said, in that authoritative voice she uses when I question her source, "and the first person I thought about was that dadblame Georgia Hawthorne. I bet my bottom dollar that man-eater has something to do with it."

"Slow down, Sista Sherlock," I told Paulette. "I think you give Georgia's charms too much credit. There's got to be more to this story." And indeed, before the single ladies in the reading group fan out into a massive man hunt to be fruitful and multiply as the Good Book says, let me hasten to add that I read the article in question and the lady doc did say it may take another five million years for the process to be complete. I think it's fairly safe for us all to take a moment and collect ourselves.

As a matter of fact, in the way that only the Internet can, that article led me to another article which led me to another article where I discovered an opposing and somewhat irate male expert who vehemently disagreed with his female colleague's assertion that the Y chromosome is in any danger at all. (I'm not suggesting that there is any connection whatsoever between the two doctors' genders and the positions they're taking on this issue. I'm sure it's nothing more than a coincidence.) I would cite that source for y'all, what with this being an important how-to and advice book, only I didn't bookmark it—which means I'd have about as much luck finding that article again as Ralph Nader would have trying to win a presidential primary, bless his optimistic heart. The important thing is that Doctor Number Two is offering a completely different take on the future of the male species.

Mr. Genetic Expert admits that while the male chromosome has been under attack in the past millennia from "random mutations" (why am I picturing Mel Gibson in *Braveheart*?) the news is not all bad. He contends that his studies prove the Y chromosome has been secretly creating backup copies of its most important genes. Interesting . . . So the little Y guys have been busy storing mirror images of what they consider to be their best stuff?! If he's right, this could explain a lot. Some of my theories of what special abilities the Y men deemed worthy of securing will henceforth go unnoted here in the interest of what is and what isn't an appropriate topic for public conversation. However, I will say that if there was ever a gene marked "context clues," there is good reason to suspect that it never got write protected.

"What You Say Can and Will Be Held Against You"

Context clues are words or phrases that can help the listener decode the meaning of a given word that the listener does not know or did not hear. Let me spell out a conclusion born of personal experience and countless exhaustive reports from the belles in my case studies: *Bubbas don't do context clues.*

There is little evidence to suggest that bubbas are more limited in their vocabulary than their female counterparts, so their not recognizing the missing word doesn't seem to be at the root of the problem. Personally, I believe the fault lies more with their hearing, and yet even this theory is fraught with inconclusive data. For instance, do they not hear well because of all the work they do around heavy equipment (while this would explain the behavior of bubbas in the agricultural field, it wouldn't explain the hearing-impaired office bubba), or is it because hearing = effort and our bubbas don't see the need to exercise that sort of supreme exertion when they can just ask their sweethearts to repeat themselves? Ding, ding, ding—we may have a winner!

I'm not saying I have it all figured out, but I do have a theory. I don't think it's so much that they don't want to hear us the first time as it is that they aren't *ready* to hear us. I know this because my own sweet man will often say "What?" before I get halfway into my question or statement—and I've documented similar behavior in other bubbas. I know this is going to sound strange, but for some reason our men need a head start to hear, you know, kind of like advance warning that communication is about to begin. This is why it often helps to get your man's attention *before* you start talking. Many belles have reported success in training their bubbas to focus quicker by opening their remarks with words that are completely unrelated to the desired topic, like "hunting club" or "play-offs."

Now, to be fair to both sexes, I'm willing to admit that my fellow belles and I must share responsibility for the communication challenges that exist between the genders. Sometimes, ladies, we can be a bit, well, touchy.

One Saturday evening my friends Julia and Larry Sr. were watching TV when their son, Larry Jr., came in from his date much earlier than his curfew. He plopped his long-legged self down on the couch and slid as far down into the cushions as possible.

"Hey, handsome," Julia said. "You're in early tonight. Everything all right?"

"No," came her baby boy's response.

Julia elbowed her husband and gave him a you-try look.

"Where's Christy?" Larry Sr. asked.

"Her house," his son replied.

Well, they had doubled the word count, but they hadn't acquired a lot more information.

"Come, on, honey," Julia said. "What happened? Did y'all get in a fight?"

That seemed to hit a nerve! Larry Jr. started spilling his guts.

"I reckon so, Mama," he began. "I still don't know what happened. I thought we were having a good time. We were at the Sonic getting an ice cream and she asked me if I could explain love. I told her I couldn't, but she kept begging me to try, and so, I did."

Larry Sr. started laughing. Julia glared at him and turned back to her son.

"What'd you say then?" she prompted.

Larry Jr. continued his story, "Well, I started out by saying that suppose a boy is sitting there and a pretty girl walks by—but that's all I got out before she said, 'Why does she have to be so pretty? Why can't she be an average-looking girl with freckles, huh? Tell me, Larry! Why can't a boy love an average girl with freckles?'"

Big Larry laughed harder. Julia punched him. "Go on, sweetie," she said, encouragingly.

"So," Larry Jr. says, "that's when I said, 'Well, I guess he could.' And I tried again. I said, 'Suppose the guy's sitting there when an average-looking girl with a big nose and freckles walks by—' and boy, Mama, that's when she really blew up! Said she never said the girl had a big nose! And then she made me take her home and she wouldn't talk to me all the way there."

It was all Julia could do not to laugh. Big Larry, on the other hand, didn't even try to hide his amusement. "Son," he said, as soon as he could control himself. "I'm sorry, but you just learned a very important lesson the hard way. Heck, we men can't even talk about love without getting in trouble, much less explain it!"

I grew up with a girl named Ashley Jean Jackson, folks called her Sissy. Some called her a tomboy, too. She was the youngest in the family with five older brothers. That's where she got her learning. She could shoot, wrestle, chew, cuss and fight just like the boys. Of course, she stood way out with the combat boots she always wore. One day a new boy from the city moved to town, driving a fancy looking car that impressed everyone. We sort of hooked him up with Sissy for fun. I guess the joke was on us though because they fell in love and got married! Isn't it something how love happens like that?

~Gary Millwood
Missouri

Mustard Yellow Spells Barbecue

If we're honest, we will admit that there's a bit of truth to Larry's observation. But let's advance the ball in this discussion, shall we? Another of my gender's charming little quirks that might have the potential to complicate communication with our men would be our tendency to go on a wee bit long, and by that I mean we've been known to grab a subject by the neck and wring it like a chicken before we let it go. Please take that in the spirit in which it is intended. I'm just trying to contribute to the greater good here.

Through hard earned experience, I've learned that it is completely unrealistic to expect your man to hang in for a detailed discussion on the advantages and disadvantages of matchstick blinds vs. roman shades in the family room and whether or not you should paint the kitchen buttercup yellow or mustard yellow. (Note: The slight variation in hue may be vitally important to you, but as soon as mustard yellow is brought up, your bubba will be ready to grill out and you'll have no one to blame but yourself.) Communication between you and your man will be greatly improved by remembering that bubbas aren't big on lengthy discussions, and

While reading your first book I felt as though my Southern gramma was sitting next to me, imparting her wisdom on the finer points of being a good Southern belle. Here's the advice I got on training your man: "The man may be the head of the family, but the woman is the neck. A wise woman turns him in the right direction and he happily complies, thinking it was his idea. But never, never ever, nag! When a man hears a woman nag, he will usually do just the opposite of what he's being told just to prove she ain't the boss of him!"

~LaDonna "Nicki" Sanchez
Woodway, Texas

might I add that this is true regardless of who's in charge of the dissertation.

I'm reminded of a family story harking back many years ago to a Sunday morning service being held at Riverside Baptist Church in Natchez, Mississippi. The preacher, my Papaw, Brother Marvin Stone, had worked up a bona-fide sweat in the pulpit that morning. He'd been going at it hard and heavy, I mean he was really shucking down the corn, when he took a moment's pause to wet his whistle from the ever present water glass setting at his right hand. That's when he heard it! Someone was snoring. It only took Papaw a minute to locate the source. One of his fine upstanding young sons-in-law was catching some winks in the middle of his sermon.

Unfortunately for Uncle Stan, Papaw was almost as much comedian as he was preacher. Inspiration hit him quickly. Papaw put a mischievous finger up to his lips to signal the congregation to be quiet. Then he slipped down from the pulpit and crept over to his unsuspecting son-in-law. Uncle Stan was just about to get another log sawn in two when Papaw dipped his fingers in the glass and flicked a little water in Uncle Stan's face. Uncle Stan shook his head and repositioned. A low giggle went across the congregation, which only encouraged Papaw. He flicked again. This time the church folk lost it and Uncle Stan woke up to the sound of hearty laughter.

To be sure, Uncle Stan was a good sport about the whole thing. Later, after church, when everyone was ribbing him pretty good, he told his side of the story. "It's like this," Uncle Stan said, "I know y'all have heard that it's not polite to fall asleep when your wife is talking, haven't you? Well, for goodness' sakes, people, a man has to sleep sometime."

How to Choose and Train a Bubba

But I have seriously digressed this time, haven't I? Before we got sidetracked balancing our bubbas' context clue challenges with our tendency toward information overload, we were talking about those two doctors and their different takes on the future of the male gender.

To be honest, I'm not all that concerned about the likelihood of us ladies outlasting the male sex, but many of my single girlfriends insist there is already something of a man shortage. I don't know about that, but then, I have my own sweet man and haven't been doing any serious looking. However, if you ask me, I think it's less a question of quantity and more about quality. My mama always used to say a good man is hard to find. Sugar, ain't that the truth! And this, dear readers, is what concerns the good Southern women I know.

So before we get into the science of understanding and training your man, I feel a certain responsibility to address the careful selection that should go into choosing a bubba of your very own, as rushing through this critical process can be disastrous for all involved. I do ask that you bear in mind that what one belle sees as a negative quality may be exactly what another belle is searching for, and vice versa. The trick is in understanding one's own expectations. That being said, here are some helpful tips on identifying the various breeds of bubbas available on the market today. Most bubbas fall into one of three main categories: **Stray Bubbas**, **House Bubbas**, and **Yard Bubbas**. For our purposes, we'll need to take them one at a time.

Stray Bubbas: These bubbas are easily identified by their friendly personalities. Stray Bubbas are freewheeling, fun—and hard to offend. You can rant and rave at a Stray Bubba and he'll simply distance himself and return once you're out of ammunition. However, if you're looking for a long-term relationship, this may not be the bubba for you. Try as they might to change, in the end, you should know Stray Bubbas love the open road. It's the call of the wild and it's quite strong. As a matter of fact, country music exists in large part to chronicle the stories of Stray Bubbas and the broken hearts often left in their wake. That's not to say that Stray Bubbas can't be trained, but it does take a woman of incredible patience, like the legendary Lou Anne.

To recount Lou Anne's story will necessitate a short explanation and a couple of introductions. While "bubba" can be a generic term used to describe the Southern man in general, it is just as often the given name of an individual male. Almost every Southern community has at least one man that everyone knows simply as Bubba. Ours is no exception. The stories of our Bubba and his best friend, Buford, reach the *All Things Southern* porch on a regular basis.

Buford and Bubba have been thicker than thieves since grade school. They made a pact way back in junior high that they would never get married, and they stuck to it. For years, those two were content with working, hunting, and riding around the town square like teenagers. Girls came and girls went until that fateful night. Cue the music. That would be Lou Anne, stage right, running just fast enough to get caught. She and Buford have now been dating exclusively for about five years. It didn't take Lou Anne any time at all to decide that Buford was the

> Whenever I was upset over unrequited love, my mother would tell me what her mother told her: "We don't want anybody that doesn't want us."
>
> ~Janie Elizabeth Horne
> Bossier City, Louisiana

one for her. She's been turning up the heat ever since. Buford, as you can imagine, has been a tad slower coming around.

I can't count the number of times I've heard Lou Ann say she'd better have an engagement ring on her finger by the time she turns thirty-five or it's over. Although some of us think thirty-five has come and gone a couple times, when she gets worked up and repeats that ultimatum, to our credit we just let it go.

Well, bless her heart, it took a while, but Lou Anne's persistence has paid off. Buford has finally asked her to marry him. One of the town's oldest never-in-a-million-years-will-I-get-hitched Stray Bubbas is headed down the aisle—sooner or later. It should be noted that the date has yet to be announced. (Right now Lou Anne's trying to keep the boy's cold feet from turning into a block of solid ice.)

Rumor is that the couple's big news can be directly traced to Buford's good corn crop. Lou Anne had gone out to ride the combine with Buford that magical day. Harvest was going really well for Buford, and Lou Anne's man was in high spirits. Lou Anne said they were just finishing unloading into one of the grain carts when Buford suddenly turned to her and said, "Lou Anne, let's do it! Let's get married!"

"Oh, Buford—" Lou Anne said. "Yes! Yes!" The grain cart pulled off and they started back down the field. Lou Anne was talking a mile a minute, already planning when, where, how, and what (she knew why), when she realized Buford had grown quiet, very quiet. "Sugar Plum," she said, "aren't you gonna say anything else?"

Buford shook his head. "Naw, Sweetie," he said in a low voice. "I'm kinda thinking I've said too much as it is."

Again, this story illustrates that even though Stray Bubbas can be domesticated, their impulsive tendencies should never be underestimated. When considering something more permanent, many belles opt for a House Bubba.

House Bubbas: These bubbas are equally friendly but far less likely to roam. A House Bubba is a great choice for the belle seeking companionship, but be warned: House Bubbas like to be with their belles 24/7. This works for some couples, but it can be a challenge for others. If a belle is afraid she may find a high level of camaraderie stifling, a Yard Bubba may be just what she's looking for.

Yard Bubbas: Please don't let the common-sounding name mislead you. A Yard Bubba is a quality choice for any belle! Yard Bubbas clean up well and are equally comfortable in and outside of the home. Far from needy, this charming bubba is capable of staying busy with his own interests while exhibiting unwavering loyalty to his sweetheart. He's protective, loving, and dependable. When fully grown, Yard Bubbas are often referred to as Family Bubbas and only increase in value with age. If you find a Yard Bubba, move quickly, Sugar. They don't stay on the market long.

Early Training and the Need for Consistency

Early education is critical when it comes to your bubba's training. To reiterate, you can not begin too soon. Actually, I recommended that you conduct a few tests with any potential bubba before taking any sort of legal ownership. One way to do this is to see how he responds to your people. If your bubba demonstrates curiously high levels of anxiety around them, there could be a problem with his breeding, or he could've been subjected to previous experiences that will make him hard, if not impossible, to train.

There are other pre-ownership tests, but for brevity's sake, let's say you've chosen your bubba, filled out all the necessary papers, and brought him home. From this point on, you must be consistent with your training. Inconsistency is unfair and confusing to your bubba. He needs to know you're a woman of your word.

By way of illustration, once during the early years of their marriage, Aunt Marleta and Uncle Stan were in a huge fight when he announced that he was leaving.

"Don't do it!" Aunt Leta said. "If you walk out that door, I'm not letting you back in."

Uncle Stan left anyway and in such a hurry that he crashed his pickup between two trees a little piece down the road. Limping, bruised, and bleeding, Uncle Stan made his way back home to the wrong side of a chained door.

"Let me in, Leta," Uncle Stan said, "I'm bleeding."

"That's not my fault," Aunt Marleta said. "I told you what'd happen if you left!"

Aunt Marleta left her bubba outside bleeding for the better part of the night, too, and as she likes to tell it, "Once I opened that door, Shellie, he never left me again."

I realize that story may sound harsh in some circles, but you can't mess with those kinds of results, girls, and it does underscore the truth: Consistency in communication with your bubba will pay great dividends, as will clarity. My fellow belles, it is crucial that we take responsibility for our own shortcomings in this area. Many problems arise because our men, bless their hearts, don't always know where the land mines are.

My kids have both been happily married for several years now, but all four of these young married people will admit that there has been a rather steep learning curve in communication. I remember the day shortly into her marriage when my daughter, Jessica Ann, called home with her lip run out. Her sweet husband had come home from work raving about some brownies his female coworker had brought to the office. Being the observant male that he is, Patrick missed the sudden temperature drop in his home. Nor did he realize it was falling by degrees in direct proportion to the extravagant compliments he was heaping on this other girl's brownies. Ice was forming on the dog bowl before he finally clued in and asked his bride what was wrong. Being female, Jessica needed to be sure he really wanted to know, which is why on the eighty-seventh time he asked she thawed enough to answer.

"What'd you say?" I asked.

"Exactly what you think," Jessica replied. "I told him throwing another woman's brownies in my face was like cheating on me!"

My son had a similar conversation with his wife, Carey, around that time. It was as puzzling to Phillip as it was to Patrick. Neither of them knew where they had gone wrong. This is where clear communication is necessary. Your bubba needs to understand that getting to a man's heart through his stomach is more than a saying to Southern women; it's the gospel we cut our teeth on. If we aren't feeding our man, we're gonna be suspicious of anyone who is. It's in our DNA.* Most of us have seen our mamas scan our daddies' plates at many a church potluck and note with only a hint of accusation, "So, you didn't get any of my potato casserole?!"

Yes, we belles may be a tad sensitive here, but this charming quirk can also partially explain

Official Guide to Speaking All Things Southern

*DNA, noun: duly noted abnormalities that tie a Southerner to his or her tribe

the popularity of Paula Deen, that queen of Southern cooking. We see in the delightful Ms. Deen a healthy married woman who loves her sons. That adorable little Rachael Ray and that curvy little Italian chick—well, they can't carry her cookbooks. I'm just saying.

Direct dialogue with your man will not only help him avoid the type of culinary catastrophe noted here, it will also help you and your man in navigating other male/female land mines. Take shopping, another legendary area of difficulty in the training of your bubba. Without setting unrealistic expectations, it's important for us belles to guide our men through what they often consider to be hostile territory. Take the cute young couple I observed shopping for a gift for their friend. I didn't get much background information, but I gathered they'd been shopping a lot longer than Mr. Shopper had bargained for, or was conditioned to endure—say, at least five minutes.

I watched as Mr. Shopper paced in circles and checked his watch while his sweetie chatted on her cell phone and conducted a simultaneous examination of every article of clothing in the ladies' section. I wasn't the least bit surprised when he reached his limit.

"How about this?" Mr. Shopper asked, holding up a random blouse.

Mrs. Shopper finished her call before giving her man her full attention. "That's ugly," she said.

"Okay," Mr. Shopper said, holding up another shirt. "What's wrong with this one?"

Mrs. Shopper rolled her eyes. "Look at it, Honey. It's way too small."

Desperate Mr. Shopper turned to another aisle, inadvertently crossing into the maternity section before picking up another selection. "This'un's good and roomy," he said.

Mrs. Shopper glanced up. "Yes, but it's a maternity blouse."

"So?" Mr. Shopper asked innocently.

"Duh," Mrs. Shopper said, rolling her eyes, "she's not pregnant."

"No, duh," Mr. Shopper said, getting pretty fed up himself, "but she's big! And it'll fit!"

Mrs. Shopper propped her hands on her young hips and glared at her sweetie. "You do not give a maternity outfit to someone who isn't pregnant!" she practically growled. Then she gave a big huffy breath and dismissed Mr. Shopper to the food court, with this zinger: "Please. Y'all should have to take classes."

I was tempted to laugh out loud, but then I remembered my dog wasn't in it. Besides, I'd never advocate classes for our men.

My husband once gave me a $15 Chili's gift card and a seriously humongous flannel nightgown for Valentine's Day! Yes, I was expecting triplets, but I wasn't anywhere close to being super humongous—yet. He actually thought I might want to buy myself some take-out chips and salsa and had no clue why I burst into tears upon receiving the "You're-a-real-fatty-so-I-bought-you-a-fatty-nightgown-and-a-gift-card-to-Chilis-so-you-can-get-even-FATTER" gift. I locked my blubbering self in the bathroom, and when I finally came out, I called Mama to tell her that my husband didn't love me anymore. (She was probably laughing, but she calmed me down).

~Leslie Moore
Tyler, Texas

They wouldn't show up. It's far better for us to understand that our men see things differently. FYI, I'm preaching to myself on this one. For illustration (and your enjoyment) I offer you the following story at my own expense, in which one of my dearly beloved bubba friends offered me yet another opportunity to practice the generosity of spirit I recommend when it comes to making rash judgments as to our men's intentions.

Help Me Make It Through the Night

I was feeling particularly perky that fine summer morning. Not only had I "made it through the night," but the scales showed that I had come through a wee bit lighter. That's always a delightful surprise, isn't it? In the event that you aren't from around here, I should explain that making it through the night is a Southern phrase.

I was just a little thing the first time I noticed that there was more to this daylight deadline than met the eye. Where I come from, making it through the night was obviously much more than a barometer of health. It was also used to assess a family member's concern, or lack thereof, as in "Why, she hasn't even called to see if I made it through the night." Oftentimes I watched people shake their head sadly and shrug their shoulders as if little could be done for someone who didn't care whether or not their own family member made it through the night. As far as I could tell, Southern people were much more likely to pass on during the night, because it wasn't nearly as necessary to make sure people made it through the day.

Forgive me if I should sound flippant about surviving till dawn, but just thinking about that morning requires a bit of an attitude adjustment on my part. See, I had been gunning for a level of fitness slightly more ambitious than making it through the night. I hadn't been forcing myself to walk three brisk miles a day and willing myself to push away from the table just to shoot for a discernible pulse rate, but, alas, it would seem my exercise program had fallen shorter than I had realized. And, for the record, those firearm metaphors are purely coincidence. They have nothing to do with that morning's realization that I needed to ramp up the exercise program. Nor are they directed at the person who helped me see the light. That would be my dear friend's husband and one of my best bubba buddies who, upon seeing me cross the parking lot, hugged me tight and commented on how nice it was to see his "beautiful full-figured friend." Full-figured friend . . . God love him, the thing is I know he meant it as a compliment.

That's what his friend and my husband told me. "Calm down, Shellie, you know that's not what he meant. It just came out wrong." I'm sure Phil's right, but all the same, I decided to leave it up to him to see if his buddy made it through the night. However, in the spirit of forgiveness and fostering healthier relationships, I will be happy to offer y'all a free Man Tip that came to me around this same time.

Men, let's say your woman is growing upset for reasons you may or may not have caused, and you'd like to de-escalate things because if Mama ain't happy, ain't nobody happy. Whatever you do, please don't fall back on that standard male response: "Calm down." Telling a smoldering belle to calm down is like wearing a good fake fur to a PETA convention. You may be entirely innocent, but you're still gonna pay for it.

A Word of Caution

We are almost ready to begin our work in earnest by looking at the field of Bubba Whispering, an applied science whereby a belle uses proven training methods to overcome the communication barriers between the sexes and achieve the desired behavior in her beloved bubba, but first, a word of caution.

Not long ago I received a letter from a bride who was new to our Southern region. Eva wrote, "Dear Shellie, I knew Southern men were fond of their trucks, but my husband's gone crazy. First he insisted on buying a four-wheel-drive truck and we live in the city. He washes it constantly. Now he wants me to park on the street so he can park in the garage. For the record, I drive a fairly new car. Is there anything I can say to get through to him?"

I told Eva that I seriously doubted it. See, part of bubba training is knowing when to pick your battles, and girls—this is not the one you want. When it comes to bubbas and their trucks, your best bet is to lower your window, crank up the radio, and go with the flow.

I'm reminded of the day my friend Paulette asked to borrow her husband's new truck to run an errand. Her man reluctantly agreed but not until he had put her through a ritual as serious as their wedding vows.

Shellie, why do you girls (my wife included) have to slam the door of a brand-new truck so hard? Truck doors close just like car doors. Please tell the girls to quit it. In grateful appreciation . . .

~Steve Nelson
Jonesboro, Louisiana

"Do you promise to park at the end of the parking lot so no one will ding the door?"

"I do."

"Do you promise not to ride the brakes?"

"I do."

When she was finally allowed behind the wheel, Paulette found Jerry Don tapping on the window. When she lowered it, he said, "Use the back roads. They're working on the highway and I don't want to pick up any tar."

"Honestly," Paulette huffed. "I'd rather not take this thing if it's gonna make you so crazy."

"Me?" he asked, innocently. "I'm fine. Go on."

She'd barely begun backing up when Jerry Don put his hand up. Paulette cracked the window, again. "What now?"

"Just remember," her bubba said with a big grin. "If you have an accident, the newspaper will print your age."

When it comes to their trucks, ladies, our bubbas' skills should not be underestimated.

The Science of Bubba Whispering

It should be noted that not all belles will become successful Bubba Whisperers. However, most successful Bubba Whisperers are belles. This can be attributed to ancient secrets carefully handed down through generations of Bubba Whisperers.

Southern Mamas begin teaching their daughters the finer points of whispering early on, beginning with this foundational teaching from The Official Belle Doctrine: *A belle must control her own behavior before she ever attempts to train a bubba.* It's a critical part of the educational process and why Southern Mamas say things like "If you want that boy to act like a gentleman, you need to act like a lady." And that includes dressing the part (if it's not on the market, don't advertise it). And by the way, no one interprets the message of a girl's dress-code message any more accurately than other belles. Even the youngest bellerinas can be quite the savvy little observers.

We have a young belle around here on the *All Things Southern* porch that we've watched grow up now for the past seven or eight years. She's become something of a mascot, and her appeal is mostly rooted in her tell-it-like-it-is observations. Savannah Grace minces no words.

The story I have in mind happened one evening a couple summers ago now, when everyone's favorite little Southern belle turned twelve. Her older brother, Larry (he of the earlier "attempting to explain love" story) was fifteen. They were fighting like cats and dogs and their poor mama was worn slap out* from refereeing. That evening Julia was cooking a special supper for Larry's new sweetheart. This girlfriend thing was a pretty big milestone for Julia, but she was handling it well. Neither set of parents were actually letting the kids date, but the two lovebirds were allowed to spend time at each other's house, under supervision.

Savannah Grace had made it abundantly clear that she didn't think much of the older girl. As I remember it, she told her mama that "Missy wears her shirts too tight and her skirts too short—and she shows too much of her belly." Savannah, much to her mother's delight, is growing up into quite the conservative young lady. Her mama thinks she is also a might possessive over her brother, however much they may battle. Julia says she doesn't think that in Savannah's eyes any girl would be good enough to date her older brother. Naturally, Savannah Grace strongly denies any such thing.

Savannah was setting the table for her mama that evening when Larry waltzed into the kitchen smelling like he broke a bottle of his daddy's cologne.

"Sure smells good in here, Mama!" Larry said as he got the dill pickles out of the refrigerator and helped himself to a big one with his fingers.

Savannah rolled her eyes as if he was the most disgusting creature she'd ever seen. Julia didn't like it, either.

"Larry Allen!" she said, sternly. "If I catch you with your hand in that pickle jar one more time, I'm gonna slap you nekkid and hide your clothes."

Just then the doorbell rang and both kids ran to get it. A minute later Savannah came back to the kitchen, alone. "It's Larry's new girlfriend," she announced, sarcastically. "And it looks like somebody caught her in the pickles . . ."

Developing an Effective Bubba Command

For our purposes, we will suppose that you have already disciplined yourself and you are now endeavoring to train your bubba. Dear ones, Bubba Whispering shouldn't be undertaken lightly. It's a delicate science. Novices or poorly trained whisperers often cause more problems than they solve. Case in point: multiple whispering. If a bubba is listening to his dear Mama and his Sweet Thang whisper conflicting instructions at the same time, he will become increasingly anxious and confused. This is unfair to the bubba. There must be a dominant whisperer, and if vows have been exchanged, this should be his spouse.

A belle's effectiveness as a Bubba Whisperer can often be gauged by the strength of her Bubba Command, a signal heard on a unique frequency recognized only by her bubba. If she can give him a signal in public, without

When a young college boy from the city came to town to be the music director at our local church, we immediately struck up a friendship. Since I was the farmer's daughter, it was my responsibility to teach him the ways of the country life. Everyone needs to know about "tromping" cotton! So, one wonderful fall evening we were having a lesson in cotton tromping when we fell back into the soft cotton and he proposed! We've been happily married for 35 years.

~Donna Goodman
Delhi, Louisiana

disrespecting him, and with no one else being the wiser, she is well on her way to becoming a good whisperer. Sadly, however, we've all seen this test fail. When a belle gives a Bubba Command in a crowd and her bubba says something like "Why are you looking at me like that?" you can bet your sweet baboo their progress has just taken a major hit.

While this type of embarrassing incident can happen and often does happen to many potentially skillful Bubba Whisperers, it need not spell the end to your man's training. Consider it an opportunity to discuss with your bubba the importance of not opening issues in public that should be handled in private. Be warned: Sometimes your bubba will need a remedial lesson with this one. I well remember the last time Paulette's Bubba Command was tested.

It so happens that it occurred in April, which for the uninformed, is officially Southern Belle Month, a time to appreciate the Southern belle! (And no, I didn't make that holiday up, but I do milk it for all it's worth.) Not surprisingly it was also, cross-my-heart-hope-to-die-stick-a-needle-in-my-eye-saw-it-on-the-World-Wide-Web, Informed Women Month. This cannot be a coincidence! Like Paulette likes to say, "We know things." To wit, Paulette referenced an article she emailed me recently about some research coming out of a university in California.

"Remember, Shellie, they were plum proud of themselves for discovering that when it comes to judging beauty, men only use part of their brain while women use their whole brain!" I remembered. Apparently, they had found it surprising that men judge beauty spatially (meaning they see objects), while women access the objects along with verbal cues. Paulette and I feel we could've saved 'em those educational expenditures.

"Why," Paulette said, "I could even give 'em an object lesson! Last week Jerry Don and I were at the mall picking out a birthday present for his mama when this shapely young sales-girl tried to help us in the lingerie department. I thought Jerry Don's eyes were gonna fall out of his head." I gave him a look Stevie Wonder would've been able to see. That man not only kept staring at what he shouldn't have been staring at, but he actually had the nerve to ask me—out loud—what the prob-lem was! Don't you worry, though, I fixed his little red wagon."

I was almost afraid to ask, but I did. "How's that?"

"On the way home I said real casual like, 'That salesgirl sure was pretty, and nice, too.' Jerry Don just stared at me like a deer caught in the headlights."

"Smart man," I said.

"Not so much," Paulette said. "I went on to say that I couldn't understand anything she said what with that heavy accent of hers. And do you know what my man said? He said, 'She had an accent?'"

I tried not to laugh. "Go, ahead," Paulette said, "laugh. I know you want to. Just make sure you tell your readers that it took a bit of time, but once I got through with him, that man's been real busy appreciating this belle and he didn't need a spe-cial holiday to do it."

Exactly what Paulette did that was so effective, why that, gentle reader, is an area of Bubba Whispering that is highly personal and of a much too private nature for me to print. I'll merely say that it's a time-tested tactic that is by no means unique to our region. Here are a few ladylike hints from across the globe: "no mas," "nein," "nyet," and "nea." If you still aren't there, think along the lines of drought and deprivation. It'll come to you.

While a belle can achieve a strong Bubba Command if she is persistent, caution should be taken to keep in mind that the signal is not transferable. Bubbas will rarely respond to commands from anyone other than their own belle. Case in point: A couple Christmases ago, my son and his wife rode with my man and me to visit my daughter and her husband in Texas. Together, we all set out to enjoy a much anticipated holiday meal. We make it a point not to go to Houston without eating at this restaurant. We'd been looking forward to it all day.

That evening we were seated next to a couple men and their elementary-age children. The kids were fine. I can't say the same for Amplified Man, who talked loudly and continually. By continually I mean without breathing. By loudly I mean we were treated to every aspect of his life. It was our own TMI episode: Too Much Information.

Among other details, we were treated to updates on his extended family. We learned he was a high school jock who blew his knee out before he could play college ball. We were treated to details of his latest promotion at work and we learned he volunteered for the Red Cross. Kudos on that last one, but still. We also learned his wife didn't feel like joining them for supper. We envied her.

Her absence explained a lot, however. For during the course of our tortured meal we tried to give the loud stranger polite signals. We began by glancing in his direction and smiling. Then we glanced his way without smiling. As our headaches intensified and his booming voice reverberated in the small room, we glanced his way and frowned. Amplified Man, his friend, and the male children present were totally oblivious. They needed a female. Had his wife been with him, she would've caught the first fleeting look. I do not know how she would have responded. She might have defended him. She might have smacked him (one can hope), but she would've surely caught our signals.

Instead we played our own version of Holiday Jeopardy. I'll

take family trivia for three appetizers, Alex. Amplified Man's favorite aunt. Who is Amber? You got it! And then, without warning, we beheld a Christmas miracle. His food arrived. Oh, Silent Night . . .

Advancing Your Bubba's Career

I'd like to conclude our bubba chapter with thoughts on advancing your man's career. Granted, in today's two-income families, a belle can find it daunting to keep her own head above the job waters, and manage the house and the kids, all while supporting her bubba's professional goals—but this is the type of loving effort that will eventually pay great dividends in your relationship. Don't be discouraged if this gratitude isn't immediately apparent. Unfortunately, you may not get the appreciation you are due right off, especially if you use novel methods, as did the belle in our following story.

This illustration is based on true life events somewhere in the South. Names have been changed to protect the not-so-innocent, for this is the story of a good church lady. We'll call her Glory Jean. Our tale begins with Glory Jean leaving Wal-Mart. She had just finished loading her purchases into her car and checking out all of her mirrors, when she promptly backed out and into a vehicle coming down the aisle. Oh, dear.

Glory Jean exited her vehicle to speak to the other driver and exchange the necessary information. And that's when it hit the fan! Before Glory Jean could say, "I'm sorry," the woman started swinging. She attacked Glory Jean like a crazed person, name calling, hair pulling—the whole nine yards. Well, now, there was nothing for our good church woman to do but defend herself.

Glory Jean loaded up a hard right, connected with her assailant's chin, and coldcocked her right there in the Wal-Mart parking lot. By the time the woman came to, the police had arrived. They threatened to handcuff both women and haul 'em to jail. Glory Jean's attacker, who happened to be driving without any identification, went mute. Glory Jean did not.

"Please," she begged the officers. "You can't do this. I'm Sergeant John's wife. He'll just die."

The officers quickly exchanged glances. Sergeant John, head of the Alcohol and Drug Task Force—that Sergeant John—was this really his wife? Could it be? A hasty phone call confirmed that yes, indeed, it was.

After some consultation between the two of 'em, the officers decided to allow Glory Jean to follow them to the police station, where one very irate Sergeant John met them at the door and began to read his Sweet Thang the riot act. What was she thinking, fistfighting at Wal-Mart?! He wasn't interested in Glory Jean's story. He didn't let her explain that the fight wasn't her fault and that she had witnesses. Oh, no, Glory Jean's vindication came much later—after her assailant's fingerprints came back—after they matched up with those of a woman on the Alcohol and Drug Force's Top Ten Most Wanted List. Yes, indeed! Glory Jean had inadvertently apprehended the drug dealer her husband had been trying to bust for months.

Dear reader, Glory Jean is still waiting for a thank-you from Sergeant John, but these days the Church Lady is singing a brand-new song, "Bad girls, bad girls, whatcha gonna do? Whatcha gonna do when I come for you . . ."

Bubba Training Tips

THUS SAITH THE BELLE DOCTRINE . . .

* Endeavor to give thy Bubba a heads-up when communication is about to begin by using highly charged men words to get his attention.

* To retain your Bubba's interest in the conversation at hand, thou shalt limit thy tendency toward information overload.

* Proper identification of Bubba breeds will greatly enhance thy chances of a satisfying relationship, as not all bubbas can be successfully domesticated.

* Unrealistic expectations concerning thy bubba's public behavior can best be avoided with direct dialogue.

* Bubba Whispering shouldn't be attempted without proper supervision from an expert in the field.

* While supporting thy bubba's professional goals may require a sacrificial effort, it will pay great dividends in thy relationship.

Main Dish Recipes to Make
Him Sit Up and Beg

Contrary to the stereotypical media image of toothless red-necks, all my family and friends have back teeth and we know how to use 'em. We belles cook for men who work long and hard, men who think a meal without meat is called a snack. And yes, we've heard the hysteria about cows ruining the planet, but we think it's not only a pretty serious charge, but also largely an unsubstantiated one, and repeating one side of the issue all day long with a serious expression and a knot between your eyes doesn't make it so. So if you're a conscientious carnivore looking for help in the care and feeding of your bubba, this chapter is for you. If you're hungry for tofu, Sweet Cheeks, you're flat out of luck. You might try Chapter Seven: "Rein It In, Geraldo: Regional Issues with Side Dishes and Vegetable Recipes to Iron Out Our Differences."

Maple Mustard Tenderloin

(SERVES 6–9)

To be fair to the cows, I've included a couple fish, a few chickens, and a pig or two among the offerings. This tasty pork tenderloin recipe uses Dijon mustard and maple syrup to make a tangy sauce. And serving it with fresh sliced apples just sends the flavor over the top.

> 4 Granny Smith apples, peeled and sliced thin
> 2–3 pound pork tenderloin
> 6 tablespoons maple syrup, divided
> 3 tablespoons Dijon mustard
> 1 teaspoon dried rosemary
> ½ teaspoon each of salt and black pepper
> Cooking spray

Preheat oven to 425 degrees. Slice and peel Granny Smith green apples and set aside. Trim fat from the pork tenderloin. Prepare the glaze by whisking two tablespoons maple syrup with mustard and seasoning it with dried rosemary, salt, and pepper. Place tenderloin on a broiler pan that's been coated with cooking spray and brush with glaze. Bake for twenty-five minutes, or until the meat registers 160 degrees on a meat thermometer. Meanwhile, cook sliced apples over medium heat for about five minutes. Reduce heat, add remaining maple syrup, and cook until tender. When the pork is ready, slice it and spoon the apples over the top. Have mercy! That's good eating!

Cajun Blackened Fish

(SERVES 4–6)

Every cook needs a blackened fish recipe in her repertoire. Kudos to legendary Louisiana chef Paul Prudhomme for giving us this remarkable dish! Its simplicity is only matched by its flavor.

½ stick butter

2 teaspoons garlic powder

2 teaspoons cayenne pepper

2 teaspoons black pepper

2 teaspoons lemon pepper

2 teaspoons salt

8 fillets (we used catfish)

2½ cups bottled Italian dressing

Heat your oven to 350 degrees or, better yet, fire up your grill and save yourself the cleanup. Melt a half a stick of butter in a small saucepan. Combine seasonings in a separate mixing bowl. Dip your fillets first in the butter, then the seasonings. Place fish on the grill, or if using the oven, coat a pan with nonstick cooking spray before adding fillets. Cook fillets eight to ten minutes on each side, brushing lightly with the Italian dressing when you turn them. They're ready when they're flaky and white. Serve with fluffy rice and French bread for a fabulously simple meal.

Southern Steak Potpie

(SERVES 6)

My Southern Steak Potpie is a favorite of my meat and potato–loving farmer husband. I'm willing to bet that it'll be a hit with your group, too. We're going to cheat just a little by using a prepackaged pie crust. That might offend our grandmothers, but it doesn't hurt my feelings at all.

    1 medium onion, sliced
    4 tablespoons vegetable oil
    ¼ cup all-purpose flour
    ½ teaspoon paprika
    ½ teaspoon red pepper
    1 teaspoon season-all
    Pinch of ground allspice
    Pinch of ginger
    Salt and pepper
    1 pound boneless round steak, cut up in ½-inch pieces (I use
        deer steak)
    2½ cups boiling water
    4 medium potatoes, peeled and diced
    1 ready-made Pillsbury pie crust

Preheat oven to 450 degrees. Sauté sliced onion in vegetable oil over medium heat and remove to paper towels to drain, reserving oil. Prepare meat seasoning by combining flour, paprika, red pepper, allspice, ginger, salt, pepper, and season-all. (I use Tony Chachere's, Panola, or Slap 'Ya Mama.)

Dredge steak pieces in seasoned flour before browning in the reserved oil over medium heat. Add boiling water, cover, reduce heat, and simmer. Once the meat is tender, toss in potatoes and cook another twenty minutes, until potatoes soften. Pour the meat-and-potato mixture into a 1½-quart baking dish and spoon sautéed onions over the top.

Finish potpie by fitting the premade pie crust over the top and sealing the edges. Make small slits in the crust to allow the air to escape, and bake until the crust is golden brown. (I like to serve this with corn fritters.)

Shellie's Stacked Tortillas

(SERVES 4–6)

I suppose it's my raising, but I hate to waste food. I made this recipe up one day to use some leftovers before I had to throw 'em out. My husband raved about it and wanted me to make sure I remembered what I'd done. I tried, but to be honest, I think I make 'em a little different every time—and that's another product of my early education!

1 pound ground beef
¼ each of a red pepper and a green pepper, diced
1 small white onion, diced
1 (14 oz.) can black beans, rinsed and drained
1 (14 oz.) can diced tomatoes and green chilies
1 teaspoon chili powder
1 teaspoon garlic powder
1 teaspoon cumin
Salt and pepper to taste
6 flour tortillas
1 cup shredded sharp cheddar cheese
1 cup Monterey Jack cheese

Preheat oven to 350 degrees. Brown hamburger meat with diced red pepper, green pepper, and white onion. Once meat is no longer pink and veggies are soft, drain and return to skillet. Add black beans (excellent fiber addition) and can of tomatoes with green chilies. Season well. We like spicy around here, so I use a teaspoon of chili powder, a teaspoon of cumin, and salt and pepper it to taste.

Layer a third of the meat in a casserole dish. Place two tortillas over the meat and sprinkle about a third of cheddar and Monterey Jack cheese over it. Repeat layers two more times. Bake about thirty minutes until everything is heated through and your cheese is bubbly. I like to serve it in nice-size rectangles with a good green salad. Enjoy!

Honey Bunny Easter Ham

(SERVES 12)

My Honey Bunny Easter Ham tastes like it came from a famous chain (which will be left unnamed lest they don't appreciate the comparison and I have to spend next Easter in court), but I found it easy to prepare and a whole lot cheaper.

> 1 fully cooked ready-to-eat ham (about 5 pounds)
> ¼ cup whole cloves
> ¼ cup dark corn syrup
> 1 pound honey
> ⅔ cup butter

You'll need to set aside a little time for this one. It's not difficult, it just requires steady basting. Begin by preheating your oven to 325 degrees. Place ham cut side down in a foil-lined pan and stud with whole cloves. Using a double boiler, stir up glaze with syrup, honey, and butter. Once the glaze is warm, baste ham and slide in the oven. Leave your glaze warming on the stove. The rest is easy. Just bake your ham for about an hour and fifteen minutes, being careful to baste it every ten or fifteen minutes with your honey glaze. During the last five minutes of cooking, slide your ham under the broiler to caramelize the glaze for a beautiful and tasty finish! That's good eating, from my kitchen to yours.

Busy Day Chicken

(SERVES 6)

It has come to my attention that not everyone's mama taught them how to do Busy Day Chicken. I not only feel the pain of your misfortune, I intend to do something about it. Pull out a casserole dish or roasting pan and gather round, busy little people, this is about as easy as it gets.

    2–3 pounds chicken pieces
    ¼ cup butter
    1 cup rice, uncooked
    1 package dry onion soup mix
    1 can cream of celery soup
    Salt and pepper

Preheat oven to 325 degrees. Sear your chicken pieces in a little butter in a pan over high heat. Place uncooked rice in buttered casserole dish and place browned chicken over rice. Sprinkle with onion soup mix. (Believe it or not, we're almost through!) Combine the celery soup with two cans of water and pour it over the top of chicken and rice. Salt and pepper to taste. Bake uncovered for about two hours, or until chicken is done. You know—while you do the clothes, help the kids with their homework, call your mama, etc. Of course, your family needs to appreciate all you do, so make sure you act like you've been cooking for hours. I mean, you have—kind of.

Chicken Crescent Rollups

(SERVES 4)

Are you in a rut with supper? I've been there. Let me give you a little inspiration. Here's another of my tasty chicken dishes to save the day, and you won't have to be in the kitchen all evening to pull it off.

3 chicken breasts

2 teaspoons butter

¼ cup diced celery

¼ cup diced onion

1 ounce cream cheese

1 teaspoon lemon pepper

1 (4 oz.) jar chopped mushrooms

1 tube refrigerated crescent roll dough

1 can cream of chicken soup

½ cup milk

Preheat oven to 350 degrees. Boil chicken, cool, and pull into bite-size pieces. In a different saucepan, sauté celery and onion in butter over medium heat. Mix chicken pieces with cream cheese and season with lemon pepper. Add cream cheese and meat mixture to sautéed vegetables along with mushrooms and stir well. Place a generous helping of this meat mixture in the middle of an uncooked crescent roll and roll into a crescent starting at the long end. Place in a buttered baking dish. Combine canned soup with milk and pour over the stuffed rolls. Bake until the rolls are golden brown. Serve with a nice salad for a complete meal. Your family is going to love you tonight!

3

Normal Crazy vs. Straight Running Crazy

Southern Insight on the Absurd with Bread
Recipes That Rise to the Occasion

In my last book I gave a brief definition of a condition I often speak of called straight running crazy, or SRC.* It has since become clear to me that more clarification is needed in this area. Many of you have contacted me out of concern that you or someone you love may be suffering from SRC, and you are eager to know where the line is between normal crazy and Straight Running Crazy.

While the legal department here at *All Things Southern* (comprised of my immediate family who don't have a law degree among 'em but are still legitimately concerned because they have, if you will, a dog in the

Official Guide to Speaking All Things Southern

*SRC, acronym for Straight Running Crazy: used to describe the actions of someone who is no longer detouring from more lucid behavior, but going full steam ahead

fight) would like me to make it abundantly clear that I am speaking in jest and not proposing to diagnose or treat those that are truly mentally ill, I believe I can still offer a certain level of service to society by shining some Southern insight on the absurd.

Although the notion to include just such a chapter in my next self-help book had been floating around in my head for some time, I remember exactly when the idea crystallized. I was in Houston, Texas, with my daughter, who the day before had given birth to my first grandson, Grant Thomas Maher. My son-in-law and Baby Grant's father, Patrick, had left to put in an appearance at work. Jessica and I were alone in her hospital room when one of the nurses came in to take Jessica's vitals. (By law, hospitals are required to take your vitals every two minutes. It's been my experience that some institutions relax this rule, content instead to take your vitals every hour on the hour unless they find you sleeping, in which case they will happily wake you up to take your vitals immediately.)

The nurses from the previous shifts had been nice enough, but they hadn't been spending a great deal of time visiting with us. This was about to change. After giving Jessica Ann a thorough once-over, her new nurse began making small talk. The visit was pleasant enough, but the longer she lingered the more I realized that she had something in particular on her mind, something she felt compelled to share. Finally, after covering the weather, the news, and what was worth watching on TV, she got down to it.

My daughter and I listened closely as the nurse began to run through what appeared to be her standard "new mother operating instructions." Jessica, remember, was just hours past the birthing experience, and laughing didn't feel so good to the insides, so her sense of humor wasn't in full appreciation mode, but even she had to agree with what I'm about to tell you. That pretty little nurse's "what to expect when you get home" routine was spot-on and perfectly delightful.

"You're happy now," the nurse said, all serious like, "*but when you go home*"—at this point, she began frowning and gesturing with her hands to heighten the drama— "baby will cry! You will cry! Baby will scream at you. You will scream at your husband. This is normal for new mothers. Hormones everywhere. Don't be scared. Tell yourself, you aren't run-in-street-wave-bra-in-air crazy, you're normal crazy."

Good advice, yes? I thought so, too. I got to use it several days after I came back home to Louisiana. Jessica Ann called from Texas. She was trying valiantly to hold it all together, but I've been there, people, and I could sense those new mama hormones bubbling right there below the surface, just waiting to explode. When Jessica took a breath, I said, "It'll be okay, honey. Remember—you're normal crazy!" Jessica laughed and the mood passed.

And that's when I decided we should take a closer look at this thing, for normal crazy is where I think most of us are most of the time. Straight running crazy, again, that's what we want to watch out for. Here are just a few demarcations to get the ball rolling.

Normal crazy is getting up hours before dawn, leaving a cozy warm bed, and strapping your body to a tree to wait out the monster buck. Straight running crazy is that eager fellow I saw on the Outdoor Channel stalking that wild boar with nothing but a spear. Normal crazy is piercing your nose. Straight running crazy is piercing your private parts.

Of course, some people might say normal crazy is being an

author and straight running crazy is trying to be an author, motivational speaker, Web mistress, radio host, newspaper columnist, wife, mother, and grandmother. But for the record I have never waved my bra in the street. Not yet anyway.

Knick-Knack Paddy-Wack, Give a Dog a Prozac

I have found the best examples of straight running crazy are often found in these three places: (a) the news, (b) the news, and (c) the news. Being a trained observer, I can normally sniff out the stories that are going to cause the biggest disturbance on the *All Things Southern* porch. Those are the ones I usually address. Just kidding. What I meant to say is that those are the ones I try to avoid. Really, I do. For instance, the first time I came across the following little hot potato topic, I schooled myself to avoid it. I knew it would rile up somebody on the porch, but when it resurfaced a few months later, I just couldn't help myself. Here's the headline that grabbed me: "Growing number of suicidal pets being treated with Prozac."

Yes, indeed, apparently "Give a dog a bone" is old school advice. Today's answer is beef-flavored Prozac. Now, I love my chocolate Lab, Dixie Belle, as much as anyone has ever loved a pet, and I try to care for her overall health, but we may need to file this one under Straight Running Crazy.

I'm not saying animals don't have mood swings. My Dixie can sulk with the best of 'em. And I'm just now reminded of a certain cockatiel my family and I once owned. We named him DeGray after the Arkansas town where we had purchased him. In our early enthusiasm for DeGray's mimicking skills, we taught him to say, "Praise the Lord!" Little did we know DeGray was going to see the light in a big way! In the end that bird got so full of the spirit we had to flat-out give him away to a man who was raising a shed full of cockatiels, because our dear pet had taken to praising the Good Lord 24/7 nonstop: "PraisetheLord-PraisetheLord-PraisetheLord." To be honest, I felt like a fair-weather friend, but I still think of DeGray fondly. I hope he was able to convert enough of his buddies to hold a decent weekly service.

My point is that I realize our pets can get out of balance every now and then. I'm just suggesting that we use caution here. Let's make sure we exhaust the diet and exercise solutions before we go prescribing poocher-uppers, okay? By the way, as you can imagine, I did find experts on both sides of this issue. One animal behaviorist said that she will prescribe the drug in extreme cases but she much prefers treating her clients with aromatherapy and soothing music. I'm *pretty* sure she meant the dogs, not their owners, but I can't put money on it.

And, after mentioning this on the porch of *All Things Southern*, I heard from some of the most intelligent, balanced people around (my readers), who testified straight up that they'd had some dogs that needed medicating in the worst way, like Leslie Moore in Arkansas. The poor thing had a dog named Mr. Wilson who flat-out lost it. She still seems somewhat traumatized by memories from the day he cornered her in the laundry room.

Therefore, despite my reservations about the possible misuse of Poochie Prozac, and out of mutual respect to my readers, I've decided to resist my immediate tendency to label this an SRC outbreak. Instead, in the interest of fair and balanced reporting, I've come up with five signs to watch out for that may indicate your dog is suicidal:

Number 5: He plays in the road.

Number 4: He sleeps a lot.

Number 3: He insists on riding on the toolbox rather than in the truck bed.

Number 2: He takes up with strays.

And the top way to tell if your dog may be depressed, he sings the same sad song all night long: "Woof, woof, woof, woof, woof, woof."

The good news is that after evaluating Dixie Belle, I've decided she's fairly stable. The bad news is that she may actually support assisted suicide. I've personally witnessed Canine Kevorkian helping a number of birds end it all.

Kudzu Overlords

Many times a news report itself will provoke someone into SRC activity. Such was the case the last time kudzu claimed the media spotlight. I say the last time because kudzu cycles in and out of the headlines about as often as the Hollywood "B" list. Kudzu has not only been proven to hold a certain fascination in our national psyche, but here in the Deep South the poor overgrown weed is like everyone's favorite eccentric relative. It may be a nuisance, but it's our nuisance thankyouverymuch.

The last time kudzu had the world's attention, it was once

again being promoted as the biofuel of the future, only this time it wasn't just a theory. Oh no, a biofuel firm in Tennessee was actually producing the stuff. And they still are. They call it Kudzunol. Isn't that catchy? Course, you just know that regardless of what you set out to do, there are gonna be naysayers, and the kudzu battle lines are clearly drawn.

Those against using our vigorous plant for fuel are cautioning their opponents against growing dependent on a resource we could exhaust in three years. I ask you in my best Johnny Mac voice, "You can't be serious?!" My Southern soul grows weary of explaining the obvious, but here goes. We're talking Kudzilla, people, the Vine That Ate the South. Our insatiable green monster is growing a foot a day, threatening to swallow entire towns and, it has been rumored, showing an evil tendency to sneak into Southern bedrooms at night to steal small children. In other words, news flash, y'all: It grows back.

As my friends and neighbors can attest, our kudzu has been rooted up, cut down, and cussed out, but it's yet to be controlled. Even if, God be willing, someone could eradicate it through overharvesting, the problem with that would be what exactly?

Another argument is that kudzu will prove too difficult to gather from our roadsides. Granted, this concern does have some merit, but I'm not sure that it's going to be a problem either. We have ourselves a local case of kudzu-related SRC that may offset any anxiety over the harvesting difficulties.

It's Bubba, y'all. He didn't have the slightest interest in kudzu as a fuel source—until I told him that if Kudzunol catches on, the South could become the next Saudi Arabia. I did this accidentally, by way of conversation, and I'd like it to be known that I'd take it back if I could, as Bubba now feels we need to get a jump on this before the government gets involved.

Thus he's getting in on the ground floor, so to speak. Bubba has built himself a still (think moonshine) and he's assembling his own workforce. But that's not all. He also wants to be known as Prince Bubba of Kudzu, and just yesterday he asked me if I wanted to be in his harem! I told him, "not so much."

I know what you're thinking, and you may have a point. Sometimes the cure can be worse than the disease, but if we're talking choose your poison here, I'll take Kudzu Overlords over Middle East Maniacs any day. Course, in order for Kudzunol to catch on, we're gonna have to convince the celebrities that it's a trendy new cause, cooler even than carrying mini dogs in this season's Louis Vuitton. So here's my plan, fellow Southerners: If we can get Mr. Gore to say he invented our ancient vine, we'll all be sitting pretty and it won't be in kudzu.

SRC and the Scientific Community

Kudzu might not be the answer to all of our planet's fuel concerns, but at least we can be thankful that someone is working on this very legitimate concern. I'm afraid that's not always the case for many of the grave issues that challenge us. See, when one is a news buff like yours truly, one discovers that some highly educated and otherwise intelligent folks have some mighty strange interests. Indeed, I'm afraid my research has uncovered traces of SRC in the unlikeliest of places: the scientific community.

For instance, we would all like to think that the brightest minds in our world are busy searching for that elusive cure for cancer, diabetes, or even the common cold, and no doubt many of them are doing just that, but from what I can see, y'all, certain segments of the scientific community are otherwise occupied.

Case in point: Just recently Japanese scientists, having carefully noted the spread of bird flu, having considered Big Al's global warnings, and having pondered the problem of world hunger, promptly responded by producing a genetically altered mouse that is not afraid of cats. Yes, indeed. It's not immediately clear how this is going to help the rest of us, but Minnie Mouse has been quoted as saying, "Take that, Cat Woman." Meanwhile, South Korean scientists put their collective genius to work and produced white cats that glow red when exposed to ultraviolet light, which rarely happens even accidentally, but should your beloved feline use the sun-bed when you're at work, you'd know immediately upon your return, and as a plus, you might be able to use Kitty as a backup generator in the case of a major blackout or national fuel shortage.

> When my kids fought in public I would make them hold hands until they stopped. It worked EVERY time.
>
> ~Mary Barton
> Bossier City, Louisiana

What most people don't realize about the scientific world is that they are a very competitive bunch. This must be why, upon hearing the news, Taiwan's brilliant scientists wasted no time announcing their own success in the Field of Animal Night-Lights. Their contribution to this exciting area of study was to give the world glow-in-the-dark pigs, which only served to goad those determined Japanese into yet another remarkable accomplishment—see-through frogs. Side note: My older sister Cyndie and I used to enjoy making our middle sister choose between kissing a regular run-of-the-mill frog and professing her love for some boy whose name Cyndie and I were in charge of supplying. Of course, it had to be someone we all found revolting. I left a message on Rhonda's voice mail asking if she would like to go on record as to whether or not she would have preferred kissing see-through frogs, but she has yet to return my call. Some people have no interest in science.

To be fair, in addition to what seems to be SRC research, there is every bit as much legitimately important scientific work being done in laboratories around the globe. In light of our own long history with the pesky mosquito, I suppose all of us Southerners should be thankful for the effort being undertaken to develop a genetically engineered mosquito to assist in the fight against malaria. Because of the dedication and hard work of certain scientists, we now have newly altered lady mosquitoes so designed that they can feed on blood infected with malaria without picking up the disease. Scientists claim these wonder females will mate with Average Joe males and pass this disease-preventing trait to their offspring. It sounds terrific, right? I thought so, too. Had the article ended there, I'd be high-fiving right along with the good researchers, but yours truly has uncovered a bit of SRC in the details.

Apparently, the scientists decided to make the girls' eyes glow red so they'd be more identifiable in the dark. That's freaky enough, but it gets worse. Perhaps to prove that they do have a sense of humor, the researchers also introduced a gene in the males that makes their, um, their "parts" glow in the dark! (Yes, Mama, those parts.) They hope to introduce these mutant mosquitoes into the larger population to begin controlling infectious diseases. Forgive me if I sound ungrateful here, but I could possibly be speaking for the entire Southern region of these United States when I say, "*Thank you, but no thank you.*"

Under this new plan, not only do we get to hear that blood-sucking mosquito dive-bombing us in the night, but now she even looks evil with her glowing red eyes, and what's worse, her Sweet Thang's over there in the shadows lit up like the Fourth of July waitin' to make more devil babies. Alfred Hitchcock himself couldn't have dreamed this stuff up. If they must tinker with Mother Nature, and I'd rather they didn't, but if they must, I'd like to suggest they spend some time rethinking that eye color, perhaps a nice blue instead. And since they're introducing behavioral genes, maybe they could try and nudge her towards a vegetarian lifestyle like her other half.

Perhaps y'all are wondering where this train of thought is headed. I understand. I'm generally as curious as the next person, but trust me; I'm going somewhere this time. It's my humble opinion that we'd all benefit if these brilliant scientific minds would exert less effort on things like Animal Nightlights and more time on the biggies. Of course, this means we'll need someone to talk to them about their priorities, and for this very important job I would like to nominate Mama. Southern Mamas are big on prioritizing, and mine is certainly no exception. These are the women who taught us the fine art of prioritization by saying things like "Don't you dare come back in this house before supper unless you're bleeding—profusely." The only other recourse I can see here would be for us to contact PETA (which I'm pretty sure stands for People Against Eating Trees and Animals), and seriously, do we really want to get them all stirred up? Exactly. I'll call Mama.

This Isn't Your Bubba's Camouflage Culture

Regardless of prevailing stereotypes that would suggest otherwise, my research has proven time and again that SRC is not limited to any one particular region. Crazy lives everywhere. Exhibit A: I read about a development in Japan called

Camouflage Culture, but surprisingly, it had nothing to do with deer hunting. It seems the Japanese folk are so concerned about street crime that they're entertaining a brand-new and somewhat SRC concept in outer wear: clothes with secret panels that can immediately camouflage the wearer so as to hide him or her from approaching street thugs. One particular designer was even offering a dress with fold-out panels intended to disguise the wearer as a vending machine. Talk about thinking outside the box! We can draw two conclusions from this story. One: The fashion world has been pulling our leg this whole time, which explains those funny catwalk costumes. And two: Stupid criminals are a universal phenomenon.

The way I see it, this is going to require an unusual amount of coordination between potential victims and incredibly dumb crooks. Before activating your vending machine disguise, you'll need to point at something behind your attacker and scream, "Look behind you!" In theory, with practice, and providing that you are convincing enough, you should be able to pull this off in time to hear the hapless thug say, "Whoa—she was right here a minute ago and now there's nothing here but this stupid vending machine." There's also a kid's backpack that can disguise your child as a fire hydrant. True, there's a good chance that passing dogs may relieve themselves on Yoshi Jr., but you can't put a price on safety, people.

> My Southern Mama always said, "If I catch you smoking, you better be on fire!"
>
> Sarah Holt
> Daughter of Debbie Bagby Fortenberry
> Lake Providence, Louisiana

As teenagers, my sisters and I once tried a similar disguise-and-divert ploy. This was back when our whole gang was trying to sneak around and smoke cigarettes, despite our parents' fierce warnings of what would happen if we got caught. We were in a back booth of the Pizza Hut, jamming to the juke-box and puffing away, when in walked an adult who knew our folks. Instinctively, we all handed our cigarettes—still lit, mind you—to my cousin Jimmy Ray, whose parents knew he smoked and had long since given up on breaking him of the habit. There sat Jimmy with five lit cigarettes and a weak smile, looking every bit as believable as, well, as a human vending machine. I don't know how well the Camouflage Culture is working in Japan, but I can tell you what our weak little diversion tactic taught me and my sisters: Cigarettes might hurt people, but parents hurt people, too!

The SRC Seasons of Our Lives

Clearly, SRC knows no borders, nor is it bound by time, and yet there do seem to be certain seasons when it becomes easier to spot the absurd. We can usually count on the wedding sea-son to uncover a certain amount of madness, even if we don't reach the level of bizarre we saw when Elvis's daughter married the late Michael Jackson.

Oftentimes the season will begin with stories that are downright sweet, but if you keep your eyes open, as a trained observer you can eventually detect varying levels of SRC. One of the more recent seasons opened with a precious story about a New Jersey man who took the romance prize by hacking into his girlfriend's favorite video game and reprogramming it so that when she reached a predetermined score a diamond would appear along with his proposal. Cool geek move, right? I thought so, too. He should've stopped there.

The article went on to say that Mr. Geek admitted having covered his bases when he set it all up by "making sure the winning score was pretty low." Uh, oh—bad geek move! I'd say there's more than an outside chance that he's still paying for that one. I bet Lady Geek got her panties twisted when she heard that! Can't you hear her now: "You made sure it was low enough?! *Low enough?!* So what are you saying?" (Note to female readers: My research at *All Things Southern* has proven that few men are ever saying anything more than what they're saying. While there is the rare fellow, like my friend Bubba, who thinks innuendos are those tight swim shorts, most all males are familiar with the word, they just don't play the game.)

I can't speak as to whether or not Mr. Geek's proposal style caught on in the gaming community, as the last video game I played was on (warning: obscure reference ahead) an Atari Game System, but it may have happened. One can always count on the wedding season to bring us new trends. Some of these have staying power, others thankfully disappear. If we're fortunate, the lasting developments are positive, like "Save the Date" cards. Now, there's an idea that Southern girls have totally embraced. Not only do these pre-invitation cards give their guests plenty of notice, they're also a great heads-up to other area brides to steer clear of the chosen weekend, *and* they give belles license to extend the drama tastefully. We belles admit unashamedly that we are quite fond of drama, especially when we're the main attraction. For these and other reasons, Save the Date cards are a win-win. Again, this can hardly be said of all of the latest developments. Some trends are just downright tacky.

Like my fellow Southerners, I'm quite fond of the word "tacky." We use it as often to address what someone is doing as we do to address what they may be wearing. Short regional elocution lesson: To say the word "tacky" like a bona fide Southern belle, one should adopt a slightly pained expression and draw out the first syllable, as in taaaaa-cky. Unfortunately, society seems bent on serving up opportunities to practice your pronunciation. Why, I remember a time in the not so terribly distant past when custom dictated that the bride not wear white if the whole community knew she'd been having supper without saying grace. (We've been over this, folks. Having supper without saying grace will explain itself if you let it.) Sadly, today's brides will wear white with their bellies stuck out to there! This is without question a taaaaa-cky development but it has recently morphed into full-blown SRC. I shall now take pains to elaborate for the betterment of polite society.

Dear readers, let it be known that even a white dress on a used bride is preferable to a sheer dress on a new one. That's correct. Reread it if you have to, I'll wait. It's possible that one of the craziest fashion trends I've ever uncovered out of the halls of high fashion is the sheer wedding dress. Sheer. Wedding. Dress. I can imagine Southern Mamas from years gone by searching heaven's dresser drawers with that development and exclaiming, "Lord, have mercy! Michael, honey, did you see where I put my smelling salts?" I know when I heard about it I got on my radio program and promptly offered my audience a public service announcement. "Girls," I said, "if ever there was a time and place to leave something to the imagination, it's when you're parading

Occasionally driving through the country, we'd pass a rundown house with a "porch couch," skinny diseased dogs playing with saggy-diapered babies, and some unfortunate big-boned gal smoking in the yard. Momma would turn around, give me "that look" and remind me that ladies do NOT smoke. Of course as soon as I was old enough I tried smoking, but I always had the image that one day it'd be me wearing that dirty housedress and ratty flip-flops out in that yard.

~Sandi Bourne-Hayes
DeRidder, Louisiana

down the aisle in front of God and everybody." Thankfully, I haven't heard a lot more about that particular style. Now I'm not saying I should get credit for nipping it in the bud with that little PSA. I don't need the props. What's important here is that the sheer wedding dress didn't gain a foothold. Like my friend Paulette said, "Naked comes the bride" just doesn't have the right ring to it.

Belles Don't Emit in Public

While we're talking about both crazy and *taaaaa-cky*, it seems as good a time as any to ask y'all a personal question that's been weighing heavy on me. Please forgive me if this sounds too forward. I'm terribly curious, that's all. No one else has to know. So, here goes, have y'all really been offsetting your emissions?

Mama, if you're reading this, I have not forgotten my raising. I know proper Southern ladies do not discuss their, um, emissions in public, but this is a different kind of thing entirely, and besides, desperate times call for desperate measures, and times, they are desperate—just ask the celebrities. And like my good friend Paulette says, all you gotta do is look at those frozen eyebrows and plumped up lips to see that those people know a thing or two about desperation.

I'm not making fun, here. Okay, scratch that. I'm making a little fun, but I can't be expected to quit everything cold turkey. I've been looking into this carbon-neutral lifestyle everyone has been proposing. I feel confident that I can break it down for you. Here's what I've learned, y'all: Carbon dioxide is bad and we produce too much of it. Celebrities are good because they're willing to show the rest of us how to cut back.

Fortunately for the celebrities, there appear to be at least two ways to be carbon neutral. One can limit one's use of electricity, or one can buy offsets to ease one's guilt for producing said electricity while jetting around with one's mean green friends, instead of having to choose whether to eat or buy tennis shoes for one's kids. Now, who we do we suppose can afford to do which? Well, I swanee. Y'all are a smart group, aren't you!

The thing is I have a gnawing suspicion that there is more talk of emission offsetting out there than there is the actual practice of it, but if you're interested, I have found all sorts of websites where you can calculate your family's emissions and conveniently purchase offsets, right there at the same place. Yes, indeedy. One can do everything online these days. I'm convinced that many of these sites are quite legitimate, but do be careful. I thought the suckerborneveryminute.com site looked a little questionable.

Darn it all, it'd be really great marketing if I could send you to my website for your emission-reduction guilt program instead, but I'm afraid I'll have to ask y'all to bookmark my place and check back in. I'm still putting the finishing touches on my solid gold, I mean green, plan. But, what the heck, since you bought this book and all, I'll give y'all the inside scoop. At first, I considered having my own ATSCOP (*All Things Southern* Carbon Offset Program). I thought it could work something like this: If you wanted to take a trip in your car, you would calculate the mileage and pay me a proportionate amount to save an equal number of my emissions by staying home. Just like that, you could be carbon neutral.

I'm no rocket scientist, but the only answer I could come up with when someone asked me about offsetting emissions was to tell them that's what my husband does regularly when he says, "Wasn't me, Casey (the poodle) did it!"

~Faye Bryant
Knoxville, Tennessee

I know, brilliant, huh? (Hey, I'm just one person, but I'm doing everything I can.)

Then, while working on my ATSCOP I got distracted. It happened after I got a massive amount of email from mentioning the whole carbon neutral thing on my radio program and website. After categorizing the feedback, I did some reevaluating. In retrospect I now see that "neutral" might not have been the best choice of word for our region. I should've known Southerners don't feel neutral about anything. My inbox box almost crashed with folks ready to take a stand and fight—if I would kindly clarify what it was they needed to fight about.

I had to explain that carbon offsets had everything to do with calculating one's carbon footprint and nothing to do with sneaker size or Bubba's unintentional—or intentional—release of offensive bodily emissions. To be honest, it still hasn't been easy to get folks to give the boy a break and concentrate on their own emissions. For this reason, I've decided to go an entirely different direction with this thing. (Me and Elvis, we do things our way.) Don't despair, Mr. Gore, I'll still be saving the environment, but instead of having my own carbon offsets exchange, I'm developing something I like to call my own Stupid Celebrities Offsets Program. Stay with me, now. While similar, this program should be much more fun for the rest of us. Theoretically, when celebrities say something really stupid, they'll have to purchase offsets to benefit the hardworking people who pay their bills.

For instance, not long ago a certain celebrity whom I'm somewhat reluctant to name because he does have the cutest dimples ever (although I am dropping clues for those paying close attention) weighed in on global warming. Mr. Greased Lightning admits he isn't the best spokesperson as he does own and fly five personal jets, but he'd like to remind us that he's in the entertainment business. I suppose that means he has to have the jets for business purposes. Well, now, that's different. Not!!! In my program, that type of reasoning would cost Mr. Greased Lightning two hundred crawfish boils for needy families. Y'all can register your party, I mean, needy family at www.allthingssouthern.com.

Honestly, I was all set to give Mr. Greased Lightning some slack, 'cause of his dimples and all, but then he up and exhibited some classic symptoms of SRC. He suggested that we begin looking into living on other planets and putting domes over our cities. Domes—over our cities . . . Earth to Dimples, this will require you to give up five jet trips to Europe. With the money you save you must purchase an equivalent amount of commodities from American farmers. Oh, and you'll be required to run those jets on kudzu from now on. Granted, I'm still working out the kinks. I'm gonna need considerable time to calculate what some of these other celebrities owe us, but I think the program holds great promise.

When I first heard people talking about offsetting their emissions, I thought they meant saying something nice for every time you said something ugly or catty. I about wore myself out keeping up with that one.

~Cari Faanes-Blakey
Sarasota, Florida

Pass the Tofurky?!

Somehow I know this line of discussion is going to get me in trouble before it's all said and done, but it fits much too well in our SRC discussion and, silly me, I can't help forging ahead. You'd think I would've learned my lesson when I wrote my first book. That lesson being that there are certain topics practically guaranteed to make somebody, somewhere, mad as a hornet. My work here has taught me that those topics are, in no particular order: (1) anything, (2) some things, and (3) everything.

I'm still doing damage control from that valuable experience. Of course, my loyal readers and listeners at *All Things Southern* basically know that half of what I say is a joke and the other half is just me rambling, but faster than you could say "Shoot a monkey," I was thrust before a larger audience who didn't quite know how to take my good-natured humor. Several new Internet visitors, who had obviously spent valuable research time in the archives of allthingssouthern.com, went so far as to suggest that I, your happy hostess, am not taking the need to save this planet seriously enough, and get this, I'm encouraging a throw-away mentality that's filling up our landfills!

Well, for the love of *All Things Southern*, that's about as silly a something as ever came across my desk. I mean, heaven forbid, y'all! I was raised to understand that wasteful was right next door to sinful. The Southern women in my family have made an art out of stretching groceries. Honestly, not being wasteful is so engrained in my DNA I have never allowed myself to throw away those weird soft drinks that Jones Soda Company sent me two years runnin'. I'll have you know I kept those

It was obvious my Yankee hubby didn't know how to appreciate Southern food. He looked at biscuits in horror, thought grits and gravy were too fattening, and considered casseroles mysterious and inedible. What was a good Southern girl to do? I learned the trick was to slowly influence him away from his mother's cooking by introducing new dishes at family gatherings and getting his family to like them first. He followed naturally. Today they all like Southern-style banana pudding, sweet tea, and deviled eggs, so my stealth operation must be working. On to corn bread . . .

~Dana Mosley Sieben
Oak Forest, Illinois

silly things in the door of my fridge for months like I half-expected someone to drag themselves into the kitchen, prop their weary selves on my snack bar, and say, "I'd give my last dollar for a swig of Green Bean Casserole Soda!"

Trust me. We know how to stretch food down here, not to mention we are mighty proficient at reinventing leftovers. And that reminds me, my friend Paulette suggested I could go a long way toward redeeming myself in the eyes of the global community by announcing a change to my traditional Thanksgiving menu. She thinks I should serve Tofurky. Yeah, that's what I said. Talk about your straight running crazy . . .

Paulette said Tofurky is a loaf of tofu (creamed soybeans) shaped like a turkey. Yum, yum, kids. I did some research of my own, and color me confused here, I found that hundreds of thousands of Tofurkies are served in American homes every Thanksgiving. Let me be clear, it won't happen in my dining room. Look-a-here, I'm as interested in saving the planet as the next person and I do like to get along, but by golly I'm cooking a real bird. If it makes anyone feel better, ya got my word on this: We will not waste a sad bite!

This Little Piggy Destroyed the Planet

I could go on to describe a host of other SRC sightings, but it occurs to me that nothing I might offer here would really be able to draw a line for those of you looking for a definitive distinction between normal crazy and run-in-street-wave-bra-in-air crazy. This is because the biggest problem I've found in my efforts to help identify and treat those suffering with SRC lies in the fact that this field is anything but an exact science. Simply stated, SRC is relative. And I don't mean that in a family way, although that can often be true as well (as Paulette likes to say, "Sometimes the line between the family as an institution and the family needing to be in an institution is a fine one"), I'm simply pointing out what we all suspect. There are causes, crusades, and crazies, and it's up to everybody to figure out where they fit.

To stay on the right side of normal crazy, one needs to shoot for some perspective on the latest fashion trends, the end-of-the-world dramas, and the news alerts. Take swine flu for example. As of this writing I don't know if it's gonna get us all or if it is just another overblown media frenzy. And, what's more, I don't know if anyone knows, but it'd behoove us all to have a little more perspective here. Drama sells, but if I may be so bold as to speak directly to the media, crying wolf too often can have disastrous effects on your credibility and it can come back to bite you. Allow me to illustrate.

Official Guide to Speaking All Things Southern

*six ways to Sunday: phrase meaning to go off in all directions. The Southerner's way of explaining the sort of haste that is often undertaken to address work that has piled up during the day of rest

I remember the day my friend's daughter called with a frantic announcement, "Come quick, Keggie! [Keggie being my nickname.] The horse bucked Mama and she's broken!" I, Rescuer in Charge, took off at breakneck speed. I tore down Red's quarter-mile drive throwing dirt and rocks six ways from Sunday,* as my broken friend choked on my dust and waved vainly at me from the accident scene near the road. "Ruh, roh—there she is!" Wheeling my vehicle around, I flew back in the opposite direction. To hear Red tell it, she was more concerned at this point that I was going to run over her than whether I was going to rescue her, but she isn't telling this, now is she?

My stomach rolled when I saw Red's foot lying in a direction God never intended. After a few painful attempts to lift her into my vehicle, we both realized we needed help. My first call went to her husband. "Lamar, this is Shellie. We need you. Red fell off the horse. Her leg's broken—bad."

The busy, overworked farmer was having none of it. "That's not funny, Keggie. I can't deal with y'alls nonsense right now."

"I'm serious, Lamar. I need help—"

I may have been able to convince him, but we'll never know; the injured one jerked the phone from me and hung up on him. Honestly, Red and I have pulled our fair share of practical jokes. No doubt it was our fault her husband didn't believe us, but trust you me; he is still the one that paid for it. And therein lays my point. If this swine flu piggy turns out to be another wee one, the media will be guilty, again, of squandering the public trust in their rush to market. But what's worse, one day a real threat could catch the rest of us crying—all the way home.

Choosing the Moment

We'll leave this subject now with one more insight and a final warning. First, the observation: My studies show that sometimes a perfectly normal crazy person can have short-term bouts of SRC should outside forces (like deadlines and well-meaning relatives) converge at just the right moment in time. This is especially true if said writer spends way too much time on the Internet searching for bizarre stories to work into future articles. And no, I'm not bringing this up merely to provide a defense for the voices in my own head, although several of them have suggested that we may need the cover by the end of this sequel. I simply believe the record should show that SRC can be temporary.

It may have been because I went to sleep after reading about the seventieth anniversary of *Gone with the Wind* and trying in vain to tie it into a column. It could've been the cold pizza scarfed down at midnight. Regardless, the next thing I knew I was smack in the middle of that famous movie. Only it wasn't a movie exactly, it was more like a talent contest/reality show, and actress Sherri Shepherd was talking smack while trying to stuff me into one of those ridiculous whalebone corsets. "Girl," she said. "You best listen to your own advice and suck that stomach in else all the color in the world ain't gonna get those folks to text your number in."

Indeed, my version didn't exactly follow the original premise. For example, in my movie Rhett had been forced to withdraw from competition in order to defend himself against sexual harassment charges. One of my sisters was playing sweet Melanie and the other one was playing Belle, that notorious lady of the night (and you can forget it because I ain't for the life of me gonna tell y'all who was playing which part). Oh, and in my show, Mama wasn't dead and Papa wasn't losing his mind, although here in the real world both of them seem to have lost touch with reality, which is where this dream ties into my thoughts on relatives, deadline stress, and borderline SRC. (And you thought I was just rambling.) Should those you love inadvertently contribute to your temporary SRC moments, it is important to remember that *they mean well*; thus saith my Southern Mama.

Not long ago I mentioned to my dear sweet parents that I'd love to learn the fiddle one day—if I could find the time. Voilà! The next thing I knew those two had bought me an old fiddle from Antique Alley in West Monroe, Louisiana. Papa is nothing if not a bluegrass fan.

It seems the parents aren't pleased with my progress, however, and by progress I mean the way I propped the fiddle against the wall beside my desk. I know this because they just brought me some new rosin and a couple Teach Yourself the Fiddle books with my very own play-along DVD.

As God is my witness, I'm gonna learn to play those two a song on this fiddle if it's the last thing I do, just not right now. Deadlines await, and as my predecessor would say, "Tomorrow is another day."

And now the warning: Consider it an advance notice, if you please. Looking at my schedule for the next few months, it is all too clear that I'll be in a lot of airports. It's just as clear that, thanks to the increasingly tighter restrictions on air travel, I'll also be waiting in even longer lines. Bummer.

I'm gonna try hard not to complain about the extra security measures. Poke fun at 'em? Probably so. Complain? Not if I can help it. It's not that I think going blanket-free is the answer, but I'm beginning to think drawing attention to myself isn't such a wise idea, what with everyone getting so testy. Don't misunderstand me here, I think testy is a good thing! I'm glad those in charge of protecting us aren't taking this thing lightly. But as I told my husband, I'm gonna try to be good, but if someone insists on patting me down in places where no one's hands should be, it's gonna be ugly. I realize I may make the No Fly list in record time, and yes, I could even be looking at a brief stay at the Po Po. But hey, a girl could get a lot of writing done behind bars. And just think about the material one could gather! Besides, someone once said that "no one is sane who does not know how to be insane at the right moments." Hear, hear.

Tips on Staying This Side of Straight Running Crazy

THUS SAITH THE BELLE DOCTRINE . . .

* Thou shalt give new mothers a wider than usual berth between normal crazy and SRC.

* Thou shalt be careful to remember that celebrities aren't immune from SRC and they're often carriers.

* Thou shalt take special care to guard against SRC during its most prevalent period, the wedding season.

* Perspective is needed to protect thyself and thy loved ones from media-induced SRC.

* It's possible for thou to recover from temporary SRC brought on by well-meaning loved ones.

* When thou are confronted with certain circumstances, a certain amount of normal crazy is expected and even encouraged.

Bread Recipes That Rise
to the Occasion

By maintaining a healthy perspective, you should be able to take a good look at the causes, crusades, and crazies out there and decide for yourself who among your family and friends is normal crazy and who has a touch of SRC, but here's something to keep in mind: If you don't like bread, you'll be hard-pressed to find a Southerner who doesn't think that your own butter has slipped off your biscuit. It's not about limiting yourself. We're trying to do that, too. I'm just saying, if you don't eat some amount of bread on a regular basis, well, we're worried about you. As a region, we've managed, for the most part, to give up trash bread (white bread) in favor of whole grain, but we will always be bound to and nurtured by the staff of life. Here are just a few wildly diverse bread recipes you'll find in a Southern kitchen.

Pecan Mini Muffins

(SERVES 12)

Prepared in mini tins, these muffins make a great presentation for a bridal shower, but they're just as delicious stirred up to enjoy with a steaming cup of java. Keep these ingredients on hand and go from stirring 'em up to enjoying 'em with your morning coffee in twenty minutes flat.

2 eggs
½ cup self-rising flour
1 cup light brown sugar
½ cup melted butter (1 stick)
1 teaspoon vanilla extract
1 cup chopped pecans

Preheat oven to 350 degrees. Beat eggs in a medium-size mixing bowl. Stir in self-rising flour, brown sugar, and melted butter. Add vanilla extract and chopped pecans. Spoon the batter into buttered mini muffins tins (or standard size if you prefer). Slide 'em in the oven and bake for fifteen minutes. Don't forget to put the coffee on. They'll be ready before you know it.

Peachy French Toast

A simple can of peaches takes everyday French toast up a notch. This recipe makes a sweet morning treat for those holiday mornings, or just to show your family some love. You can prepare this dish the night before and slip it in the oven the next morning when everyone begins to stir.

1 cup brown sugar
½ cup butter or margarine
2 tablespoons water
12–14 (1-inch-thick) slices French bread
1 (29 oz.) can sliced peaches (drain and reserve juice)
5 large eggs
1½ cups milk
3 teaspoons vanilla extract

Melt brown sugar and butter in small skillet. Stir in two tablespoons of water and cook until the butter, sugar, and water form a thick brown sauce. Allow to cool. Slice French bread into one-inch slices and arrange in a 9×13 casserole dish. Drain peaches (being careful to reserve the juice) and layer over bread. Top with brown sauce. Whisk eggs well; add milk and vanilla extract and pour over brown sauce. Refrigerate overnight if desired. Cook in 350 degree oven for 35–40 minutes. Oh, and that peach juice? Right before serving, heat that juice in the microwave and pour it over your Peachy French Toast. Enjoy!

Firecracker Biscuits

Southern cooks often have more than one biscuit recipe in their repertoire, but if you like to walk on the spicy side of life, these are the biscuits for you. They're great with grilled steak or chicken, but please, don't serve 'em with any wimpy food. These biscuits would be plum offended.

2¾ cups biscuit mix
½ teaspoon crushed red pepper
1 teaspoon garlic powder, divided
1 cup milk
1 cup shredded cheddar cheese
2 tablespoons butter, melted

Preheat oven to 425 degrees. Season biscuit mix with crushed red pepper and ½ of the garlic powder. (If you're feeling especially spunky, you can up that red pepper to taste.) Take a fork and cut milk into biscuit mix along with the cheese. Mix just until it forms a soft dough ball (overmixing will make your biscuits hard) and drop by spoonfuls onto a greased cookie sheet. Combine two tablespoons of melted butter with remaining garlic powder, brush over the tops of your biscuits, and bake 10–12 minutes, or until golden brown. That's good eating straight from the *All Things Southern* kitchen.

Beat the Heat Spinach Bread

Here's a recipe for those grill masters out there who would just as soon cook everything outdoors. Spinach leaves and mozzarella cheese partner with the zest of lemon to offer a flavorful bread to serve with that grilled-to-perfection steak, fish, or chicken.

1 stick unsalted butter, softened at room temperature

3 teaspoons chopped garlic

2 tablespoons chopped fresh parsley leaves

2 tablespoons fresh lemon juice

1 teaspoon black pepper

1 large loaf French bread, halved lengthwise

2 (6 oz.) bags baby spinach leaves

1½ cups mozzarella cheese

Take butter and stir in garlic, parsley, lemon juice, and black pepper. Brush butter mixture on both sides of French bread and layer with spinach leaves. Top with shredded mozzarella cheese. Put the slices back together, wrap the whole loaf in foil and throw it on the grill for about fifteen minutes. Have mercy, that's good eating!

Stuffed to Perfection Crescent Rolls

Perhaps you're looking for a bread that acts more like a meal? I've got that, too! This recipe stuffs crescent rolls with sausage, onions, and over-the-top flavor. Put this in the oven and watch the aroma lure everyone in the house to the kitchen in record time.

½ pound Cajun smoked sausage, cut into bite-size pieces

¼ cup chopped onion

⅓ cup coarsely shredded carrots

1 (8 oz.) package cream cheese

1 (10 oz.) package frozen, chopped spinach, thawed and drained

⅓ cup chopped pecans

¼ cup bread crumbs

1 teaspoon chopped chives

Salt and pepper to taste

2 cans refrigerated crescent rolls

2 teaspoons melted butter

Preheat oven to 350 degrees. Brown sausage with onions and carrots in skillet over medium heat until the vegetables are tender. Stir in cream cheese, spinach, pecans, and bread crumbs, and season with chives and salt and pepper to taste. Unroll crescent rolls onto greased baking sheet and form dough into one big rectangle. Spread with meat-and-veggie mixture and top with the second can of crescent rolls, again keeping the dough in one big rectangle. Seal the edges and bake in the oven for fifteen minutes, or until the bread is nicely brown. Finish by topping with melted butter. Serve it with your favorite spicy mustard and a great green salad. Yum!

Festive Cranberry Bread

Maybe it's the orange juice that sends my festive cranberry bread up the charts. I don't know. But one thing's for sure. It's a great breakfast or coffee bread, and it's perfect for gifting. Make a few extra recipes to share with those you love and tie 'em with a big pretty bow. Nothing says "I love you" like homemade bread.

1 cup cranberries (fresh or frozen, washed and chopped or
    halved; I use my food processor)
½ cup chopped nuts
2 cups flour
1 cup granulated sugar
1½ teaspoons baking powder
½ teaspoon baking soda
½ teaspoon salt
1 beaten egg
3 tablespoons vegetable oil
1 cup orange juice

Preheat oven to 350 degrees. Send nuts and cranberries through the food processor. Now take a large mixing bowl and sift together flour, sugar, baking powder, baking soda, and salt. Add berries and nuts.

Stir together beaten egg, vegetable oil, and orange juice. Add to flour and stir just until moistened. Pour into a greased loaf pan. Bake for 1 hour, or until a cake tester inserted comes out clean.

Stop and Drop Easter Rolls

While bread finds a place at the Southern table all year long, its status is elevated for the Easter meal. My Stop and Drop Easter Rolls celebrate the resurrection of Jesus, the bread of heaven. So why the catchy name? Well, when some folks hear "yeast rolls," they immediately think it must be a difficult recipe, but it doesn't have to be. If you've got a moment, you can stop and drop some beautiful rolls for your holiday table.

1 package dry yeast
½ cup sugar
4 cups self-rising flour
2 cups lukewarm water
1 egg, beaten
1½ sticks margarine, melted

Mix yeast and sugar and flour in a large bowl. Stir in lukewarm water, egg, and melted butter. No need to knead. (I thought that was fun wordplay, but what I mean is, it isn't necessary to work the dough.) Drop dough by large tablespoons into greased muffin tins. You'll want to fill the individual tins up to the halfway mark. Let 'em sit at room temperature for several hours, and they'll rise up beautifully all by themselves, just like our Lord! Bake 'em at 425 degrees until brown and top 'em with a little more butter right before serving.

Mexican Cornbread

I cannot tell you why this cornbread is called Mexican Cornbread, it just is. I honestly don't know that it'd be recognized as a cultural staple south of the border. What I can tell you is that some version of this dish is served all across the South, and those who put their feet under our tables don't care what you call it, as long as you call them when it's piping hot!

1½ cups plain cornmeal
3 teaspoons baking powder
1 teaspoon salt
2 eggs, beaten
1 (14 oz.) can cream-style corn
1 cup sour cream
2/3 cup cooking oil (scant)
2 jalapeño peppers, chopped
8 ounces grated cheddar cheese

Preheat oven to 375 degrees, letting empty pan preheat in the oven.

Combine cornmeal with baking powder and salt in a large mixing bowl. Stir in beaten eggs, cream-style corn, and sour cream. Add cooking oil, chopped jalapeño peppers, and grated cheddar cheese. Pour into the preheated pan, coated with cooking spray. Bake for about 40 minutes. Delicious!

4

Self-Cleaning Underwear, an Idea Whose Time Should Never Come

~⊃

Time Management and Business Development Tips with Casserole Recipes to Beat the Clock

From the first day I discovered that letters made words and words made sentences and sentences made books, and books could be freely obtained at the end of our driveway from the East Carroll Parish Bookmobile, I've been a bona fide card-carrying bookworm. Fortunately for me, I also came into the world in multitasking mode. I was the kid who appeared at family meals with my nose stuck between the pages of a book, feeling for direction with my empty hand. To this day I love reading with my meal (and yes, I do realize that's frowned on by dieticians but so is most of my diet), because it was never allowed at home. "Shellie Charlene, get your nose out of that book and join us," Mama would say, a line I disliked even less than Papa's favorite contribution, "Yeah, and spill your milk now so your mama can clean it up before we eat." Of course, I couldn't manage to wet my whistle* before my milk was all over the table. I blame every one of those accidents on Papa. He prophesied it, don't you know?

While balancing Mama's "haste makes waste" dictate with my need for speed has never been easy, and I do so love to check things off of the to-do list, there are things I will and will not do to streamline the schedule. With that in mind, let's begin our time management discussion.

One day in the not so distant past my phone rang while I was making coffee. It was Paulette. She'd been surfing the Internet again. This is never a good thing. The quiz began as soon as I said hello. (Paulette's phone calls always make you feel like you're a rookie contestant on a weird new game show and you have zero chance of winning.)

"So," Paulette said before I could clear my throat and speak. "Do you have on clean underwear, you know, just in case you get in an accident? Tell the truth, Shellie, I promise not to tell your mama. And just how many days do you go without changing them, huh?"

"Pardon me?" I said. "Is that you, Paulette? What in heaven's name are you talking about now?"

"I'm just asking," Paulette said. "It says right here that scientists have invented self-cleaning underwear. They're all excited 'cuz you can wear these new undies for weeks without changing. They put something called 'nanos' on 'em that repels bacteria—article says dirt and liquids just bead up and roll off."

Trying hard to ignore the visuals forming in my head from that last detail, I told Paulette that this was entirely too much information before breakfast. She ignored me. "They're saying it will save time. Please, I'm as busy as a cat in a roomful of rocking chairs myself," she said. "But really, how long does it take to slip on some new drawers?" I had to admit that it didn't take long at all. "Exactly," Paulette said. Then she started laughing. "Hey— do ya reckon Britney I'm-Running-Low-On-Underwear Spears knows about this? It might just save that poor child's career."

I, of course, don't have the foggiest idea if Britney Spears knows about self-cleaning underwear, and from what I've read she isn't the only commando-loving celebrity out there. Besides, I'm not so sure Ms. Spears's career is dead, and if it isn't, pro-fessional advice from Paulette is the last thing the poor thing needs. For these and other reasons, I attempted an early redirec-tion in the conversation.

"Well, Paulette, look at it this way. It'll be good news for toilet-training mamas. Wouldn't it have been great if they would've had this fabric when our kids were that age?" It was a nice try, but Paulette barely broke stride.

"I don't know," she said seriously. "It might have worked with our daughters, but I haven't forgotten how hard it was to train Jerry Don Jr.! Heck, Shellie, if our boys would've had self-cleaning underwear, they'd still be in training pants!" Paulette . . . the girl ain't right, but then again, she's seldom wrong.

I didn't tell Paulette, but the thing that bothered me most about her article was that line about the repelled stuff just "beading up and falling off"! Excuse me?! And where does it go

Concerning the panties rule, I remember that growing up, Mama did stress wearing clean panties (no holes) in case we were in a wreck. God forbid the doctors and nurses saw our dirty "draws." So my thinking has always been that not wearing them might lessen my chance of getting in a wreck. You know, have 'em on, you wreck . . . no panties, no wreck.

~Tanya Dillon
Baton Rouge, Louisiana

exactly? And how are we supposed to avoid stepping in it—or worse, sitting in it? Let it be known that I'm fully prepared to defer to our mamas on this one. I know, I've joked as much as the next person about their constant admonitions to wear clean underwear because "one never knows when one will be in an accident," but there is something to be said for everyone keeping their repelled stuff to themselves, if you know what I mean.

By the way, when I was little and Mama was always harping on our underwear, I used to think that clean undies would be the last thing on one's mind if one got in a serious accident, but my sister Cyndie has worked as an emergency room nurse for years, and she has personally witnessed folks coming in worried every bit as much about the state of their Fruit of the Looms as they were about the status of their vitals. Mama considers that vindication. That sort of thing is happening more and more the older we girls get.

Now that I think about it, Mama seemed unusually preoccupied with the vast array of potential accidents back then. I guess raising three tomboys gave her plenty reason to fret. She often said things like "If you fall out of that tree and break your neck, it won't be 'cause I didn't warn you." My sisters and I never understood how Mama being absolved of responsibility would've improved a situation like that, but we knew better than to ask. We might've been country kids, but we weren't stupid. I'd like to think we're not just older now, but wiser, too—wise enough to know that self-cleaning underwear is a time-saving technique whose time should never come.

Self Checkouts and Fatal Exceptions

While some time-saving efforts are just plain nasty, like the aforementioned self-cleaning underwear, others have the potential to be downright dangerous. I, your dutiful hostess, feel compelled to offer y'all a heads-up on what could be an impending disaster, all in the name of time management, but first, an illustrative story to set the mood.

I was running late that day, as usual, and facing long lines at my favorite We've-Got-Everything–You-Need-So-Why-Should-We-Actually-Talk-to-You store." After surveying the shoppers grouped at the mercy of the human checkers and taking a quick tally that revealed two checkers per ninety-three customers, I briefly considered giving the dreaded self-check counters another go. No doubt, you are familiar with those hateful machines. You may even check out without incident. I, however, am not meant to use 'em. I've tried, but lights inevitably start blinking, bells begin ringing, and I can feel everyone looking at me like I'm trying to steal a plank off the White House. Besides, those machines say ugly things to me, in CAPS. I have witnesses. I've been with people who claim, "It's easy! I do it all the time!" until they try self-checking with me. Once that machine sees me, all bets are off. Not that I always have the most positive experiences with human checkers, but I like my odds, most of the time. For this reason, there deep in my heart of hearts I knew where I belonged that day—with the huddled masses.

I appraised the two sole checkers like the experienced

customer I am. I've never won Choose the Fastest Line either, but I refuse to quit playing. I decided against Attila the Hun, a grizzled veteran looking like whowouldathoughtit,* who I felt pretty sure had never been saddled with an employee-of-the-month distinction, in favor of Little Miss Happy, who at the very least seemed to be aiming for the title. Unfortunately, it soon became obvious that she was shooting blanks, bless her heart. When she giggled and pulled the chain of her "I need help" sign for the third straight customer, I silently concurred and switched my allegiance to Attila's line.

I was much older by the time I stood across from Attila watching her manhandle my purchases. I said hello. She grunted. Our relationship showed little promise, but I persevered, arranging my goods helpfully on the moving counter. When Attila reached the end of my items, she picked up that little rubber thingy the man behind me had put down to separate my stuff from his and started searching it from top to bottom. Just as it dawned on me that I was witnessing a brain cramp and that dear tired, overworked Attila was looking for the bar code, she let out a big huffy breath, looked in my general direction, and mumbled, "Do you know how much this is?"

I know I shouldn't have, but by then I was having too much fun to stop. "I think it was $9.99," I said, "but I've changed my mind. I don't want it after all." Poor tired Attila rolled her eyes at me and put the rubber thingy under her counter. I wish I

Official Guide to Speaking All Things Southern

*whowouldathoughtit, adjective: an observation Southern women make about one's appearance. It suggests that they wouldn't have thought anyone would leave the house in the condition in which one was sighted in public!

could've hung around to closing time and watched her try to restock it. I have a feeling she was grunting, in CAPS!

Of course, the big box stores aren't the only ones pushing us to use their inanimate little kiosks. The airline industry is all about 'em. And, to be fair, I do have a better track record with their self-serve stations than I do the big box checkouts, but not even that modicum of success can ease my concern over the arrival of the next wave of do-it-yourself terminals. I'm not sure you're ready for this, but ready or not, here they come. Friends and relatives, prepare yourselves for Self-Serve Emergency Rooms!

Yes, Virginia, they do exist and they're already in use in a number of institutions. You simply type in your personal information and choose the button best describing your symptoms. Hospital spokespersons say the terminals "speed up service and make one's emergency room experience less painful." No doubt they would've been happy to elaborate had they not had to hurry off to their *Last Comic Standing* auditions.

These systems are being billed as user-friendly, but I have my doubts. Supposedly, the patient chooses from a list of complaints ranging from "I stubbed my toe" to "There's an elephant sitting on my chest." This information then appears on the nurses' screen, allowing the true emergencies to receive top priority while the not-so-serious folk wait their turn. At least it does in Perfect. Here in the real world I smell lawsuits. While it may be frustrating to have a machine misread your toilet paper bar code, it'll be tragic when dear old grandpappy thinks he keyed in heart problems only to have the staff crack the window and offer him some Beano. Friends, we're skiing downhill on a slippery slope. One hospital I'll refrain from naming is so pleased with their self-serve kiosks that they've cheerfully announced,

"Plans for self-serve surgery are already on the drawing board." Well, Yippy Skippy!

Surely I can't be the only one who thinks we could be taking the time-management/do-it-yourself craze a tad far with this one. I can see the ad campaign now: "You can do it; we can help!" You're right, that one's taken. Oh, well, I do hope none of you dear readers find yourselves in a self-serve emergency room anytime soon, but should the occasion arise, take a deep breath if you happen to get that "fatal exception" error message. It could just be a poor choice of words.

When DYI Projects Go Wrong

Please understand: I'm not helpless. Over the years I've tackled plenty of projects with a yellow book for dummies and the Cable Guy's now famous "get 'er done" mentality—all to save time, money, or both. I'm just suggesting that not everything is suited for the do-it-yourself approach, although I will be honest enough to admit that this realization has come with age. As a young mother, I once became oh-so-obsessed with do-it-yourself projects. This was the eighties. DIY was all the rage, and I went at it with gusto!

I taught myself to sew and set out to make everything my family wore. The kids were much too young to notice the extra sleeves on their little jumpers, but only true love can explain Beloved Hubby wearing that sad work shirt out of the house, unless he had a change of clothes stashed in the pickup. (You can come clean, honey. The statute of limitations will clear you.) I also made curtains for every window in the house, and I mastered the hottest crafts demonstrated in my mommy magazines. I gardened, I learned woodworking, and once, on a do-it-yourself high, I wallpapered the hall of our tiny starter house in contact paper from the dollar store because it "looked" like wallpaper, and because I could. And yet I knew my limits. Not everyone does.

I've recently learned of a do-it-yourself trend that I cross-my-heart-hope-to-die-stick-a-needle-in-my-eye would never have considered, no, not even in the throes of my obsession. I'm talking about Do-It-Yourself Childbirth. Take a moment to let that sink in. I'll wait . . .

This mother of all do-it-yourself projects is also called unassisted labor, or free birth. There are no doctors, no nurses, and no drugs. To quote one advocate, "The birthing mother simply chooses a comfortable place in her house, gets out of the way, and lets her body give birth." Well, now. Kinda sounds like her body is in one room giving birth while she's in another folding laundry. Neat trick if you can pull it off!

All joking aside, I'd like to go down on record here. Not only am I flat-out impressed by these gals' "Me Woman" attitude, but I'm not worthy to be counted in their number. In the interest of full disclosure, I birthed my first child in the hospital without pain meds. With the second one I wanted two of everything they had, and I'm not proud of it, but I may have threatened my supplier if he didn't deliver. (Of course, if I did do such a thing, which has yet to be proven beyond a reasonable doubt, I'm 100 percent sure I apologized once things calmed down, and I probably even stitched up his torn lab coat.)

For sure, where and how to give birth is a personal decision, but I would like to offer a tip to any fathers out there who may be involved in this intimate drama. I read where one expert suggested it was helpful if the birthing mother could retain a sense of humor during the event. Oh, ya think?! Dad, I'd be very careful about when and how I brought that recommendation up, but that's just me.

My point is simply that DYI projects can go wrong. For illustration I offer you a story that can be traced back to my grade school years and the school bus altercation that left a piece of #2 pencil lead embedded in the shin of my right leg. We won't go into the details of that disagreement other than to say that I still maintain my innocence. Instead, we'll fast forward a decade or so. Beloved Hubby and I were in our twenties, several years and a couple kids into married life. We were short on time and money and, by all account, brains. But that will be apparent soon enough.

By now, that piece of lead had worked itself into a vein in my lower leg. The blasted thing was discoloring my shin and creating a possible health danger, so surgery was scheduled to remove it. I went to sleep believing I'd have one scar several inches above my ankle. I awoke with five incisions and four dozen staples marking up my shin. Over time, the scars have faded, along with my desire to staple the doctor's stethoscope to his chest, but the do-it-yourself-gone-wrong project that followed it stays with me. See, when it came time to have the staples removed, Beloved Hubby suggested he could save us a doctor's visit by taking them out himself. It sounded reasonable at the time.

If you'll quit laughing, I'll explain: (a) The staples appeared to be working their own way out anyway, and (b) we had yet to consider that the unseen ends were angled into my flesh. We assumed they went straight down like those from your regular staple gun. Phil retrieved pliers from his truck, I hopped up on the kitchen counter , and he tested one.

Whoa. That smarted.

Believe it or not, we actually decided that one wasn't "ready," but after my beloved's second staple removal effort failed, I peeled myself from the ceiling and recalled his medical license! I'm slow, but I get there.

Do-it-yourself projects with your spouse, fun.

Do-it-yourself medical projects with your spouse, questionable.

Do-it-yourself medical projects with your spouse using farm tools, deadly for all parties.

Actual Time Tip Straight Ahead

Even now I can hear the angst filled voices of my agent and editor (both of whom are serious book type people who feel strongly that my chapter headings should have something in common with their content) fretting over when, if ever, I plan to include an actual time-management tip. Bless their hearts. I suppose they do have a point. To ease their minds, I shall now offer you three tips for the price of one with a bonus story for illustration.

If, like me, you are the type of person who feels the need for speed, it will be necessary for you to (a) choose your friends wisely because some people make turtles look like Olympic sprinters and will make you want to thread a sewing machine with the needle running, (b) understand that slowpokes are God's children, too, and

My police chief husband tells me to always tell the officer who I am and who he is before the officer starts writing the ticket. Once, after being pulled over in Bradley, Arkansas, I quickly said, "I'm sorry I was speeding, Officer, but my husband is the police chief in Maumelle, Arkansas." He replied, "Lady. Do you know how many times a day I hear that?" I said, "Well, then, we have two problems." (P.S. He wrote the ticket.)

~Terry McBroom Williams
Arkansas

(c) convince these people that you must drive because the shotgun seat makes you car sick.

My friend Rhonda and I have logged a lot of miles the last few years both with my speaking engagements (on which she is so kind to accompany me, and it is going to be a real shame when I rat her out here in just a minute) and in touring with my first book. By the way, we long ago nick named my buddy Red to differentiate her from my middle sister Rhonda. Through it all, I would like to say that I did not get a single speeding ticket. I'm feeling so reformed—not to mention a little proud. (Red would like to add lucky.) Now, in the event that any of you sweet, precious, policemen are listening, I'd like to offer a disclaimer at this time: I try very hard to obey the speed limits. It's just that I was born with a heavy foot. And that's not my fault, either. I got it from Mama's side of the family. I realize some of you may discount the likelihood of such a gene, but not if you're Southern. The scientific community might limit genetic markers to physical resemblances and medical histories, but Southerners can trace most every trait straight through the family tree.

I can honestly say the heavy foot gene is missing in my friend's family. Rhonda and I have vastly different driving styles. She thinks I drive too fast; I know she drives too slow. Over the course of our friendship, Rhonda and I have learned to plan our departure time and resulting ETA according to who's going to be at the wheel. If Rhonda's at the controls, I tack on thirty minutes per every hundred miles. If I'm driving, she subtracts . . . a few . . . 'Nuff said on the grounds that it may incriminate me.

One day we were on an interstate somewhere going some-place for something. Rhonda was at the wheel, and the more the girl talked, the slower she drove. This was far from Thelma and

Louise—heck, this wasn't even Oprah and Gayle's Big Adventure. I was doing my best to pay attention to Rhonda's story line, but the truth is I had gotten a bit preoccupied. I was seriously wondering if I could beat her home on foot when she caught me looking at the speedometer.

"What?" Rhonda said. "Why are you looking at the dashboard?"

I feigned ignorance. "I don't have the slightest idea what you're talking about."

"I guess you think I'm driving too slow!" Rhonda said.

I shrugged.

"That's it, isn't it?" Rhonda asked.

When I grinned in spite of myself, Rhonda said, "I know that's what you're thinking,

I was about seventeen. My girlfriend and I had been hanging out at Desoto Lake in Rena Lara, Mississippi. On the way home I got pulled over for doing 71 in a 55. My heart started racing. Being a typical teenager, my daddy didn't know I was at the lake. A ticket was going to be bad, but where I received it was going to be worse. Thankfully, I happened to pull over on the side of the road beside a dead dog that must have been there awhile as he had a really good stench to him. When the officer could barely hold down his cookies to ask for my license, he decided to let me go with a warning. Saved by the dog! RIP, Fido.

~Amy Self Braswell
Transylvania, Louisiana

Shellie, but at least we won't get a ticket for speeding!"

"I'll have to agree with you there," I told her. "We are in no danger of getting a ticket for speeding." I really would've left it at that, but Rhonda just had to give me a self-satisfied smirk. "Of course," I added, "We might get one for loitering!" Poor Rhonda, if the gene pool holds, her grandkids will have to speed up to fall behind . . .

Carmen the Garmin Gets a Name Change and an Attitude Adjustment

Another of my fine business development ideas came during the release of my first book. Notwithstanding the times we fought over the wheel, Red and I totally enjoyed the *Suck Your Stomach In and Put Some Color On!* book tour or the *Suck It Up* tour, as we aptly renamed it after the fourth city in as many days. Red and I skipped all around Louisiana, Mississippi, Alabama, Arkansas, and Georgia without once getting lost, though I suppose the credit should go to Carmen the Garmin, the GPS navigator Beloved Hubby bought me just for that trip. God be with Carmen, wherever she is today. (*There will be a brief explanation on Carmen's unknown location immediately following this section.)

Carmen was a wealth of knowledge during the tour. She knew it, too. I'm sorry if that sounds ungrateful, but it's like Mama always said: "No one likes a know-it-all." Frankly, after the new wore off, Red and I grew tired of Carmen getting her undergarments twisted up whenever we chose a turn that wasn't on her preplanned and highlighted route. If I didn't turn exactly when and where she wanted me to turn, she'd cop an attitude. "Recalculating" she'd say politely but pointedly, and with a noticeable sigh that sounded more like "What part of *take the next exit* confused you girls the most?"

Once, in Mobile, when she was acting particularly snippy, Red and I were in the middle of suggesting that perhaps she needed an attitude adjustment when Carmen up and announced in her curt little way, "I have lost my satellite signal." True, we were in a tunnel at the time, and it was the same tunnel she'd just tried to warn us not to take, so I suppose her prissy little announcement could have been legit, but I swanee, you could almost hear her snickering, and that brings me to my grand idea.

I have considered marketing a Southern GPS, you know, one with a good double Southern name, some new and improved manners, and a more pleasing personality. Red and I were thinking that Mary Elisabeth sounded nice. Not only would she be more considerate and understanding when you missed your exit, but she'd help prevent such unfortunate mistakes way ahead of time by saying things like "Pardon me for interrupting, Sugar, but you need to be getting in the right lane. Y'all gonna have to turn up the road a piece—right beside that house where the little boy with the big ears is riding his bicycle in the driveway. Good Lord, I wonder if his mama has ever thought about having those things fixed. You can, you know."

Shellie, I love that Southern GPS idea you were talking about on the radio. I mean, forget the technical mumbo-jumbo that was probably programmed in India and give us something that talks and thinks like we do. Tell us to go a far piece, over yonder, a country mile, past the bend in the road, etc.

~LauraBeth DeHority
A Southern Girl in San Jose, California

Think about it! Wouldn't it be nice to have a bit of encouragement after a successful exit in the middle of heavy traffic, like maybe "You go, girl!" Of course, being Southern, Mary Elisabeth would tack on some free fashion advice, which, I believe, would make her an instant hit with our fellow belles. "You are now arriving at destination on right. Have a nice time and don't forget to suck your stomach in and put some color on."

Thank you. I thought the idea was brilliant, too, but I lost my will to live over the details necessary to actually pursue my ingenious product. Just joking—what I meant was, I lost my focus. Seriously, I may be all good on the creative part, but my mind does wander on the business end. It wasn't nearly as easy as I thought it might be. That's why I decided to just change my GPS's name to Mary Elisabeth instead and hope for the best.

Unfortunately, the name change didn't work out so well, either. Perhaps I should've listened to Puff Daddy, or P. Diddy, or plain Diddy, or is it Sean John now? The point is that Husband and I went to Destin, Florida, shortly after Carmen's moniker makeover, to attend a family wedding, and despite her newly christened Southern double name, my GPS had a small stroke trying to find the condo where we were supposed to be staying. (A rose is a rose is a rose.)

Our plans were to stay in the same condo that was housing Mama, Papa, Aunt Judy, Uncle Wayne, and their grandson Jackson. While the GPS was blowing a gasket with Destin's revamped coastline, I was on the cell phone with Aunt Judy and Mama. God love 'em, both of them were trying valiantly to direct us to the condo.

"We're standing right out front on the corner," the sisters said. "Do you see us?"

Phil and I strained to scan both sides of the street while the cars behind us urged us to keep it moving.

"No, ma'am," I said.

"Do you see a big cream building?" they asked in unison.

"Yes'm, we see twenty-five big cream buildings."

That's the type of rejoinder that could stymie some people. The Golden Girls were undeterred. "Our condo's pink, Shellie, and its right beside a blue one." I casually mentioned that pink and blue seemed to be a popular condo theme down there. "Oh," they said, only briefly dejected.

"Listen sweetie," Aunt Judy said. "We're waving really big. Do you see us now?"

"No, ma'am, I'm sorry . . ."

And that, y'all, is when my aunt, whom I have known and recognized from my earliest memory, standing with the woman who birthed me, offered the following helpful directions. "Look-a-here, Shellie, I have on a white tank top shirt with blue shorts and your mama's wearing a little tee with orange shorts."

For the life of me, I still can't imagine why those two thought I needed help recognizing them, but it's just the type of humorous logic I hope to work into my Southern GPS idea if I ever get back to it. That sort of thing might not help you get where you're going, but I guarantee you'll enjoy the ride!

While visiting my daughter in Houston, Texas, a thief, or thieves, broke out the passenger window of my car and made off with dear old Mary Elisabeth! It has been my prayer that they'd type in pawn shop and she'd direct them straight to police headquarters instead. I miss you, Mary Elisabeth, bossy voice and all. Traveling has not been the same without you.

When I would ask for something unattainable, my mother would say, "Spit in one hand and wish in the other and see which gets full the fastest."

~Renea Winchester
Roswell, Georgia

Top That, Blue Collar Boys

Another business development idea that has been kicked around the porch recently was an all-female comedy tour with Southern style humor. It seemed like a good idea, as the entertainment field appears rife for belleisms.* Not long ago a few of us took a stab at it.

No doubt you've heard of the Blue Collar Comedy Tour, an act comprised of four famous comedians, but have you heard of the Pink Collar Comedy Tour? No? Well, give it time, just give it time. You may yet. It's been a couple years now since three female author friends and I made our stage debut at the Pulpwood Festival/Girlfriend Weekend in Jefferson, Texas, but we haven't closed the door on an encore. Our show was comprised of Kathy Patrick, the original Pulpwood Queen, Suzanne McLennan, author of *Praise the Lord and Pass the Biscuits*, River Jordan, author of *Praying for Strangers*, and yours truly. There was no lack of big hair, tiaras, and rhinestones. Top that, Blue Collar boys!

With absolutely no practice and scant preparation, we girls took the stage and our seats in those four metal lawn chairs, tossed out a subject, and took turns milking it. Segues were nice, but they weren't considered a prerequisite. We slid from funeral missteps and family eccentrics to blessing hearts and garden club dropouts, without nothing more than a "that reminds me" to tie 'em together. Suffice to say a number of our revelations evolved accidentally.

For instance, River Jordan and I discovered that our extended families share a strong commitment to drug preservation. Let the rest of the world preserve the environment, the Southern women in our families are bent on rescuing leftover pain medicine. Have surgery, save medicine. And if the prescription says fill twice,

Official Guide to Speaking All Things Southern

*belleisms (bell-is-'ems), noun: witty observations born from the southern persuasion

well, for goodness' sakes, girl—fill it twice. You never know when somebody in the family will need it.

The more the crowd laughed, the heavier our Southern accents became, until I thought for sure they'd have to shovel us out of there when we were done. Why, even the Pulpwood Queen, a native of Kansas, was developing a faint drawl. Which reminds me, Mr. Foxworthy, one of your foursome—that cable guy—he's from Nebraska, which is kinda like Kansas, almost. I think it's a sign myself, and you know how we Southerners feel about signs. Come on, Jeff. Have your people give our people a call and we'll open for y'all, unless of course you're worried about four middle-aged women upstaging you. If that's the case, you may be a redneck boy . . .

Dear readers, the only thing holding the Pink Collar Comedy Tour back at this point is a little clamor. If y'all would be so inclined to start some clamoring, we may be able to pull some sponsors together and get some wheels on this thing. The way I see it, the material would take care of itself. Like I told my Pink Collar partners, all we really have to do is listen to your stories afterward at the book table while we're signing authographs, polish 'em up a bit, use our storytelling licenses, and voilà—we'll be set for the next city. At least, that's how it works for me.

My previous book tour yielded material at every stop. I met the most interesting Southern women that summer. In Jackson, Mississippi, I enjoyed visiting with Amie, a pretty young belle who'd graduated college and taken a job in her hometown despite the promises she'd once made herself about moving as far away as she could from "The Compound," a street heavily laden with the married women of her family, their husbands and off-spring, anchored by Grandma the Matriarch and recently joined by Amie's older sister, who built a new home directly across from their mom. As of this writing, Amie is still managing to hold out

I knew Mama was unique in some ways but I didn't know she was part of a breed until I read your first book. Here are some of her words of wisdom. On travel: "There are only two rules: Keep your knees together and your purse zipped." When we were on her last nerve: "I'm going to pinch your head off and spit in the hole." (Once my sister and I foolishly asked why she'd spit in the hole and she said, "Because spit burns!") She also liked to say, "I'm going to skin you alive and tack it to the wall!" (She never did anything of the sort but my cousin had a bull skin tacked to his wall, so the possibilities raised some fear in us.) I'm glad to know others appreciate a raising some experts say left us scarred for life. If that's so, I wear my scars proudly!

~Leslie Smith
Thomson, Georgia

against The Compound, which she swears is something akin to a cult. She says she will never ever move there. But after all her vehement disclaimers, dear Amie left me in stitches with her parting words of resignation: "Course, you just know I'm gonna be there in five years!"

And then there was Rita in Atlanta, Georgia, who charmed me with stories of her Southern mama, a healthy belle in her late eighties, living alone and growing feistier by the day. Her mother's favorite ploy is to put the house on the market. Indeed, whenever she's feeling neglected she likes to pull a lawn chair out to the curb and prop up a homemade "For Sale" sign. While she never intends to follow through, her time-tested SOS is a well-developed signal that never fails to get her girls' attention. Remember when our mamas asked our daddies, "Do you know what your child did today?" Now, like siblings everywhere, Rita told me that she and her sisters take turns pulling their hair out over their dearly loved mama's endless antics and calling one another to ask, "Do you know what your mama did today?" I think they call that payback.

And, who could ever forget the Alabama belle I met who was reclaiming her sass after losing well over two hundred pounds! She said her teenage daughter was astonished at how prissy she had become since her makeover. Miss Alabama told her child that she hasn't really changed on the inside, explaining that it's just hard to be prissy at four hundred pounds. At that point Miss Alabama lowered her voice and added that she did intend to leave some meat on her bones because—and I'm quoting her now—"Southern men don't wanna have to shake their sheets to find their women." Indeed.

Deer Urine and Marketing Magic

Be at peace, friends. I realize that so far these have all been business development ideas for yours truly here at *All Things Southern*, and you may have been hoping for advice as to some moneymaking products of your own. That's a perfectly reasonable expectation, especially since the powers that be insist on shelving my books in the self-help section. And for the record, might I just add that this is not of my doing! I'd prefer to be in the classics aisle with fellow Southerner Mark Twain, but I don't see that happening anytime soon.

Let it not be said, however, that I'm insensitive to your needs, dear reader. With the economy on the skids, I, too, have been casting about for moneymaking ideas to supplement the family income, you know, beyond my written work at *All Things Southern* so trust me, I feel your pain. I mean, there are only so many times I can work the title of my last book into a column, blog post, or porch chat, regardless of how important it is to Suck Your Stomach In and Put Some Color On. I've tried to explain to the hubby that we should just spend our way out of financial stress like the government is so fond of doing, bless their hearts, but I have yet to sell him on the theory. Whatever.

To prove that I care about y'all, I'm about to share what I consider to be the greatest single marketing frontier out there today. And no, I'm not even worried about letting y'all in on my intentions, as there is ample room for each of us on this promising bandwagon. Here it is in a nutshell: We need to sell stuff to hunters. Deer hunters, duck hunters—it doesn't really matter. It's like six of one and half a dozen of the other here. Trust me, my friends, hunters will show us the money!

Okay, so you'll need an idea. The right one hasn't hit me yet, either, but I'm optimistic. I remain convinced that there's a creative product out there I can develop and sell to hunters. I know this because our men pay good money for deer urine—fresh deer urine. Indeed, the hunter shopper is an interesting study in relativity. The same man that is worried about the high cost of cleaning supplies for your home will purchase a tiny bottle of special detergent—for $17—that will remove all trace of scent from approximately two whole loads of hunting clothes. Later on, during the real hunt, this same man will bathe in non-scent soap and shampoo and pack his scent-free clothes in scent-free bags, just so he can get to the woods and douse his surroundings with deer urine. And not just any deer urine, but a carefully chosen aroma of doe-in-love urine blended with mighty buck urine and guaranteed to permanently affix itself to whatever it touches. I can vouch for the mighty and permanent claims. Last year, Beloved Hubby dropped a bottle of that potent stuff in my laundry room, and for a time there, I considered killing him and telling the Good Lord he died.

Hubby orders this stuff from his precious Cabela's catalogs.

You may want to pick up one of these publications for your own research purposes. They can not only yield important data about your potential customers, but I've found them to be good sources of comic relief. For example, I enjoy reading the advertisements from the competing urine companies, all boasting of how fresh their urine is based on how recently their samples were collected. I can't shake the visual of two deer holding those little cups you get at the doctor's office and saying, "But, seriously, I just don't need to go . . ."

We Oughta Be in Pictures

Do not despair. If you're unable to come up with a good product for this lucrative hunter's market, I may be able to offer you an opportunity to get in on the ground floor of another of my brilliant business ideas. In the past few years, a family of good old boys from my neck of the woods here in Northeast Louisiana has made quite a name for themselves in the hunting industry. The Duck Commander and his boys have even launched their own show on the Outdoor Channel. Yours truly was honored to have a bit part in their television debut, even if it was only a matter of being in the right place at the right time. I interviewed them on my radio talk show, *All Things Southern LIVE*, during the time they were taping their first season. Prince Willie, the Duck Commander's son, and his mama, Queen Kay, showed up in the studio of FOXFM92.7 with their film crew in tow.

They were very entertaining guests. I had a great time visiting with them, and I enjoyed hearing from my readers around the South a few months later. They were as surprised to find me on the Outdoor Channel as I was to be there. But the whole experience also gave me another of my brilliant ideas. I mention it here because I could be tempted to take on partners.

In the past, I've expressed my severe distaste over the emergence of reality TV. Well, no more. If people wanna eat cockroaches, that's their business. I still have no interest in joining 'em, but it has occurred to me that there may be a way to ride this wave, folks. I'm looking at developing my own television series, combining the most popular crime-stopping shows with the draw of the Outdoor Channel and mixed with a little reality TV. It'd be sort of like *Fear Factor, Without a Trace*, and *Survivor* all rolled into one.

In the pilot, Dixie Belle, my chocolate Lab and esteemed associate, would join me to investigate the disappearance of a local hunter. We'd begin by retracing his steps and documenting his recent purchases. That's the *Fear Factor* part. His spouse's expression when she calculates the dollars he has spent on his hunting loop should be must-see TV. I can't give the ending away, but there's a reunion scene between our supposed "vic," his wife, and a stack of sales receipts where someone needs an immunity necklace. Brilliant, I know, but if that pilot doesn't get picked up, I have another idea.

How about Last Hunter Standing? The contestants could all be avid deer hunters. As the season approaches we can see who is able to go the longest without hunting. Each week our guys will be forced to watch as actors, pretending to be "inept hunters" go about hunting from our contestants' own deer stands! These fake hunters won't use deer urine, or dress in camouflage, and they'll laugh and talk while they are "hunting." Watching the real hunters reactions should make compelling TV. I expect we'll see who the real survivors are! Stay tuned. We may be coming to a television set near you.

Time Management and Business Development Tips

THUS SAITH THE BELLE DOCTRINE . . .

* Time required maintaining thy clean panty status is both necessary and nonnegotiable.

* Murphy's Law on time management and checkout stands holds that the line thou aren't in is the quickest one.

* If saving time or money involves pain, the savings isn't worth it if the pain is thine own.

* Consider mining thy belleisms in the entertainment field.

* When considering product development, hunters are likely to be thy most promising demographic.

Casserole Recipes to Beat the Clock

When faced with a squeezed schedule, make like a Southern cook and turn to the one-pot wonder. We Southerners are accustomed to taking a good bit of ribbing for our casseroles, but we don't mind, not really, because we know that with a repertoire of these dishes we're always just a few steps away from delivering a complete meal to a friend or relative in need. And that's a worthy cause in our book. Whether its bad news striking at your neighbor's house, an anticipated visit from the stork, or a bit of unexpected company, the right ingredients in the freezer and pantry mean you can show up with a steaming dish in record time. Sometimes we make a double recipe just to freeze that extra casserole for an emergency. By the way, if you're cooking for someone who doesn't like the idea, take a page from my darling daughter's book. Her sweet husband isn't big on casseroles. Jessica handles this by avoiding all use of the "c" word, and her man just raves over her cooking. Here are a few popular casseroles from my house to yours.

Awesome Artichoke Casserole

(SERVES 6–8)

We're all indebted to the soul who looked at the artichoke and saw more than a pretty face. The edible flower is a standout ingredient in many a dip recipe, but it's just as willing to shine in a host of other dishes. For instance, here's a flavor-packed recipe that will make the standard green bean casserole green with envy.

- 2 cloves garlic, chopped (or a tablespoon from
    the refrigerated jar)
- 1 tablespoon butter
- 1 (16 oz.) can cut green beans, drained
- 1 (14 oz.) can artichokes, drained and chopped
- 1 small bunch green onions, chopped
- 4 ounces grated Parmesan cheese
- 4 ounces shredded mozzarella
- ½ cup olive oil for drizzling
- 1 teaspoon Italian herb seasoning
- 1 teaspoon red pepper
- Salt and pepper to taste
- ½ cup bread crumbs

Preheat your oven to 400 degrees. Sauté garlic in butter. Combine with green beans and chopped artichokes and green onions. Stir in both cheeses, spread in a lightly greased 9×13 baking dish, and season with Italian herb seasoning and red pepper. Salt and pepper to taste, and top with crushed bread crumbs. Drizzle with olive oil and bake for thirty minutes.

Frito Pie Shellee

(SERVES 6–8)

I call this dish Frito Pie Shellee because it sounds like a party, which is exactly what happens whenever I whip this baby up for my circle of loved ones. If you add it to your recipe book, feel free to substitute your name where you see mine!

1 pound ground beef

¼ cup chopped onion

¼ cup chopped green pepper

1 (16 oz.) can diced tomatoes

1 (12 oz.) can whole kernel corn, drained

1 (8 oz.) can tomato sauce

½ cup sliced black olives

½ teaspoons chili powder

Dash of oregano and cumin

1 cup crushed corn chips

1 cup shredded cheese

Preheat oven to 350 degrees. Brown ground beef with onion and green pepper. Drain well and combine with diced tomatoes, corn, tomato sauce, and sliced olives. Add chili powder, oregano, and cumin, stir well to blend the seasonings, and finish by sprinkling with crushed corn chips and a cheese of your choice. Your ingredients are basically cooked. Bake finished dish in oven until it is heated through and through.

Tomato Pesto Pasta

(SERVES 6)

Speedy cooks have a lot of secrets. Here's one of the best. If you're trying to save time, you can't fail by reaching for the pasta! Its versatility as a hot or cold dish is well known. Here's another of those simple and satisfying dishes that's happy at either temperature:

1 (16 oz.) package of your favorite pasta
2 tablespoons extra virgin olive oil
½ cup chopped onion
2½ tablespoons store-bought sun-dried tomato pesto
2 tablespoons grated Romano cheese
1 small can chopped black olives
Salt and pepper to taste

Cook pasta according to the package directions. Drain. Heat olive oil in a cast iron skillet and sauté chopped onion with sun-dried tomato pesto. Cook over medium heat until the onions are soft and clear. Combine in a casserole dish with cooked pasta and chopped black olives. Salt and pepper to taste and top with cheese.

Sausage and Cornbread Pie

(SERVES 6–8)

I suppose you can make this hearty dish year-round, but it's one of those family favorites I tend to reach for when the temperature starts dropping. My group considers it soul-satisfying comfort food on a cold winter's day.

1 pound ground pork sausage

1 cup chopped onion

1 (28 oz.) can tomatoes, undrained

1 (4 oz.) can chopped green chilies, undrained

1 cup frozen whole kernel corn

1 teaspoon chili powder

1 teaspoon garlic powder

1 cup yellow cornmeal

⅔ cup self-rising flour

½ teaspoon salt

2 teaspoons sugar

1 egg, beaten

⅔ cup milk

¼ cup vegetable oil

Preheat oven to 375 degrees. Brown sausage and onions together, breaking up sausage with the back of your spoon. Drain off fat. Add tomatoes, green chilies, corn, chili powder, and garlic powder. Spoon into a lightly greased baking dish and set aside. Stir together cornmeal, flour, salt, and sugar before adding wet ingredients: egg, milk, and oil. Pour this cornbread mix over the sausage base and bake for 40 minutes.

Crawfish Pie

(SERVES 6–8)

A refrigerated pie crust delivers an easy and pretty presentation to this homemade crawfish pie, but once it's sliced and served, the flavor takes center stage. This delightful marriage of crawfish, sausage, and corn will deliver the goods and have you basking in the compliments.

1 bag of frozen onion, bell pepper, and celery

2 tablespoons butter

1 (15 oz.) can whole kernel corn, drained

1 (15 oz.) can cream-style corn

1 can cream of mushroom soup

1 tablespoon tomato sauce or salsa

1 pound crawfish tails

½ pound smoked sausage, cut in ¼-inch slices

½ cup seasoned bread crumbs

1 egg, beaten

1 cup milk

¼ cup minced parsley

¼ teaspoon lemon pepper

⅛ teaspoon red pepper

⅛ teaspoon celery salt

Salt and pepper to taste

1 refrigerated pie crust

Preheat oven to 350 degrees. Take a large cast iron skillet and sauté onions, peppers, and celery in butter. Once the vegetables are tender, add drained whole corn, cream corn, and mushroom soup. Stir in tomato sauce, crawfish tails, and smoked sausage. Cook ten minutes and remove from fire. Add bread crumbs, beaten egg, milk, and seasonings. Pour mixture into a greased casserole dish. Spread a refrigerated pie crust out flat and cut into one inch strips with pastry knife. Use the strips to make a pretty plaid pattern across the top of your pie. Beautiful! Bake for 35 minutes, until lightly brown, and dig in. Or, as we say in the South, "Amen, Brother Ben, back your ears and dive in."

Creamy Crab Casserole

(SERVES 6–8)

This Creamy Crab Casserole is one of my family's favorites. And with a slight twist, it's also a great recipe for parties. Just omit the pasta, keep warm in a pretty chafing dish and offer with your favorite cracker or toast points.

1 cup cottage cheese

1 cup sour cream

6 ounces cooked and drained pasta, your choice of shape, but I usually use bowtie

½ cup chopped white onion

½ cup chopped green pepper

12 ounces imitation (or fresh) crabmeat, chopped

Salt and pepper to taste

1 teaspoon garlic powder

1 teaspoon Worcestershire sauce

Dash of hot sauce

1 cup Parmesan cheese

Preheat oven to 350 degrees. Combine cottage cheese and sour cream with pasta in large mixing bowl. Stir in onions and peppers and imitation crabmeat. (If you have fresh crabmeat, that's all the better!) Season well with salt, pepper, garlic powder, and Worcestershire and hot sauces and place in a greased casserole dish. Sprinkle with Parmesan cheese and bake for 45 minutes. This is also good with crawfish tails! Enjoy, folks! That's good eating, Southern style.

One Pot Chicken Spaghetti

(SERVES 6–8)

My married daughter encouraged me to share this dish. In the interest of full disclosure, neither of us Southern cooks start with the more involved roux version anymore. We also suspect, even if we can't prove it, that we're not alone. This one's so much easier and it delivers the same big taste with half as much fuss. Starting with bone-in chicken always delivers more flavor but we've been known to use boneless, skinless breast in a pinch!

32 ounces vermicelli

5 to 6 boneless, skinless chicken breasts

1 bag frozen cut-up onions and peppers

2 cans seasoned chicken broth

1 stick of butter

1 can RO*TEL tomatoes

1 small jar pimientos

1 can cream of celery soup

1 small can sliced mushrooms

1 pound Velveeta cheese

Salt and pepper

Garlic powder

Top with Parmesan cheese

Place chicken breasts, onions, and peppers in a large pot. Add seasoned chicken stock and bring to a boil. (If the stock doesn't cover the chicken breasts, add extra water until it does.) Lower heat and simmer until your chicken is no longer pink, then remove to cool. Don't overcook the chicken. You'll add it back to the pot shortly. Once your chicken is cool, pull it into bite-size pieces. Meanwhile, bring broth to a rolling boil, add vermicelli, and cook 6 minutes. Turn the heat down and stir in a stick of butter, a can of Rotel tomatoes, a jar of pimentos, a can of cream of celery soup, and your sliced mushrooms. Add Velveeta cheese and stir well. When the cheese melts, return your chicken to the pot, season with salt and pepper and garlic powder and cook on low for twenty or thirty minutes, or until it's heated through and bubbly. When you're ready to eat, top with shredded Parmesan and enjoy!

Tater Tot Casserole

(SERVES 6–8)

Here's a dish my mama has served since way back when. It was a favorite then, and it was a big hit with my own kids when they were small. If you have any finicky little eaters at your house, whip up this Tater Tot Casserole and watch them respond. I've never seen a child that wouldn't try it (or, for that matter, a man that wouldn't eat his fair share!).

1 pound ground beef
1 small onion, chopped
1 can cream of mushroom soup
1 cup shredded cheddar cheese
½ teaspoon salt
½ teaspoon pepper
1 (32 oz.) bag frozen Tater Tots

Preheat oven to 350 degrees. Brown ground beef with chopped onion. Drain off the fat. Layer in the bottom of a 9×13 casserole dish and cover with cream of mushroom soup, undiluted. Sprinkle with a cup of shredded cheddar. Top with frozen Tater Tots and bake for 30–45 minutes, or until the casserole is heated through and the Tots are done. If they're serving to adults, some people like to add a can of Veg-All under the tater tots. For those small kids, might I suggest you leave well enough alone and add whatever vegetable dishes you'd like on the side. They're only young once. Sometimes, you just need to cater to the little darlings.

5

Ya Southern Mama Is Following You on Twitter

Thoughts on Manners and Social Media
with Snacks to Please Any Crowd

Long, long ago, in a land that time has forgotten, well-mannered children were trained to answer the phone with a polite greeting and a formal inquiry, "To whom do you wish to speak?" Yeah, I'm not exactly sure when that was either, as no kid I know ever talked like that, but at least my friends and I had the teenage pleasure of running to answer the phone full of hopeful anticipation. Is it for me? And is it who I want it to be? Sadly, that's something our grandchildren will never know. Answering a phone on your hip that's equipped with

My grandson is a real child of the South, maybe even a throwback to another time! Once, when he was in preschool, I got a call from his teacher that P.J. was sick and needed to be picked up early. Naturally, I rushed over. Once I had him in the car, I asked what was wrong. His answer, "Grandmama, I've taken ill."

~Gail Weickhardt
Port Royal, South Carolina

caller ID has a way of taking all the mystery out of whether or not it's for you.

But enough complaining, friends. This type of change brings choices. One can embrace it and move on, or resist it and get left behind. It's far better to repeat after me, "Technology is our friend." Of course, I suppose there is another more painful option. One can always fall out and get run over by the tech train. Tragically, this is what seems to happen to far too many of the poor souls in my parents' generation. They have a difficult time bonding with technology no matter how hard they try. Take my friend, Mrs. Nancy, who recently had an experience that taught her two things: (a) she is ignorant when it comes to computers, which she already suspected, and (b) she can't trust her own children, which she also suspected, but now she has proof.

The other night Mrs. Nancy was going through her email when she began hearing a series of musical notes, sort of like her laptop does when it's starting up or getting mail, only it wasn't doing either, and she couldn't locate the sound's origin. After completely exhausting her troubleshooting skills, which took at least five good minutes and consisted mostly of her staring at the screen, she was forced to call tech support (or what I fondly refer to as Customer H-E-Double L) to try and communicate with those very smart people who speak very broken English. As time wore on, and Mrs. Nancy wore down, their relationship deteriorated. Soon Mrs. Nancy was going through techies faster than Paula Deen goes through butter. One of the consultants tried to convince her that he was state-side and one of 'em actually *hung up on her*, which I think could be a first in customer service history.

Mrs. Nancy finally ended up with a nice young girl who was determined to identify the laptop's mysterious sound, a combination of musical notes that came at regular three- to five-minute intervals, even with the computer off! They tried everything, including taking the battery out, but the sound continued to play. Tech Girl's last-ditch effort was to have Mrs. Nancy locate a tiny screwdriver and remove the memory card. She wanted Mrs. Nancy to operate on the computer, but that's where my friend drew the line. She wasn't about to go there! Instead, she made an arrangement for Dell to call back the next morning to talk to her more computer-literate husband.

And so it was that at one-thirty in the morning, some six hours after that first unidentified sound, Mrs. Nancy and Tech Girl broke fellowship.* My friend grabbed her purse and began stuffing her paperwork inside it as she limped to bed, disgusted and worn out, only she couldn't sleep because the message notes could still be heard chiming from the computer in the other part of the house. Mrs. Nancy had gotten up to close the bedroom door when she realized that the sound

Official Guide to Speaking
All Things Southern

*broke fellowship: phrase meaning to agree to disagree and go your separate ways with no ill feelings

was actually coming from her purse and, in particular, the cell phone within. You guessed it. Someone had sent her a text message, only Mrs. Nancy doesn't text, bless her heart, so she had no way of knowing that her phone's text alerts sounded much like the notification signals on her computer.

The next morning, Mrs. Nancy sent her son, Michael, a sheepish email about her experience, asking him not to tell anyone else about it. All she needed was to figure out what to tell tech support when they called and how to put her husband's laptop back together before he found it! Her darling son, however, not only repeated the story, he forwarded it to his siblings *and* his work associates. Oh, and did I mention that Michael works at Microsoft?! Poor Mrs. Nancy, she didn't just meet the enemy, she may have birthed him.

Click This!

Computers hold way too much power over some of us, and they know it, y'all! I'll never forget the horror I felt the first time mine told me I had performed an "illegal procedure"! Why, I've never done anything illegal in my life, except for those occasional little speeding tickets, and maybe those road signs we took when we were teenagers, but really, isn't there a statute of limitations on that kind of thing?

My computer doesn't just sass me, either. It also threatens me. Sometimes it says, "If you repeat the error, this computer will shut down." I resent that. It sounds like one of my mama's lines, "Do that again and I'm taking you to the back room." I think they should reprogram it to say something nicer, something Southern like "Oops, sorry, Sugar, wrong button. But that was a good idea. You just try again, you hear?" Come to think of it, I wouldn't even mind a little humor thrown in. It might lighten the mood a little if one of those boxes popped up with something like "Honey, you can't play slick'em with a bar of soap, can you, now?"

So far, I've managed to avoid the "worry gene" that runs rampant in my family's female DNA, but my computer seems bent on fixing that, too. Not a day goes by that my email box isn't flooded with things I'm supposed to be worrying about. Many of these concerns have a Chicken Little feel, only the senders know the sky is falling because their "mother's sister's cousin-in-law's uncle's aunt had X and Y happen to them and this isn't just a forward and you have to pass it along lest you be guilty of accelerating the extinction of mankind."

Whoa—it's right powerful stuff! I swanee, many a day I'd crawl right back into bed if I were the worrying sort—which I'm not. If anything worried me, it'd be my inability to worry, which suggests that I don't know enough to worry, but I'm not worried. I'm a Tigger and proud of it. Indeed, this is a character flaw to those dedicated emailers trying to alert me to the dangers of _____. (You fill in the blank.) Fortunately, many of these ominous emails have places where I can donate to their cause to ease my mind or buy their products to protect myself. Lucky me, or is that "lucky them"?

Not that I'm questioning everyone's motives. I'm sure the Chicago woman who developed the gas mask brassiere did it for the good of mankind. That would be the female undergarment that's ready to be deployed at the first sign of chemical attack, or perhaps even the germs of a fellow human. When threatened, the wearer can simply snatch off the undergarment and detach the individual cups, each of which can now double as a gas mask—one for her and one for the lucky bystander of her choice. (Bubba said if his Aunt Clydette had one she could save half of the town all by herself, but I told him that was flat-out ugly and he should stop. Besides, if anybody other than Uncle Amos buried his face there, that poor soul would soon discover that a nuclear attack would be a much preferable way to go! Uncle Amos has a right nasty jealous streak.)

As strained as the relationship is between me and my computer, here's a fact that will make the techies at my ISP fall out of their chairs laughing: In my family, I'm considered the computer wizard. It's true. Papa thinks I can fix anything. But then,

Papa makes me look like Bill Gates. You should see the way that man works a mouse. His style is quadruple-click quick. He works that mouse like a madman and can't understand why the computer freezes up. On the other side of the family, my husband's dad employs the stealthy, yet forceful, mighty click method. His index finger hovers over the mouse waiting for just the right moment to strike. WHAM! What can I say? Papa and Grand Buzzy—they don't do windows—95, 98, or XP!

Texting, One-Two-Three

In light of all this computer angst, the following admission may come as a surprise, but yours truly here is quite the little texter. At least I have been since I traded in my old flip-top phone for my sweet BlackBerry with its handy dandy keyboard. In the ancient days of B.B. (before BBerry), my kids would text me a complete novella in subsequent messages in the time it took for me to respond on my ancient cell phone with a laborious y . . . e . . . s . . .

As college kids, Jessica and Phillip were initially delighted with my new skills, but as sometimes happens to those who are involved with people like me (translation: people who do not come with a filter), they have lost some of their enthusiasm over the past couple years. To be honest, I may have gone a little overboard with the hospital texts the day I had my first grandchild. Of course, I didn't actually have my granddaughter, my daughter-in-law did, which is how it should be, y'all. I read about that woman who had her daughter's triplets and I think she must be a real stand-up type of gal for doing that for her loved ones, but I'm glad I didn't have to birth my grandbaby.

It's been a couple decades now since I've pulled an all-nighter at the hospital waiting on a baby to arrive, but I can tell you one thing straight up. It's a whole lot more fun when you're not the one doing the heavy lifting.

From start to finish my trusty BBerry and I kept up a running text with the friends and family who couldn't be there in person, giving them periodic updates on our progress. Once, I even caught myself texting Carey, the laboring mother to be, with the following exciting message, "We're at SEVEN CENTIMETERS!" Thankfully, I caught myself before hitting send. I'm pretty sure it wouldn't have come as much of a surprise.

All in all, my son and daughter-in-law did a fantastic job. Throughout the birth, I found myself thinking how such an event could be so unique, so personal, and so individual while echoing the experiences of people everywhere. For instance, once, as the birth neared, I was standing at Carey's bedside watching my son watch his laboring wife with a tender, how-can-I-help look that made me say, "It hurts you, too, doesn't it, Phillip?" He nodded. "Makes you want to do something, doesn't it?" Before Phillip could answer, Carey said through gritted teeth, "He's already done something. That's why I'm here." Carey didn't laugh. The rest of us couldn't help it.

A few short months after Emerson Ann was born, my daughter gave birth to our first grandson. Pops (Beloved Hubby) and I (known as Keggie for the wee ones) would've been totally shut out of the second birth were it not for the beauty of texting. Let it be known that we had a plan worked out where we would be there for the big event, but Jessica didn't work the plan. Or, should I say, Grant Thomas didn't work the plan. As we all know, when the little ones decide it's time, the rest of us are just along for the ride!

As Pops and I sped down the interstate from Louisiana to Texas, my sweet son-in-law kept us informed with regular texts from the delivery room. Things were happening oh so much faster than anyone had anticipated. I relayed the messages to Phil as he drove and scolded myself when I realized I was hoping the birth might take just a wee bit longer. I felt quite sure Jessica would never forgive me for wanting to stretch it out. About that time Patrick called and put us on speaker phone so I could speak to Jessica briefly. The doctor had said it was time to push. Tears strolled down from my eyes when I realized I wouldn't be there with my firstborn daughter during her big moment, but as I bid her our love and God's great blessings, I knew that I'd never been more thankful for the technology that helped in some small way to bridge the distance.

In all seriousness, gratitude would be one of the manners that sorely needs to make a comeback in our society. I think learning to be grateful is a lot like making banana nut bread. Mama taught me that I should never throw out old bananas just because they look bad. They may not look appealing, but they're just right for making the best banana nut bread because the broken-down sugar in the bruised fruit lends the bread an extra sweet flavor. Likewise, gratitude is one of the nicest manners we can cultivate, because a healthy sense of appreciation can often squeeze the sweet out of what would otherwise just seem sad.

Twitter Dee, Twitter Dumb

For all of its advantages, technology has also brought us to a whole new standard of strange. Methinks we need a course in civility and a little brushing off of the old manners now more than ever. As The Belle of *All Things Southern*, I'm willing to avail myself to help sort out these new challenges by drawing on the tremendous body of knowledge passed on to me through my Southern heritage.

It may behoove us to begin with a story to illustrate just how much our world has changed. Not long ago I read where this Japanese woman was arrested for allegedly killing her husband, only he wasn't her real-life husband, he was her virtual husband in this online game and they weren't really married, not anymore. See, he had virtually divorced her without giving her any virtual notice—which is why she stole his log-in information and whacked him—the virtual fellow, I mean. The real guy who operated him is alive and kicking, but she was hauled to the not so virtual slammer. Are y'all still with me?

I think there's a bit of Southern soul somewhere inside of me. Believe it or not, there are some traditionally-minded people up here who wish to impart some good old-fashioned wisdom to our offspring. Having two daughters of my own, I'm personally using the info from your first book to mold my girls into proper women. I've already started telling my two and a half year old that "good girls don't yell at the top of their lungs" and it seems to be registering! So, thank you!

~Mrs. Iva Musa
A Northern Reader

Granted, this kind of thing can lead one to believe the whole world is going straight running crazy, but my fellow Southerners, I'm here to tell you that we can not afford to give up on 'em. They have us outnumbered. No, if we're gonna beat 'em, we're gonna have to join 'em. We can't help from the sidelines. We're gonna have to stay on top of the wave, which is why I'm an official new tweeter. Yes, I tweet, I post twits. In the event you've been living under a rock, tweeting is something one does via Twitter.com, a free website that also works with your cell phone and lets people everywhere stay in touch in real time—think of it as texting the whole world simultaneously!

I tweet under the name "ShellieT," although I understand there's someone else you may know on Twitter.com, too. She goes by the name of "Ya Southern Mama" and she looks suspiciously like yours truly. Go ahead. Look her up. She's stepping up to the keyboard to assist those unfortunate souls around the globe who have not had the benefit of being raised by a Southern Mama, in the hopes of learning 'em a few things.

Granted, Ya Southern Mama finds it a challenge at times, as each post is limited to 140 characters and Southern Mamas are known to use a hundred words when a handful will do, but you must give her props for endeavoring to condense her cradle-to-grave advice into sound bites. Thankfully, a good deal of our age-old Southern Mama wisdom translates just perfectly for this new media. Thus, the whole world is now getting tweets that remind them that "if you lie down with dogs, you'll get up with fleas" and "the belt goes over the butt, young man, not below it." You're welcome to follow Ya Southern Mama on twitter, benefit from her helpful advice, or ask her a question, but do be careful. If you give her any back talk, she's liable to knock you into the middle of next week; virtually, of course.

As committed as I am about taking advantage of social media's opportunities to help see to it that our manners don't fall victim to the digital age, let's not make the mistake of thinking that every failure to communicate in our relationships, both professional and personal, can be traced to technology. That kind of thinking is grounded in excuses and it won't help us modern-day belles with the responsibilities we have to pass those well-taught social graces down to the next generation. The truth is that while the explosion of technology may be hampering real-time interaction and threatening to rob us all of important people skills, lack of communication and misunderstanding can't be laid entirely at the feet of the digital age. Personally, miscommunication has long been a part of my world.

Years ago I worked at Minsky's drugstore after school along with my sister Rhonda and our cousin Carol. One evening, a football player from our local high school approached the counter where we girls were whiling away the hours until closing time. He seemed terribly embarrassed to make his request, but finally, after much stuttering and stammering, he managed to ask if we sold (and I'm trying to be delicate here) athletic support straps.

Unfortunately, my blond-by-birth sister understood only a word of his mumbled request. "Strap?" she said, all puzzled-like. Then her face lit up as a light came on—the wrong light, mind you, but a light nonetheless. "Oh! Like a collar!" she said.

And with that Rhonda somehow jumped to the conclusion that the customer before her needed a dog collar. To the paralyzing shame of that poor fellow and the delight of those of us witnessing the following exchange, Rhonda began a detailed

My 4-year-old daughter told her preschool teacher (my co-worker) before our egg hunt last Friday . . . "Mrs. Shelly, it's a sad, sad day." Shelly asked her why. She said, "The Easter bunny isn't real and Michael Jackson is dead." Shelly, who was trying her best to contain her laughter asked her, "How do you know this?" Prissy looked her dead in the eye and said very matter-of-factly, "Just check out YouTube," and walked away.

~Jamie Ainsworth McBride
Monticello, Arkansas

and lengthy description of the variety of items we had on hand, even pointing out our best sellers.

The young man took in Rhonda's sales pitch with the classic deer-in-the-headlights look as she described leather ones, colored ones, and even ones with small bells and metal studs. When Rhonda finally paused, her customer took a deep breath and announced that she seemed to have misunderstood. Speaking slowly and clearly, he repeated his request: "I need an athletic strap."

"Oh, right," Rhonda said, and promptly sunk behind the register, leaving one of us to close the deal—which wasn't right, and I told her so after Carol rang the customer up and he left with his purchase.

"Rhonda," I said, "you owe Carol a favor. She might not be an athlete, but at least she was willing to be an athletic supporter!"

Southern Pro Bono and Potty Parties

See what I mean? We don't need to demonize computers as bringing the end to all polite conversation; we just need to be better listeners, while gently sharing the type of common sense advice we got from our Southern Mamas. I may just be a voice in the wind, but I have accepted this heavy responsibility and am doing everything I can to assist the growing number of people who badly need a guiding hand.

Case in point, not long ago I learned that some busier-than-they-oughta-be people are paying other people big money to toilet train their children. These professional potty training consultants help anxious parents teach their reluctant kids how to "do the doo" for the low-low cost of $250 per consult. Paulette says these folks have too much money and not enough sense, and we should get in on it, but as the Belle of *All Things Southern*, I can't in good conscience take advantage of these people. I'm even willing to throw in a few pointers gratis, Southern pro bono if you will.

I read where one potty professional believes the secret to getting the uninterested interested is to offer the child a "Potty Party"—and let them help plan it! Dear hearts, anyone who has ever washed out a pair of soiled training pants understands clapping and cheering for their wee one's next masterpiece as if it were solid gold, but sending invitations is overkill. Besides, if Sweet Cheeks can help make out the guest list, you've already waited too long. Seriously, I've wanted to weigh in on this point ever since I first noticed the increasingly mature age of the kids in today's diaper commercials, parading gleefully in their Pull-Ups and announcing, "I'm a big kid now!" Well, I reckon so. They look old enough to drive!

I understand that the challenges presented by toilet training can lead one to do things one wouldn't otherwise consider (like secretly throwing away Underoos filled with number two because one doesn't have the heart to wash out one more pair), but the more I've looked into these potty consultants, the more ridiculous it sounds. Paulette's cousin works as a legal secretary in Washington, DC, and she told Paulette that one of the firm's fancy female lawyers recently hired such a consultant, only the woman prefers being called a coach. Here's where it gets good. The potty coach doesn't train the kid; she gets the big bucks to coach the mother! Mrs. Fancy Pants still has to do the dirty work. I was picturing the potty coach following mother and child around with a whistle and calling "fouls" on the poor kid, but Mrs. Fancy Pants says the coach is mainly there to keep her spirits up, so I reckon it's more like "You can train her, yes you can; if you can't train her, nobody can!"

Unfortunately, Mrs. Fancy Pants said her daughter isn't making much progress, so the potty coach is now suggesting she try another new trend: diaper-free kids. (I know. It just keeps getting better.) With the diaper-free kids technique you let your child run around nekkid as a jaybird* so you can watch for his or her "signal"—and rush the child to the bathroom. Well now, someone's getting trained here, and it's not the kids. I've been through this kind of thing with a puppy before, and trust me, it's hard work—and that's if you can catch 'em in the act. Remember what Mama said: By the time your wee ones are ready to potty, they'll be hiding out to do their business. Can you say, "Watch your step?"

Official Guide to Speaking All Things Southern

*nekkid as a jaybird: a Southern phrase meaning not just nekkid but really nekkid; it often brings with it the promise of impending trouble

While I realize that, in the end, every mother has to feel her own way through the toilet training maze, an abundance of patience is all you really need. They will get it, eventually. But should you go with the diaper-free idea, please allow me to leave you with a gentle word on public decency. I'm afraid you and your bare-bottomed young'uns aren't gonna feel the love at Wal-Mart, either. As a famous Southerner named Mark Twain once said, "Nekkid people have little or no influence on society."

Why Head Counts Are Important

Far be it from me to blame today's parents for looking for short-cuts, every generation does. We just need to encourage them to hang in there when the going gets tough and remember that ~~they will eventually get to laugh at other parents, too~~ this, too, will pass. Before you can turn around good, the little girl you have to coax into the bathroom will become an older girl you can't coax out of it. Remember, the only thing that ever really stays the same is that nothing ever does. Kids are little game changers that burst into our lives on a dead run out of 'em and into their own. That's not meant to make you parents sad, either. As that wise old wise saying goes, "The basic assignment of every parent is to work your way out of a job." That being said, however, you should really try to resist the temptation to take premature leave as well as creating the appearance of it. The public can be so critical, don't you know?

I'm reminded of that harsh news story I read about those parents inadvertently driving off from a theme park without one of their kids. (Apparently they had more than one, and well, who's counting, right?) I felt the reporter was leaping to conclusions and making judgments about the parents' intentions that hadn't been established. It reminded me of a similar story a few years ago now about the poor little boy in Florida whose parents accidentally left him behind at a Chuck E. Cheese restaurant! By all accounts, the parents' unusual case of forgetfulness came right after they'd finished giving the six-year-old a big birthday bash. Oh yeah, and they didn't notice he was missing until the next day.

I know, I know, it sounded suspicious to me, too, but I had to stand up for the harried innocent-until-proven-otherwise parents. I've hosted my share of kiddy parties and it's no cakewalk, people. You plan and they party, but rarely does the plan resemble the party. I once left my seven-year-old birthday girl and a pack of her giggling friends at a big room upstairs in my home church. The idea was for them to have a slumber party, supervised by two trustworthy teenage girls (and, no, trustworthy teenage girls is not always an oxymoron).

A short time later I slipped back in to video the fun. I was eager to see how it was going. Were they playing with the games I had bought, watching the videos I had stacked up—bursting the piñata perhaps? No, no, and no! The little sweeties were swinging and swaying rock-group style on the altar of my church, still dressed in their bathing suits from their afternoon swim, their little faces painted up like ladies of the night, and belting out the lyrics to one of Mr. Brooks' early hits about chasing the blues away with his beer-drinking friends in low places. In the song Mr. Brooks assures everyone that he would be okay, only I wasn't so okay. I had to sit down before I fell down!

So, I'm just saying, none of us should rush to judgment on that Florida thing, and any naive souls out there who have never hosted a birthday party for a bunch of wild Indians should reserve their opinions, period. True, it did seem to take the absentee parents a little too long to recover from their celebration enough to realize their child was missing, but I refuse to throw stones. My Southern Mama taught me to always look for the best in others. By the way, I don't know that I have ever shared that Garth Brooks birthday party story in the Lord's house with my dear pastor. If you read this, Brother Don, all I can say is, it was never in the plan . . .

Parent See, Children Do

Perhaps few areas of public discourse need a refresher course in manners as much as politics and sports, two endeavors that have a lot more in common than you might realize. In both instances everyone chooses sides and tries to yell louder than the other group while the players fight over the ball—at all costs. We'll get to the manners lesson in just a moment, but while we're on the subject of rude behavior, and before my mind wanders too far, I'd love to take this opportunity to say that my beloved country doesn't have a monopoly on this malady. Seeing as how the term "Ugly American" offends this die-hard patriotic belle on a number of levels, it only seems fair to note that civility appears to be in scarce supply around the globe.

For instance, did y'all hear about the high school baseball game in Japan that was called at the bottom of the second inning? The score was sixty-six to nothing with one out. Reread that. I'll wait. No nail-biter, that one. The losing coach said he felt obligated to call it to protect the pitcher from injuring his throwing shoulder. Oh. Okay. While it does seem he was curiously slow in reaching that conclusion, what say we set that aside for just a moment and give the poor young pitcher some props? Seriously, what type of kid is willing to stay in there and keep throwing after the sixty-third run scored against him, or the sixty-fourth, or the sixty-fifth run? We're looking at the very epitome of optimism—"Wait, Coach! Don't pull me. I'm getting in the groove. I can feel this thing!"

Despite that can-do attitude on the pitcher's part, I'm glad level heads finally prevailed and called for the mercy rule. That mercy rule is a good thing, y'all. I know for a fact that if there wasn't a mercy rule in Little League, some kids would grow beards right out there on the field. A slow game can lead to the sort of fascinating exchange I once witnessed between my six-year-old nephew, an extremely bored center fielder, and his equally bored left fielder.

The other kid said, "Hey, you, I forgot your name! Can I call you Blood?" Blake considered the request, blinked twice, and declined the nickname with a solemn head shake. To our knowledge that was the extent of their communication for the duration of the season.

If memory serves, that was also the season of The Great Clash that's still heard about around these parts. Disclaimer: The Great Clash shall not be brought forth as a sterling example of the proper sports protocol, but it is fun in the telling. That spring, one of our Little League teams was being coached by a certain husband-and-wife coaching duo who will remain nameless. Mr. was coaching third base, Mrs. was coaching first, and they'd been in disagreement in most every coaching decision from the first pitch of the season. The last straw came one night when Mr. Coach, who had a notoriously aggressive coaching style, sent a runner straight into a tag-out at home plate during a crucial play-off game.

"Did you send him?!" Mrs. yelled across the field.

"I sure did!" Mr. answered with a what-about-it-you've been-second-guessing-me-all-season look.

"Have you lost your mind?" Mrs. demanded to know.

It only got worse after that, folks. Believe you me, if we fans could have called a mercy rule on those two, we would have done it sooner rather than later.

In the event that you haven't noticed the common thread to the last couple of stories, let me spell it out so we're all on the same page: The adults were the ones displaying questionable behavior! Yes, civility begins at home. Furthermore, lest I be accused of throwing stones from a glass house, I'll go even further and tell one on myself. I offer the following confession by way of disclaimer and with the caveat that I've changed, really, but you should know that there was a time when I was a repeat offender where it pertains to sports.

Though I am now serving as The (reformed) Belle of *All*

Things Southern, I was once a passionate girls' basketball coach and I may have been a teeny-weeny bit hard on the referees. By "teeny-weeny" I mean that I once tapped the official calling our contest on the shoulder and asked him what game he was watching, because it certainly wasn't the one I was coaching. Yeah, he thought that deserved a technical, too.

But hey, the good news is that I got help. I went through a 12-step program called "Zebras Are Our Friends." I'll never forget the first time I said, "Hi, my name is Shellie and I holler at referees." Although I've come to accept that I'm only one call away from a relapse, I'm happy to say that I'm in my eighth year of sanity, thanks to this program. One of the first steps was acknowledging that I can never again hold a clipboard while standing in a crowded gym.

Granted I was wrong to be so, uh, vocal, but I still contend that I was often unfairly provoked. For instance, I remember once when my point guard was practically knocked out cold. The referee himself stopped the game and called me onto the floor. After making sure my player was okay, I asked him for the foul—well, it *was* a close game!

You won't believe his response. "Number 20 didn't foul your girl, Coach; she just hit her in the head." Oh . . . thanks for clearing that up.

To show my sincerity, the rehab program required me to make amends to all the referees I had hurt in the past. By then I had this handy dandy platform called *All Things Southern*, so I just used a television segment on the local morning show to offer an apology. "Dear referees," I said. "If any of y'all are listening, I'm sorry for asking y'all to clean your glasses, buy a ticket, and get in the game. And I never should've said those things about your mama."

Indeed, I may have been a Johnny-come-lately to the

subject, but I did have a come-to-Jesus meeting where my referee bashing was concerned, which is why I'm determined not only to encourage a return to sportsmanship, but also to be a better example when my grandchildren start competing. That's a number of years in the future, mind you, so I've been using one of my favorite times of year to practice—March Madness! In the event of a relapse or two, I will at least be in the privacy of my own home. It's better that way.

Etiquette for Life's Big Passages

To reiterate for emphasis, manners begin at home, and we must all do our part to shore up the home front. Our challenge is to shape culture and not reflect it. Much of what society is selling is bad medicine for our kids. For instance, I love a good belleabration* as much as the next belle, but I'm here to tell you that Divorce Parties, they "ain't right." That's correct, Divorce Parties, a trend that began several years ago in where else but Hollywood. But heads up, friends, they are growing in popularity. I read where Divorce Parties are spawning an entire industry. This isn't getting together with a few close girlfriends for a crying jag, either. We're talking guest lists, gift registries, and party favors! Fellow belles and/or wannabe belles, I plead with you, let's not . . .

Let me be clear, I'm not judging anyone for the knot coming untied. I've seen a number of friends and relatives through some bad divorces—and several relatives through a number of divorces. As

Official Guide to Speaking All Things Southern

*belleabration   (belle-`a-bration), noun: an impromptu or formal get-together of Southern belles

a whole, my people believe in getting married, some more than others. One of my cousins has been married eight times, or nine, depending on how many times you count the fellow she married more than once. I was among those who were thankful when her last ex managed to join the group of survivors. Annabelle had once told me she was planning on keeping that one till death did them part, even if she had to kill him.

Not long ago, at a family funeral, a group of us cousins were gathered up reminiscing about old times when we began to discuss who was coming in and who couldn't make it. Someone mentioned that Annabelle was supposed to bring Number Nine. The news shocked one of the family's sweet yet confused belles. She amused us all by exclaiming, "Are y'all telling me she's bringing all nine of 'em?" No Precious, just the caboose.

Later, upon Annabelle's arrival, she simply penned her first name in the guest book. I guess she figures she's more easily identified now without a surname, kind of like Cher and Oprah.

See, dear ones, I understand the realities of divorce. I just think having a belleabration in honor of a marriage's demise is tasteless and beneath the dignity of a belle—yes, even a betrayed belle. There are other ways to deal with your emotions. Why, I remember once when my friend Sally-That's-Not-Her-Real-Name found out her husband was cheating with her own beautician (which is wrong on so many levels). Sally left him that very day—after she went to his farm office and deleted every critical file on his desktop computer. I'm not necessarily recommending that, mind you, although I understand hitting "you betcha" every time the thing asked, "Are you sure you would like to delete this file" was very therapeutic. No, I'm just begging y'all not to contribute to the further devaluing of the great institution of marriage. I know it hurts, but this is no way to heal.

Think about your kids for goodness' sakes! It'd greatly benefit them if you managed to keep up the appearance of civility, even if that's all it is, which was the case with another Southern matriarch I know of who refused to remove all traces of the ex-son-in-law from her family's history. I thought that was a beautiful gesture and I said so. "I'm surprised that you're still displaying these pictures," I told her, "but I think it's right big of you."

"Not really," she said, earnestly. "The truth is I'm not about to get rid of all my nice family portraits. I'm gonna leave 'em right where they are and just pretend like he died." That works, too.

See, not only would said matriarch not have to redo the family portraits, but she'd have reason to expect that the distasteful subject of the ex–family member could be laid to rest even if he wasn't. Southern death etiquette dictates that one not speak ill of the dead (at least not in public). Many a Southern scoundrel has benefited from having his image polished up postmortem. We're known to give saints and sinners equal billing and trust the One True Judge to separate 'em on the other side.

While not formally dictated alongside the food prep and clothing choice rules, Southerners consider it perfectly acceptable if, at some time during the funeral ceremony or the postservice food bash, mourning turns to mirth—as long as the deceased is not the punch line. Just because it happens sometimes, accidentally, in no way means that we condone it, right, Cousin Jeffrey?

Several years ago my mother's sister passed away, leaving behind a large and adoring family. The visitation was sad, the funeral and graveside services were harder, and yet, by the time the family settled into the big feed—compliments of Aunt

Elaine's church—the solemn occasion was showing signs of morphing into a good old Southern family reunion.

Aunt Elaine was still uppermost in everyone's hearts and minds, but the grief seemed to pause somehow as the stories began flowing, tears mixing with laughter to perform that unique tonic that we all knew would see Aunt Elaine's loved ones through lonelier days ahead. I sat with my cousins as they recounted their mother's last moments on earth.

Cousin Lissa told how the three kids, all in their forties, stood clinging to one another in a tight group at their mother's deathbed. With tears streaming down their faces, the little group slipped back into the comforting and familiar sibling rivalry they'd perfected in childhood. Steve, the oldest son, and Lissa the only daughter, looked toward Jeff, their baby brother, and said in unison: "You always were her favorite."

During such times of sorrow it isn't unusual for some well-meaning soul to slip up and say something they wish they could take back and that day was certainly no different. While there were a couple other small faux pas that day, everyone agreed that Jeffrey may have been guilty of the worst choice of words imaginable when he bit into a delicious cake a neighbor brought to the house and gave it the highest of Southern accolades, "Um, um! That'll make you want to slap your mama." Horrified, Jeff tried to fix his mistake with a lot of stuttering and stammering, but he quit when he caught the look on his sister's face.

The glare was straight out of their beloved mama's page book, and it clearly said, "When you find yourself in a hole, the first thing to do is stop diggin'."

This Just In from H, E, Double L

From major life dramas to daily peeves, belles are taught that life smiles more favorably on those who learn to hold their tongue and control their emotions. Granted, this can come across as something of a contradiction early on when the teacher is having a hissy fit about the student's hissy fit (sorry, Mama), but eventually we get the message. By and large our mamas are with the great Apostle Paul on this one, admitting that while they haven't arrived, they are pressing toward the worthy goal, and by golly, they're determined to take us with 'em. The thinking is that one should practice restraint as a way of showing consideration to others.

> Here's advice from my great-grandmother that was passed to me and my sister and now to my daughter: "Be a lady even if it kills you."
>
> ~Donna Drake Anton
> Houston, Texas

The problem, of course, is the reality. We're constantly being bombarded with situations that tempt us to throw caution to the wind and have a Class A hissy fit. Why, just the other day I was picking up my Southern Living magazine at the checkout stand when I saw the most amazing headline. Someone had taken the first ever pictures from H, E, double L and sold them to one of those tabloids. Why, whatever do you mean? It must be true. It said it right there on the front of the paper. Right. And that begs my next question, who in tarnation is buying those magazines?

Who out there sees a headline screaming: "Eighty Year Old Grandmother Gives Birth to Full Grown Elvis Impersonator While Singing 'I Did It My Way'/photos inside," and thinks, "I have got to read that article!"

'Fess up, y'all. Somebody's buying it or they wouldn't keep selling it. I'm just curious. Your choice of reading material isn't peeving me at all. However, there's a second group of folks I'd love to identify who are bothering me—and your friends and neighbors—and to them I say, frankly, y'all need a whooping. I'm talking to whoever is mailing in those annoying renew-your-subscription cards that fall out of their magazines. I'm just saying. Someone's using 'em for something other than coasters or else they'd disappear as many times as the rest of us have cursed their existence.

If I had a mind to, I could have myself a for sure hissy fit over those cards, but seeing as how Mama would frown on it, I'm thinking about hiring it done. Now, there's an interesting new development hot off the Internet presses. Some genius has come up with a plan to capitalize on whatever issues you find annoying. Yes'm. You can now "rent a mob" to put on your own customized protest. Are you mad as a hornet but crazy busy? Too tired to whine? No problem, Sugar. Tell them what's bugging you, and a good-size mob of protestors will show up to do all the sign waving and name calling you'd like—for a price, of course.

The company says business is good, and I'm not surprised. As they say, we are a consumer-driven society. So hire a mob if you must, but let it be known that the day this Southern girl feels the need to hire someone to work up a good hissy fit on her behalf will be the same day she purchases a tabloid magazine featuring the first ever photos of H, E, double L!

Someone Missed the Memo

Just recently my BFF gave me another opportunity to practice the art of self-control, bless her heart. In closing, I shall attempt a ladylike discussion that will require me to proceed delicately. First a question: Who among us hasn't been caught in a situation where a public restroom was needed in the worst kind of way? Exactly—it happens to us all. My Southern Mama taught me a lady prepares for these occasions by carrying matches in her purse to show her consideration for others. Consideration for others is a theme with Southern Mamas.

Recently, I found myself traveling with Red to another city when I was struck by this very type of urgency. By the time we located a facility, my lack of matches had taken a backseat to my growing stress. I entered the public restroom in haste, noting two stalls. The first one was out of order. The door to the second one was closed, but I couldn't see any feet under the door. I knocked and waited, uncomfortably. No answer. I tried the handle while shifting my weight from foot to foot. It seemed to be locked. I wondered if a kid had left it locked as a prank. I knocked again. No answer. Being unable to shake the feeling of approaching doom, and feeling sure no one was in there, I tried the lock once more as I actually considered climbing under the stall door in search of relief.

That's when I heard a desperate, unintelligible lady's voice from within. It was weak, but it went something like "Eeeeeoooo-ouuu," which I quickly translated as "I have problems of my own. Please don't open the door and please do not crawl under it, either."

Dashing back outside, I approached the car, signaling clearly to my friend that I was still in a bad way and we must find another facility, quickly. Red's caring response—if I'm lying I'm dying here—was to lock the doors and promptly dissolve into fits of laugher. Apparently, she missed the consideration memo entirely.

Tips on Manners and Social Media

THUS SAITH THE BELLE DOCTRINE . . .

* Thou shalt use social media for the greater good by sharing thy tried-and-true Southern Mama advice.

* Thou shalt not rush to judgment on other people's parenting skills, especially where birthday parties are concerned.

* Thou shalt remember that toilet training is meant to be a family affair and not a village endeavor.

* Care should be taken in sporting situations not to talk about thy referee's mama.

* Hiring a hissy fit is considered more improper than having one of thine own.

* Carrying matches in thy purse is considered a welcome sign of public consideration.

Snacks to Please Any Crowd

Everyone appreciates tasty appetizers. Why open a bag of chips and a jar of store-bought salsa when you can wow your family and friends with some Can Do Corn Dip or my Handy Ham Spread? Every Southern belle or Southern belle wannabe needs a repertoire of snack recipes at her disposal for those all-important belleabration events or family get-togethers. Regardless of whether you have chosen to hire yourself a hissy-fit crowd, or you just want to serve up some appetizers to an equally emotional group, like say, a living room full of LSU football fanatics watching their Tigers play Alabama, you'll need some handy snack ideas to feed the rioters. Here are a few favorites from my kitchen to yours. Most of them are prepared from staple ingredients you can stash in the pantry for those drop-in guests, so you can be at your unruffled belle best!

Sausage and Crawfish Spread

It has been said that watching sausage being made will put you off the product for the rest of your natural born days. I've got a good fix for that—don't watch it. But do trot yourself down to the grocery and pick up some Jimmy Dean (or whatever brand passes muster in your neck of the woods) to use in this family favorite. Sausage married with crawfish tails and a few simple ingredients produces a belleicious spread you don't want to miss!

The Holy Trinity of Southern Cooking (1 cup each of
    chopped onion, bell pepper, and celery)
1 pound hot pork sausage
1 can cream of mushroom soup
1 medium box Velveeta cheese
1 pound crawfish tails, chopped
1 tablespoon minced garlic
1 teaspoon fish seasoning (Panola's blackened blend is best
    if you can find it)
Dash of All Things Southern hot sauce
Couple loaves of a good French bread

Topping:
1 bundle green onions, chopped

Brown the Holy Trinity (onions, peppers, celery) with sausage, breaking the sausage up with the back of your spoon. Drain and return to skillet. Stir in mushroom soup and Velveeta cheese. Add chopped crawfish tails once the cheese has melted. Season with minced garlic, fish seasoning, and a dash of All Things Southern hot sauce (or whatever poor substitute you must use). Cook over medium heat for thirty minutes and look-a-there! (Look-a-there is the southern equivalent of voilà.) Spoon over French bread, bruschetta or your favorite cracker, top with chopped green onions and serve.

Nutty Game Day Trail Mix

This one is aptly named, both for the nuts in the mix and the stressful pace of ball season. Whether you're watching your own kids or cheering on the grands, here's a good mix to bring along to help stave off the hungries at those games that will not end. You could also use it to bribe the referees, not that I'm recommending that. It's just something I've heard rumored, don't you know?

Dry Ingredients:

  3 cups oatmeal

  ½ cup slivered almonds

  ½ cup coconut

  ½ cup sesame seeds

  ½ cup pecans, cashews, or walnuts

  ½ teaspoon cinnamon

  ½ teaspoon salt

  1 cup raisins

  ½ cup dried cranberries

Wet ingredients:

  4 tablespoons unsalted butter

  ½ cup honey

  ½ teaspoon vanilla extract

Preheat oven to 325 degrees. Take a large mixing bowl and combine dry ingredients except for the raisins and dried cranberries. Set aside. Melt unsalted butter in a small saucepan. Remove from heat and add honey and vanilla extract. While hot, pour over oat mixture and stir well. Spread oats in thin layer on a greased cookie sheet. Bake for twenty minutes, stirring every five minutes or so to make sure it doesn't stick. Once the mix is cooked and cooled down, stir in raisins and dried cranberries. You may need to break the mix up if it sticks in large pieces. Make a double batch, or a triple batch, to take to the game. You'll be the hit of the whole ballpark! Get it? Hit of the ballpark!

Romano Cheese Artichoke Hearts

(SERVES 4–6)

A well-trained belle knows to keep a couple of cans of artichokes in the pantry at all times. It gives one a head start on serving up tasty and elegant appetizers faster than you can say, "Lord have mercy, supper isn't on and I don't have a clue what we're having." My Romano Cheese Artichoke Hearts will appease the hungry bunch and buy you some much needed time.

2 cans artichoke hearts
½ cup seasoned bread crumbs
1 teaspoon garlic powder
1 cup shredded Romano cheese
Olive oil for drizzling
Salt and pepper

Preheat oven to 350 degrees. Drain artichoke hearts and set aside. Mash bread crumbs and garlic powder into shredded Romano cheese. Place artichoke hearts on a cookie sheet prepared with cooking spray. Slice each heart in half, press the middle of each down with your thumb, and fill with a teaspoon or so of Romano cheese mixture. Bake for 10–12 minutes and then broil until cheese is well melted and beginning to brown. Remove, drizzle with olive oil, shake with salt and pepper, and serve.

The Handy Ham Spread

Chicken salad and pimiento cheese get a lot of attention as Southern sandwich spreads, but my Handy Ham Spread just might become one of your favorites. It can be dressed up and served with a party rye bread or spread between slices of regular sandwich bread. It's a great way to use leftover ham (like after Easter), but if you don't have leftovers, do use those big slices you find in the meat department. Starting with regular old sandwich meat defeats the purpose. You can give the spread a whirl in the food processor if you prefer, but we like it diced.

2 cups diced or ground ham

½ cup mayonnaise

2 hard-boiled eggs, chopped fine

½ cup sweet pickle relish

2 tablespoons chopped onion

1 loaf party rye bread

Combine ham with mayonnaise and chopped hard-boiled eggs, yolks and all. Stir in sweet pickle relish and chopped onion. (If you can find 'em, try substituting Panola Pepper's Sweet and Spicy Jalapeño Peppers in place of the pickles for a divine upgrade!) Chill well before serving.

Mike's Can-Do Corn Dip

I named this dish after the guy who helps me "cook" on my radio segments. Those quotes are meant to suggest that he doesn't exactly cook. He's actually the producer who doubles as my main prep guy. I told him the recipe gets its name from the fact that even Mike can do it! (Just funnin', Mike!)

½ cup mayonnaise

1 (16 oz.) carton sour cream

8 ounces shredded cheddar cheese

2 (11 oz.) cans Mexican corn, drained

1 (4 oz.) can green chilies, chopped and drained

4 green onions, finely chopped

¼ teaspoon garlic powder

Salt and pepper to taste

Combine sour cream and mayonnaise. Add shredded cheddar cheese, Mexican corn, green chilies, and green onions, and season with garlic powder, salt, and pepper. Chill in the refrigerator at least an hour to allow flavors to blend.

Hot Pecan Spread

We put pecans in everything around these parts. Here they pair up with dried beef to create a mouthwatering topping for your favorite cracker. Serve my Hot Pecan Spread at your next get-together, but do be warned. You'll need to keep the guest list to a minimum or make a double batch because it's gonna go very quickly.

2 ounces cream cheese

2 tablespoon milk

1 (2½ oz.) jar dried beef, shredded

2 tablespoons onion flakes

¼ cup finely chopped bell pepper

½ teaspoon garlic powder

Salt and pepper to taste

½ cup sour cream

½ cup chopped pecans

2 tablespoons butter

Preheat oven to 350 degrees. Blend cream cheese with milk. Add shredded beef, onion flakes, bell pepper, garlic powder, salt, and pepper. Fold in sour cream. Spread in a shallow ovenproof dish. Set aside. In a small saucepan, heat chopped pecans in butter for 2–3 minutes. Sprinkle pecans over the cream cheese mixture and bake it all for 15–17 minutes. This is a great spread to serve on Melba Rounds or your favorite snacking cracker.

Cheesy Mushroom Dip

I've heard of mushroom dips being called the poor man's oyster substitute. I, however, do not feel this is fair to the mushroom. My Cheesy Mushroom Dip is no one's country cousin. Broccoli and garlic cheese combine with the mushrooms to create a crowd-pleasing favorite. While the flavor can be ramped up even more with fresh mushrooms, experience tells me you're going to enjoy it as is!

1 package frozen chopped broccoli
1 large onion, chopped
8 tablespoons butter or margarine
1 can cream of mushroom soup
1 (6 oz.) roll of garlic cheese
1 can mushroom stems and pieces (undrained)
Dash of All Things Southern hot sauce

Cook broccoli according to the package directions and set aside. Sauté chopped onion in butter. Stir in mushroom soup and cubed garlic cheese. While the cheese is melting, add mushrooms pieces and hot sauce. Fold into cooked broccoli, mix well, and serve warm with crackers or your favorite chips.

6

Paulette the Pundit, Lord Help Us One and All

⟍⟋

Political and Economic Observations with
Soup Recipes to Stretch the Family Budget

I swanee,* it would've been a dream job. Word was the Treasury Department was looking to hire a humor coach to teach the department how to laugh. Well, "Hello, Washington!" I know some good jokes and I am an ex–basketball coach. It sounded like a perfect fit, but before I could get my spit-shined résumé in, they determined that they were no longer interested in filling such a position.

Whatever. I don't know why they had to go and pull the plug on it. Some people have suggested that the government realized there were better ways to

Official Guide to Speaking All Things Southern

*swanee (swan-ee): Research suggests the word's roots can be traced to a much longer expression the English used, as in "I shall warrant thee." Long noted for droppin' all those bothersome consonants, we Southerners have long since shortened the expression to "I swanee."

spend our money—HAHAHAHAHA HAHAHA—you're gonna have to give me a minute here.

Excuse me, but that can't be it. But, what the hay, let's just say I had gotten the job. One of the first things I would've explained to the suits is that funny is all around you. The trick is to watch for it. And one of the best places to find funny is when you're somewhere that you're not supposed to laugh.

Take funerals, for example. I don't mean to be insensitive, but funny things happen at funerals. My cousin can attest to this. He works as a funeral director and he's seen it time and again. Once, during the middle of a service, one of the town's good old boys, who hadn't stepped foot in a church since he was a child, took exception to what he felt were the preacher's rather pointed remarks about the afterlife.

The man jumped up and huffed, "I ain't listening to this." And with that he marched toward a nearby door, opened it, and stormed into what he supposed was the hall. The faithful in the congregation waited gleefully, knowing that he would eventually have to come out of the broom closet. Several long seconds later, when he opened the door, the poor man stepped back into a funeral that sounded more like a party. Not even the bereaved family could contain themselves. Mr. Huffy, however, he could've used a humor coach. Again, it is a shame there is no such a position available with the federal government, but as The Belle of *All Things Southern* I refuse to bemoan that lost opportunity any longer. My job is to use my platform to put a positive spin on the political and economic issues of our day.

Course, it's hard to know exactly where to begin with the job market. There's an awful lot of talk about jobs these days. Are we creating them, saving them, losing them, or killing them with bad policy? For the record, dear ones, that was a rhetorical question. I've no intention of opening that can of worms on this porch. Instead, I shall now concentrate on mining the good news from the bad to bring you my *All Things Southern* job forecast.

One of the most important things to remember is that it's critical to remain positive about career opportunities. As my girlfriends and I recently noted, there remain various untapped job prospects open to Southern women in general and Southern Mamas and Grandmamas in particular, or as we formally refer to them, "those who know best."

For instance, many Southern Mamas could become ventriloquists. Blessing or curse, we're each born with the ability to throw our voices. My own mama is quite proficient! I remember the day I first noticed her voice coming from my mouth. She was miles away, but she might as well have been standing behind me operating a string attached to my lips when I told my teenage daughter she "needed an attitude adjustment and I was more than willing to oblige!" I'm happy to report my own skills are coming along nicely, too. More than once this past Christmas, I threw my voice in Jessica Ann's mouth so smoothly that all the poor child could do was shake her head in mid-sentence.

My Southern Mama taught me that attitude is everything. Many times I heard "It's okay to sit on your pity pot every now and then, just don't forget to flush!"

~Sarah Hargrove
Perryville, Arkansas

Southern women could also find work as professional mind readers. Again, grandmothers are especially equipped for the position. They know whether your baby is wet, hungry, or sleepy, and they're willing and eager to interpret for your wee one. Fortunately, or unfortunately, they've also been known to share with family and strangers in equal measure.

Raise your hand if you are Southern and you have not heard

a Southern Mama say to a complete stranger's child, "Bless your heart. Tell Mama your little feet are cold!" I rest my case. Now, the real problem comes when two women get different readings, if you will, from the same baby. But that's another story.

News You Can Lose

Before I wade any further into this herculean effort to opine on politics and the economy without having my house egged by any one segment of voters, it strikes me that perhaps the time is right to take a break for a lighthearted little job bulletin, or what we refer to on my *All Things Southern LIVE* radio show as "News You Can Lose."

I'd like it to be noted that this used to be one of my specialties, laid-back news. Now serious journalists are twittering all over the place and asking us to be their Facebook friends and write on their "wall." Puts me in mind of the time someone wrote something about me on the bathroom wall at Tallulah Academy High School. I learned that girl something about wall writing, yes I did, but we won't go into that now. I'm just saying: I don't appreciate the big media infringing on my work here. Frankly, they're annoying me, which happens to segue nicely into that news piece I wanted to discuss.

I've recently discovered that the good folks in Brighton, Michigan, passed an unusual law a couple years ago right in the middle of the holidays. While we were all out buying Snuggies, they were making it illegal to be annoying in public. Indeed. You can now be arrested in Michigan for being annoying by word of mouth, signs, or motions—in public, anyway. Apparently you can still be all kinds of rude in private.

I admit to being initially intrigued. I mean, who doesn't find other people annoying at times? But then I reminded myself that these minor grievances are opportunities to practice the art of social interaction, to learn how to "pass and re-pass"* as Mama said about that long ago wall-writing episode. Besides, there is a teensy-weensy fine-print problem to consider before you start working on your Ten Most Annoying People list. Under their new law, Michiganites don't get to decide what is annoying and what is not. The police get to do that.

Official Guide to Speaking All Things Southern

*pass and re-pass: Southern Belles are taught that there will always be people you can't get along with no matter how hard one tries. With these people we are told to pass and repass. The interpretation is to speak and move on when you see 'em but don't look for or expect anything more in return.

Hmm . . . Come to think of it, friends, this may be "News We Can't Afford to Lose." If we don't pay attention, soon free speech will be so last century.

Congress and the National Beggars Association

Of course, I'm not all that worried about such a law getting passed down here in Dixie. Southerners wouldn't dream of fining annoying people; we'd just shoot 'em. Joking, friends, just joking. Contrary to Hollywood's favorite depiction of my people, we don't resort to firearms unless it's absolutely necessary. Take me for example. As The Belle of *All Things Southern*, I often find myself trying to keep the peace between all the natives and foreigners that make their way by my cyber porch. It can be quite trying, but I haven't shot anyone—yet.

People have found all sorts of things to argue about, too, but perhaps the single most recurring bone of contention on the *All Things Southern* porch has to do with the Southern credentials, or lack thereof, of different states or regions of our fine country. For illustration we'll go with the Washington, DC, debate, as it is always a hot one and it does tie in with our chapter's theme. Is DC truly Southern or is it a Northern imposter? That's the recurring question, and as is often the case, valid points have been made on both sides.

Many claim that our nation's capital is truly Northern in its pace and atmosphere. Others are just as quick to paint it Southern by contending that its very location south of the Mason-Dixon Line was chosen after The Late Unpleasantness as a way to placate Southerners. I suppose they mean it was a consolation gift of sorts. (If this is true, I feel my forefathers, or rather foremothers, should be excused if they somehow neglected to send thank-you notes.)

Surprisingly enough, my good friend Bubba may have had the last word on the validity of the capital's Southern credentials when he noted that while they aren't famous for their barbecue, Washington, DC, alone produces more pork than the rest of the Southern states combined. I would have to concur. Sometimes I'm not sure the economy can stand much more of their well-intentioned fixes.

In fact, their brand of generosity reminds me of another Papaw Stone story. One Sunday morning, Papaw Stone asked everyone in his congregation to stand during the offertory. Offerings had been down somewhat, and he had hit upon a stimulus package of his own. Papaw told the folks to hand their checkbooks or wallets to the person standing directly in front of them. The people hesitated.

"Aw, go ahead," Papaw encouraged his flock. "Humor me." They did.

"Now," Papaw said, "open the pocketbook in your hand and give as you always wanted to but never felt like you could afford."

Papaw was joking, of course, but he was on to something that I believe bears repeating: When it comes to spending the other person's money, some folks can be generous to a fault.

Personally, I think where an individual spends his or her own time and money is a much better indicator of that person's true character. That's the sort of thinking I learned from my parents, as well as my Papaw. When I was a little girl, hoboes still rode the train rails around our country. One set of those tracks roared right past my Papaw's house, and occasionally one of those hoboes would jump off for a look-see and end up knocking at Papaw's front door. If I try hard, I can still remember how they looked. Even a small child could feel the hopelessness clinging to 'em. A lot of people shunned the hoboes, fearing for their own safety, but Papaw would let 'em sleep in one of the classrooms in his church next door, and he'd make sure they had a belly full of food and whatever handout he could spare. Papaw would've helped 'em find work, too, but they always seemed more interested in moving on down the road.

Those experiences left a lasting impression on me. Some people would say I'm about to take this thing in a risky direction, but to quote my more redneck friends, "I ain't skeered." See, while I was raised to help people who couldn't help themselves, I was also taught the value of good hard work. And that, my friend, is a concept that seems to have fallen through the cracks of our society. My heart breaks for people who are willing to

Out on the Bayou Bonne Idee in Morehouse Parish, Louisiana, where I grew up in the '50s and '60s, folks said one guy was "so lazy that he wouldn't hit a lick at a snake." This implied that he wouldn't do ANY work, even to the point of not raising a hand against a snake that was about to bite him.

~George Sims
Mansfield Missouri

work and can't find a job, but I'm not at all compassionate toward those who can't tell you what type of work they're out of!

Case in point: believe it or not there is a whole host of websites out there designed to help teach people how to make a living begging. You heard right, a living, begging. These sites are quite informative in their own way. I found one where Pro Beggars gave tips on the most effective begging techniques. (I'm guessing Pro Beggars must be like amateur beggars with more gold jewelry.)

Look-a-here, y'all, somebody should be ashamed of themselves. Like our grandparents would say, "It is one thing to fall on hard times. It's another thing to wallow in 'em." Far be it from me to discourage small businesses, but pursuing begging as a career choice is a whole new level of wallowing. Indeed, times are hard and I'm serious about each of us doing everything we can to help our fellow man, but I just don't think a National Beggars Association is the answer. I mean, we've already got Congress.

Protecting Our God-Given Right to Apply Color

Obviously I have issues with able-bodied people begging for a living, but I haven't forgotten that it's a free country. Therefore, in the interest of civility, I'm willing to offer those Pro Beggars some free advice (no pun intended). If they're looking for a spokesperson with just the right look, I have a suggestion as to where they should go to conduct interviews—Hollywood! Yes'm, I saw a number of potential spokespersons in that sad little parade of rail-thin actresses at the recent Emmys. Chances are y'all probably didn't see those walking skeletons. Word is the Emmys' ratings were lower than those malnourished girls' necklines. I wouldn't have seen them either, only I was flipping channels when they came on and I paused to see those folks talking without their faces moving. That's always fun.

By the way, in the short time that I was paying attention, I heard the celebrities doing everything they could to educate us little people as to the real problems in our nation. Me and Paulette, we came up with one word for that high-maintenance crowd that we think they'll be familiar with: "Cut."

See, it's admirable for those female celebrities to want to help and all, but if they really want to sink their well-manicured claws into a good cause, I'd like to see 'em train their attention on the halls of Congress and their on-going shenanigans. In the interest of full disclosure, I should say that Speaker Pelosi and I have never exactly seen eye to eye, but I started watching that woman a whole lot closer after she made that suspicious decree that reporters must check their purses at the lobby door. If I remember correctly, the speaker said it was for security reasons, that overcoats had long been banned and this the purse ban was just about added security, but I know a power grab when I see one.

Madam Speaker had to have known a woman's purse is her everythang: briefcase, organizer, snack bar, media center—you get my point. Like I told Mama the day I saw it on the news, "She knows those women reporters will be so worried about leaving their purses unguarded they won't be able to concentrate long enough to question her about anything. They'll feel absolutely nekkid without their purses."

Mama, as usual, was way ahead of me. I thought she was gonna fit and fall out.* "Oh, they'll feel nekkid, all right! You're not seeing the forest for the trees, Shellie. No lipstick?! The woman is using the pretense of national security to strip folks of their God-given American right to reapply their color."

Mama was right. I had to sit down. I hope y'all aren't laughing. If we give up our lipstick without a fight, the terrorists have already won.

I still have no idea why those female reporters didn't scream to the high heavens, but I'm working on a theory. Perhaps there weren't enough Southern women in the group to organize a solid protest. Southern women understand that a woman's purse is off-limits, sacred ground. I have personally known marriages to come under severe duress because The Husband took it upon himself to go into his belle's purse without written consent. Yes'm. We'll go to the mat for our purses. Just ask that purse snatcher in Texas who recently grabbed the purse of that sixty-five-year-old grandmother. The aging belle promptly chased him down with her car and herded him into a crowd of civilians, who held him until the police arrived. So, okay, she did sorta kinda flip him in the air with her front fender. Please. He wasn't hurt, and as she said, "I needed my purse back."

I think my favorite part of that story was how the man ended up apologizing to Vigilante Granny before being taken to jail. I'm reading straight from the AP when I tell you that

---

Official Guide to Speaking All Things Southern

*fit and fall out: to be upset in such a way as to risk making a scene in public, something belles try to avoid

she accepted his olive branch and, in turn, offered him a sincere "God bless you." No harm, no foul, right? Take a note, reporters. Some things are worth fighting for!

Is That a Blackhawk Helicopter on My Lawn?

At the risk of oversimplifying today's serious political issues and drawing further ire from the reader who accuses me of being anti-government every time I have a little stress-relieving fun at the politicians' expense (and a nice fellow he was to warn me that the government might land a Blackhawk helicopter on my front lawn and come knocking at my door any day now), I've been proposing my own government intervention to anyone who'll listen.

What say we send a bucketload of Southern Mamas to Washington, keep the President around for that three a.m. call, and give the legislators from both parties time off for bad behavior? I knew you'd like it. The first thing our new substitute government would do is tell every politician or lobbyist (and is there really a noticeable difference between the two?) that came whining for a handout to "dry it up" and get back to work. Can't you just hear 'em, now? "The world doesn't owe you a living! You made your bed, now lie in it." Southern Mamas are big on personal responsibility. And if ever a concept needed revisiting, this is it.

The concept of tending your own business is why Southern Mamas train their offspring in the fine art of resourcefulness. Why, if it weren't for the nudity angle, my own Southern Mama would applaud the personal initiative of one of my author friends who recently shared with me her idea of how to launch her next book with a bang. Miss Get 'Er Done was contemplating going to her local mega-store, stripping nekkid in the fruits and vegetables aisle, and waving her new book about wildly. She figured it wouldn't take long for someone to twitter her picture to the media, send a phone video to YouTube, and voilà! She and her new book would get at least one twenty-four-hour news cycle. Instant exposure if you will.

I applaud her ingenuity, but let the record show that I won't be using her marketing ploy. Public nudity isn't my style. One of my greatest fears is someone finding my nekkid body in the bathroom like they did Elvis, God rest his soul. I'm not condoning Eve's falling for that apple line, but I don't mind telling you that I'm quite attached to the coverage offered by the resulting leopard prints. Which I suppose brings us back to the subject of accountability. Dear esteemed congressmen on both sides of the aisle, if I were you, I'd keep in mind that passing the buck didn't keep our ancestors from getting kicked out of the garden. It's worth a thought . . .

Chillin' with Vlad and Mahmoud

Based on the depth of political expertise I've already exhibited in this chapter, I'm sure the following admission will surprise y'all, but some of what I see happening in the political arena confuses me. For instance, wouldn't you think trying to rule the world would be a full-time occupation? Well, me, too, but apparently today's dictators are quite the proficient multitaskers. It hasn't been that long since that Russian prime minister, Vladimir Putin, released his own martial arts instructional DVD! And, not to be outdone, shortly afterward his good

Iranian buddy Mahmoud Ahmadinejad began blogging! Yes, blogging, as in: "Now don't y'all go worrying your pretty little heads about all that Death to America stuff. I'm just here to shoot the bull!" I haven't seen Vlad and Mahmoud on Facebook and Twitter, but that doesn't mean they're not there.

I realize today's world is all about instant access and having your finger on the planet's pulse, y'all, but frankly I'm a bit concerned about this blurring of the lines. Ever since news, politics, and entertainment became one big fuzzy party, I've been finding it harder and harder to tell if I'm watching the evening news or *Entertainment Tonight*. I'm so over serious-minded journalists dishing Lady Gaga updates and politicians letting it all hang out on the talk shows.

Blame it on my Southern DNA and all those warnings about being too "familiar" in public, but I wouldn't mind sacrificing a little access to the candidates this next presidential election go-round, if it means retaining some dignity to the whole process. Like my friend Paulette said after the '08 election: Seeing Hill play stewardess and hearing Huck discuss his squirrel recipe can't really help us cast an informed vote unless the next leader of the free world is gonna have to work part-time on Air Force One and sustain his or her family by shooting squirrels on the White House lawn, á la Jed Clampett. (Well said, Paulette.)

With all this chumminess in the air, one is led to wonder if anyone remembers the old dictum "familiarity breeds contempt." Hanging with Hill and Huck is one thing (and does that not sound like the makings of a fine reality show?), but we need to figure out where the line is before next season's lineup brings us Lifestyles of the Extreme Terrorists.

I, for one, would find a bit of distance reassuring. Your happy hostess here hasn't rested all that well since I read that cheery heads-up from Al Qaeda's number two man. I'm speaking of the announcement about his operation expanding their Internet use. The part that bothered me was where he said he wanted everyday infidels—that's me and you—to email questions he could then answer on his next online video. I suppose the goal there is to become a more interactive terrorist organization. Actually, I worked up a couple questions for him, but The Husband said he'd rather I not post 'em, something about suicide bombing. I didn't get it right off, but now that I've had some time to think about it, I'd really appreciate it if someone would be a dear and call 1-800-TERRORIST for me. Tell 'em this infidel has just been funning, okay? Note to self: Check on additional security for bunker.

Desert Romance Can Be a Real Killer

Heaven forbid my having a bunker should be interpreted as a lack of confidence in our military to protect us. I would hate to be misunderstood on that point. The men and women in uniform whose job it is to protect us have my utmost respect. If they're given the right information and adequate resources, I remain confident in their abilities to guard the fort. However, I do get uncomfortable at times with the priorities of the bureaucrats behind 'em. For instance, we've all heard those stories about the government spending ludicrous amounts of money on hammers and toilet seats, and we know how we feel about that sort of wasteful spending, but here's an expenditure that's a bit murkier:

I'm sure you're aware that the CIA has a history of bribing informants with things like cash, tools, and medicine. They consider it a necessary evil, and I can see that, I really can. But as the need for information in the war on terror has grown, the

CIA boys have gotten trickier. I read that they're now giving aging tribal chiefs those famous little blue pills. That's right, as in "I'll trade you ten Viagra for two terrorists." Have mercy! Reports are that one such chieftain returned the next day, gave up the goods, and put in a request for more blue pills.

At first blush, this appears to be a win/win for everyone except the really bad guys—and they aren't on our side anyway. But I have a question. Has anyone thought about the not so happy harem? Please. Just when the girls were getting accustomed to Chief Casanova falling asleep counting camels, he's there waving his tunic around his head and singing off key to Elvis Mahmoud's famous remix "Are You Lonesome Tonight?"

Maybe I'm wrong. Maybe the whole harem was hoping Chief Casanova would get his groove back, but like my friend Paulette said, "Bless the poor girls' hearts. It may not be waterboarding, Shellie, but still."

I have a better idea. Memo to the CIA: If y'all could somehow get these same pills into the hands of the terrorists, y'all might be able to keep 'em . . . well, you know, *busy* long enough to sneak up on 'em. I even came up with a cool code name for the operation: "Party Crashers." You're welcome. Oh, and one more thing. I promised Bubba I'd get word to y'all that he has some really kicking inside information on a couple high-level terrorists—if you're interested. But, I don't know, just between us, I don't trust his motives.

Hazed by the Electoral College

One can only imagine why the subject of bribes and ludicrous spending would remind me of the way we go about electing a president in this country, but I'm glad it did. There's something else that I think deserves another look. And while I have no desire to cause a stink with those outside our region, I'd like to register a legitimate complaint. On behalf of my fellow Southerners, I'd like it to be known that "we the people" below the Mason-Dixon have our lips run out about the whole presidential primary thing.

It was the topic of conversation at the recent holiday parties. Paulette said she was sick and tired of hearing 'bout y'all's electoral college. And Bubba said he doesn't know where your fancy shmancy school is even located, but y'all haven't ever been to a bowl game that he knows of, and besides if you're not in the SEC you don't matter no-how. Granted, some of us are much clearer on the details of the electoral system than others, but still, it'd be right nice of y'all to at least pretend that we matter.

It's bad enough when y'all start choosing your primary dates. Scheduling and rescheduling your parties to try and be the first one out of the blocks. Shame on you! Y'all remind me of a bunch of Southern brides-to-be trying to grab the most coveted weekend of the spring bridal season. Please. I've seen better manners at a half-price sale. But it just flat-out rubs salt in the wound when y'all start harping about how it'll all be over after the first three or maybe four primaries, as if none of the other states exist. Excuse us! We do have a dog in the fight, too, you know.

I'd like to propose a new system. I say the primaries should rotate and start in a different region every election cycle. Now, that would be much fairer. But should that not set well with y'all, I have another idea (and this is sheer genius if I have to say so myself): We could play Spoons to decide who goes first. Oh, yeah, that'd be just as civil and a lot more fun.

FYI for the uninitiated, Spoons is a regional card game we Southerners like to play. It's similar to musical chairs only bloodier. Why, Mama won't even let us, her immediate family, play Spoons on her dining room table since . . . well, never mind. Look here, y'all send a few of your delegates down here to play a few of our delegates, and we'll work out the details. Just don't send any pansies. Bubba's got his Spoons game on.

If a passionate round of Spoons sounds rough to you, chances are you're suffering from memory loss, Sweet Cheeks. I doubt it could get any rougher than the last presidential election. Shall I jog your memory? The report of a senior citizen from one campaign taking a swing at a senior citizen from the other campaign at a nursing home comes to mind as one of the more bizarre incidents. Sadly, it was a long, long campaign that left "we the people" red, white, and bruised all over.

"Angry" has been the political buzzword for some time now. Problem is, both sides keep talking about the angry voter, but in my humble opinion they still don't get it! They each speak about the righteous indignation of their own supporters while decrying the violent rhetoric of their opponents. Dear Mr. and Mrs. Politician, seeing as how you're missing the nose on your faces, allow me to spell it out. We're all angry, red and blue voters alike! And one of the things we're angriest about is your never-ending spin.

And by the way, y'all didn't invent spin, you know. It's so easy a child can do it. I'm reminded of my dear friend Debbie, who was having lunch with her daughter, Sarah, and two-year-old grandson at a local restaurant. Little Miller had finished his lunch and was playing with some other kids, when they started running. His mama called him over and explained that "We don't run in restaurants." Miller nodded. Two minutes later he was running again.

Sarah called him back over. "What did Mama tell you about running?" she asked.

And that's when Miller proved he could spin with the best of 'em. "But I wasn't running," he said. "I was skipping to my Lou."

And the Winner Is

The funny thing is that everyone knows everyone else is spinning, but it doesn't seem to keep any of the players from ratcheting up the rhetoric. I mean, once the parties have their respective presidential candidates, the attention turns to the second slot and the spin just switches gears. By the way, after much thought and a bit of that déjà vu feeling, I've finally put my finger on something that's been bothering me about that VP process, too. The revelation hit me while I was watching one of those TV talent shows and they were about to announce the winner. The host was doing the long pause thing, while the last two remaining songbirds were taking turns looking like they (a) were very excited or (b) had just eaten something that didn't agree with 'em, when I realized what's so familiar about the way that all goes down.

Those talent shows look like beauty pageants, and both of them are highly reminiscent of the lengthy process that precedes those vice presidential picks. Think about it! With the talent shows and the beauty pageants, the two remaining contestants are left holding their breath for the big news, just like the people on the short list for VP! The only difference is that sometimes, bless their hearts, the pageant girls don't seem to know who won even after the announcement.

Before I get flooded with angry emails from you sweet beauty queens (and your loyal mamas), please hear me out. I'm on your side. That little pause while y'all try and figure it out is uncomfortable for all of us, but I get it, y'all. I blame the confusion on that whole convoluted "if for some reason the winner can't fulfill her duties, the first runner-up will assume the title" thing.

Course, I could be wrong. Could be those triumphant beauty queens aren't at all confused. Could just be that Carol Beth, the winner, is wondering how Linda Kay, the disappointed runner-up, is interpreting the "if for some reason" line, while Linda Kay herself is considering her next move. Now, *that* would explain the awkward moment, wouldn't it?

And that brings me to the second-man-on-the-ticket tie-in I alluded to earlier. The vice president's job also comes with that "if for some reason" thing. Are you picking up what I'm putting down? We may have hit upon the reason it takes the nominees so long to name their potential vice presidents. I reckon they can all find plenty of qualified candidates who are willing, but perhaps they feel the hopefuls all appear a bit too eager.

Do These Campaign Fatigues Make My Butt Look Big?

The advantages in revamping the process are many, not the least of which would be a more engaged electorate, which would hopefully translate to a more informed electorate. I offer the following story to illustrate that not everyone is staying as clued in for the duration of the contest as the political establishment might hope.

We were smack in the middle of the last presidential election when my friend Paulette called. I could tell right off she'd been listening to talk radio with one ear again. (Paulette is easily distracted.)

"Hey, Shellie," she said. "What do you think about the new campaign fatigues?"

"Campaign fatigues?" I repeated, before asking, "Paulette, what are you talking about now?"

"I heard it on the radio," she said. "The candidates are gonna start wearing fatigues. If you ask me, I think it's tacky. No one knows how to dress anymore. What are they gonna wear to the swearing-in ceremony, cutoffs? They're gonna look like Jimmy Carter's brother. What was his name, Bobby?"

"Billy," I said, choosing the last question. It had finally occurred to me what the girl was talking about. "Paulette," I said, "are you sure they weren't discussing campaign fatigue, without an 's'? That's a condition caused by constant exposure to a political campaign."

Long pause. "Oh," Paulette said. "Well, I don't like that either."

I explained to Paulette that the experts were worried about campaign fatigue setting in early because the candidates had already been at it so long, and at the time, the election was still a year and a half away! It makes people lose interest in the process, I told her.

"Right," Paulette said. "Tell the truth, Shellie. Do you really think Paris Hilton was reading the Bible when she was in jail that time?"

Heaven help us all. The very possibility of Paulette being an indicator of the level of interest from the electorate sent me into high gear. Being the responsible Belle of *All Things Southern*, I immediately came up with five easy ways to help my readers determine if they or their friends were suffering from campaign fatigue. You know, so they could get help, get over it, and tune in. Perhaps I should post those here in case y'all want to print 'em out and keep 'em handy for the next go-round.

You might be suffering from campaign fatigue if:

Number Five: You believe there's a new reality show called *So You Think You Can Be President*.

Number Four: You can't believe they replaced Simon with Anderson Cooper.

Number Three: You're hoping all the candidates get an *Extreme Makeover*.

Number Two: You have tried to text in your vote after a debate.

And the Number One way to tell if you're suffering from campaign fatigue: You actually think your text vote counted.

To quote a redneck named Earl Pitts, who is rather famous in these parts, "Wake up A-murr-i-cuh!"

From all accounts, my little quiz can be quite the attention getter. As a matter of fact, it did such a good job of selling Paulette on her lack of knowledge and the importance of staying informed that she went to the other extreme, which meant that my girlfriends and I benefited from Paulette Pronouncements throughout the rest of the election cycle and right up to the big vote. We didn't mind, though, not really. We thought it was cute, even though she always got the facts backwards. It never occurred to me that I could be creating a monster until a few mornings after the election.

I was cooking breakfast when she called to tell me she was suffering from "Campaign Withdrawal." Paulette had read that experts were predicting that some Americans had become so addicted to the constant election coverage that they would likely have a difficult time weaning themselves from the twenty-four-hour news cycle.

"Maybe some people will," I assured Paulette, "but I don't

think that will be a problem for you. May I remind you that you haven't been a news buff that long?"

"That's how much you know, Mrs. Smarty Pants," Paulette sniffed. "I watch Al Reilly all the time!"

"O'Reilly," I offered.

"Him, too," Paulette said.

I tried again. "Look, Paulette, I'm getting a bad feeling about this. I hope you're not about to go off on one of your harebrained schemes."

Paulette had the gall to act offended. "I don't know what you're talking about. I'm simply planning to keep my recent finely tuned political instincts honed by staying involved at the local level."

I must admit it sounded like a fine idea, and I was tempted to say so, but I've been around Paulette's schemes before. Once bitten, twice shy. "What are you gonna do, exactly?" I asked.

Paulette wasted no time telling me her plan. "I'm gonna train to become a pundit. I plan to start small and make a name for myself down at the school board, you know like that Alaska woman did. It won't be long, and I figure I'll be right up there in the pundit pit with the big boys. Just you watch."

I asked Paulette how she planned to familiarize herself with all the issues.

"Oh, that's the best part," she said. "I know about a lot of that stuff already, and I'm not worried about the rest of it. The way I see it, to be a good pundit all you gotta do is let the other person go first and then you just get louder and louder until they give up and you win. What with my experience, I figure I'm a natural."

"Your experience—" I said.

"Oh, yeah, baby," Paulette crowed. "My experience! I've been doing that sort of thing my entire married life!"

Stuff Passing as Meat

I'll give her this much, it would be entertaining to watch someone like Paulette mix it up with those other silver-tongued pundits. Talk about rewriting the playbook! Paulette is bound to bring an interesting (not to mention hilarious) perspective to the issues. And I say that knowing I could get yet another earful from well-meaning people wanting me to know that the many problems facing our country are no laughing matter. I concur, my serious friends.

Trust you me, I've been as concerned about the economy as anyone, even before I heard that the rising cost of groceries were contributing to SPAM's record sales gains. No, not spam as in Prime Minister Butterfly offering you thousands of US dollars if you'll just send her your Social Security and bank account numbers, but SPAM, as in little cans filled with "Stuff Passing as Meat." Apparently, SPAM is making a triumphant return to American pantries. Some pantries, that is. Back on Bull Run Road, my mama fried that stuff for breakfast, sliced it in sandwiches, and hid it in cheese-covered casseroles. Forgive me if I say no to seconds.

SPAM aversions aside, however, I found another interesting tidbit about what consumers are turning to in this depressed economy that I'm just dying to share with you. Are y'all ready for this? Color! Oh, yeah! Mama and I felt plum vindicated when we read that lipstick is also seeing rising sales gains. Many of the experts quoted in my research (and again, by research I mean I googled one whole afternoon) found that confusing. I doubt very seriously that any of them were belles. Otherwise they'd know full well the advantages of facing dire circumstances with a healthy combination of steely resolve and lip color. My husband's mom has gone on to that great parlor in the sky, but I remember an incident from one of her last hospital scares that will illustrate my point. This particular setback looked like "the one."

I was trying everything I knew of that evening to rouse my mother-in-law, with absolutely no response. Suddenly, inspiration hit. Knowing full well that MawMaw Lucy was belle to the bone,* I leaned down and asked her if she would like for me to help her put on some lipstick. Lying at death's door, she answered with a most characteristic response. Without a word and without opening her eyes, MawMaw pursed up her tired and aged lips. See, folks, lipstick is our way of saying we may be down, but we're not out.

And on that note, here's a little shout-out to Washington: We've been trying to give y'all some room to work on this economy thing, but let it be known that if the girls and I have to start eating SPAM again, we're gonna be coming your way—with our color on.

Official Guide to Speaking All Things Southern

*belle to the bone, noun: a state in which a Southern female is so indoctrinated into the ways of Southern womanhood that her belleness has become deeply engrained and completely automated

An Olive Branch for Jones Soda

Please don't read that as a threat. It's more of a promise. I'm just saying that we're willing to come up there and help y'all do some brainstorming. Just say the word. You're welcome. Times, they are hard, but I feel compelled to caution everyone to remember that we are all in this thing together. No region of our country is an island. Okay, so that sounded much better before I typed it out, but I think you get my point. We should all do whatever we can to help one another succeed. Far be it from me to brag on my own generosity, but this past holiday season offered me a rather unique opportunity to do just that.

It started before Thanksgiving. I had a strange feeling that I couldn't quite place. All I knew was that something seemed to be missing. And then, it hit me, y'all. I was in the kitchen making cheese straws when, lo and behold, I realized I hadn't heard from the people at Jones Soda this entire season! Y'all do remember Jones Soda Company that made all the weird flavored sodas? There was Turkey and Gravy Soda, Fruitcake Soda, Cranberry Soda, Green Bean Casserole Soda . . . you get the idea. They've been sending me their crazy drinks free for years now, hoping, I suppose, for a good review. Bless their hearts—I reckon they've burned up a dozen good blenders on my gift packs alone. And suddenly, nothing!

I couldn't help thinking I'd finally crossed the line and had too much holiday fun at their expense so I went to their website to drop 'em a note explaining that when I said we had more guns and they should leave our turkeys alone, I was just funnin', kinda.

Imagine my shock when I discovered that, due to economic hardships, Jones had discontinued the Holiday Pack altogether! I felt like the Grinch that stole Christmas! It grieved me to think my poor behavior may have contributed to anyone's job loss. And right there at the holidays, for goodness' sakes! Besides, I almost missed 'em, the way you'd miss a weird cousin that stuck peas up his nose at the kids' table. Not that I had one of those.

In the spirit of Christmas and in keeping with my pledge to help support other businesses, I decided to offer Jones Soda an *All Things Southern* bailout. Pulling out a sheet of my prettiest monogrammed stationery, I wrote, "Dear Jones, Y'all are all invited to come on down and experience some real Christmas food—with utensils. However, I feel you should know Bubba had a really bad year on the farm, and despite considerable time spent in the deer stand, he hasn't gotten a buck yet. Translation: He's a tad trigger-happy. If any of your bigwigs mentions a golden parachute, Bubba's gonna be looking to put a hole in it. Y'all come on down, now, you hear?"

Political and Economic Tips

THUS SAITH THE BELLE DOCTRINE . . .

* Retaining the right perspective will give thee a head start in the job market.

* Before thou can be out of work, thou must know what kind of work thou art out of.

* It is understood if thou fallest on hard times, thou shalt not waller there.

* Thou shalt not hand over thy purse without a fight.

* Thou shalt closely guard thy individual freedoms lest they become a collective loss.

* Thou shalt avoid twittering with terrorists.

* Thou shalt remember that thy country rises or falls together and not by region or groups.

Soups and Sauces to Stretch
the Family Budget

Soup is the answer when it comes to dishes that make the most of your overworked dollar. Its versatility makes it easy to disguise veggies that have seen a better day and/or use leftovers that might not otherwise find their way back to the table. It's a covert art something like the one practiced by wily politicians who bury less appealing parts of a bill inside a more popular piece of legislation, only a good pot of soup won't come back to bite you in the backside. Here's a nice variety of some of my favorite soup recipes, along with a few special sauce ideas to add some zest to those weekday meals.

Simply Delicious Chunky Seafood Bisque

(SERVES 4–6)

Don't be intimidated by this recipe's name, a bisque is simply a thick, creamy, highly seasoned soup. Most bisques use pureed vegetable and the crustacean of your choice, but my family prefers it chunky. Short story, anyone? I once prepared a huge bisque for fleeing evacuees who had taken shelter at my home during the Katrina aftermath of 2006, but before anyone could partake I accidentally dropped the entire tureen, shattering it and splattering the contents over everyone in sight. Compounding natural disasters is apparently a talent of mine.

1 small white onion, chopped

3 tablespoons butter

2 (12 oz.) cans evaporated milk

1 (10.5 oz.) can cream of celery soup

1 (10.5 oz.) can cream of chicken soup

Dash each of hot sauce and Worcestershire sauce

2 teaspoons red wine cooking sherry

½ teaspoon thyme

1 teaspoon Cajun seasoning

Salt and pepper to taste

1 pound of shrimp, peeled and deveined (or seafood of choice)

Optional: ½ cup to 1 cup instant potatoes to thicken

Topping: chopped green onions

Sauté chopped onion in butter until clear. Add to next three ingredients, bring to a rolling boil, and reduce heat to low. Season with the next five ingredients. Cook over low heat for thirty minutes. Add shrimp, being careful not to overcook. They only need about three minutes. If your bisque doesn't have a thick enough consistency at this point, add instant potatoes to thicken. You basically want this to get your bisque good and hot all the way through and turn it off. Top with green onions. Serve in soup bowls, or ladle over steaming hot rice with a side salad and French bread. YUM!

Cuzin Peggy's Jambalaya Grits

(SERVES 4–6)

I just know someone is going to question me as to whether this is really a soup or if it's actually a casserole, so let me head everyone off at the pass and explain my position. Around here, if we can ladle it into one big bowl, it's a soup. If you're a puritan about this sort of thing, feel free to call it a "stoup" (a very heavy soup!) The thing is, I have a feeling that whatever you decide to call my Cuzin Peggy's Jambalaya Grits, you're going to come to the same conclusion: This stuff is lip-smacking good.

- 1 bag frozen chopped onion, bell pepper, and celery
- 1 stick of butter
- 1 tablespoon olive oil
- 1 package smoked sausage, sliced
- 2 cans of RO*TEL tomatoes
- 1 tablespoon chopped garlic
- 1½ teaspoons salt
- ⅛ teaspoon freshly ground black pepper
- ½ teaspoon cayenne
- 5 cups milk
- 2 cups old-fashioned grits, uncooked
- ½ pound cooked ham, cubed
- 1 pound sharp white cheddar cheese, grated
- 1 (8 oz.) package cream cheese
- Green onions

Using a large heavy pot, sauté frozen veggies in butter and olive oil. (The olive oil will keep your butter from scorching.) Once the veggies are soft, add in smoked sausage. Cook for

2–3 minutes before adding RO*TEL tomatoes, garlic, and seasonings. Slowly add milk, bring to a boil, reduce heat, and stir in uncooked grits. Add cubed ham and continue stirring occasionally until the grits are tender and creamy, about twenty minutes. Before serving, add cheddar and cream cheese, stir, and top with green onions.

Cream of Crawfish Soup

(SERVES 4–6)

I'm going to have to ask you not to substitute any other seafood for the crawfish in this dish under threat of prosecution. Trust me, it's for your own good. This one needs no tampering, folks. It's a deliciously flavorful soup for a cold winter's evening. Enjoy with crackers or French Bread.

1 pound peeled crawfish tails
½ bunch green onions, coarsely chopped
½ cup grated white onion
½ cup or one stick of butter
½ cup flour
2 cups chicken stock, set on stove over low heat
2 cups heavy cream
2 cups half-and-half
2 teaspoons red pepper
2 teaspoons garlic powder
2 teaspoons onion powder

Ground crawfish tails with green onions in your food processor. Take a large, heavy saucepan and sauté grated white onion in butter. Stir in flour, mix well, and cook for 2 minutes, or until thickened, before adding heated chicken stock. Simmer for another 5 minutes before adding crawfish and green onion mixture. Once soup base has simmered about 10 minutes, add heavy cream and half-and-half. Season with red pepper, garlic powder, and onion powder and simmer another 5 minutes before ladling into individual soup bowls.

Super Simple Vegetable Beef Soup

(SERVES 4–6)

I've used frozen mixed vegetables in this recipe, but now is the time to learn a Southern Mama tip: Make a habit of freezing small portions of leftover vegetables that would otherwise be thrown out. Whether or not you have a good soup bone, that lone pack of hamburger meat in your freezer will be all you need to create a big steaming pot of vegetable soup.

1–1½ pounds of hamburger meat

1 onion, diced

3 carrots, chopped

3–4 potatoes, chopped in bite-size pieces

1 (16 oz.) bag frozen mixed veggies

1 (14.5 oz.) can tomatoes

1 (8 oz.) can tomato sauce

2 cups water

Salt and pepper

Dash of hot sauce

1 teaspoon Worcestershire sauce

1 teaspoon Tony Chachere's or other Cajun season-all

Brown hamburger meat with diced onion. Drain and return to soup pot. Add vegetables, tomatoes, tomato sauce, and water. Season well with salt and pepper, hot sauce, Worcestershire, and a good Cajun season-all like Tony Chachere's, and bring to a rolling boil. Reduce heat and cook until veggies are all tender. And remember, that's just a base. Feel free to add whatever other veggies you have on hand—leftover green beans, leftover cabbage, that sort of thing. It's not high science, it's just good cooking.

Broccoli Soup Divine

(SERVES 4)

There are several different ways to enjoy this recipe. A belle may decide to add diced chicken to give it more staying power, or she may bake potatoes and layer the soup over the top if she finds she needs to stretch the recipe for unexpected company. The important thing is to have it in your repertoire. However you serve it, you'll be glad you did.

> 1 medium onion, chopped
> ½ stick of butter
> 2 (16 oz.) bags frozen broccoli
> ½ cup water
> 1 can cream of chicken soup
> 1 can cream of mushroom soup
> 8 ounces Velveeta cheese
> 1 (6 oz.) roll garlic cheese
> 1–1½ cups milk

In a large soup pot, sauté onion in butter. Add frozen broccoli and water and turn heat to high. Add soups, stir, and add cheeses. Reduce heat to medium and cook for 30–35 minutes. Depending on the consistency, it is sometimes necessary to add anywhere from a cup to a cup and a half of milk before serving. Just make sure it's warmed through and through.

Barbara's White Chili

(SERVES 4–6)

While I had heard about white chili, I must admit that I had never given it much thought until one of my readers sent in this recipe. (Chili is supposed to be red, right?) I tried it, however, and was rewarded with rave reviews and requests for seconds!

3–4 medium chicken breasts (diced in bite-size chunks)

1 tablespoon olive oil

1 medium onion, diced

1½ teaspoons garlic powder

2 cans Great Northern beans with juice

1 (14 oz.) can chicken broth

2 (4 oz.) cans green chilies

½ cup whipping cream

1 teaspoon salt

1 teaspoon cumin

1 teaspoon oregano

½ teaspoon black pepper

¼ teaspoon cayenne pepper

1 cup sour cream (optional)

Dice chicken breasts into bite-size pieces and sauté in olive oil with chopped onion and garlic powder.

When tender, transfer to stock pot and add beans, chicken broth, and green chiles. Add whipping cream and those all important spices. Bring to a boil, reduce heat, and simmer uncovered, 30–40 minutes. We enjoyed ours topped with a little sour cream, but that's optional. (Thanks again, Barbara!)

Jessica Ann's Chicken and Dumplings

(SERVES 4–6)

This is my daughter's Chicken and Dumplings recipe. Forgive me for bragging, but the girl can cook, y'all. You can see for yourself at Kitchen Bellecious, http://www.kitchenbelleicious.com. She takes a little of my ideas, some of her Nanee's, and adds her own little twists. The results are always fantastic.

1 pound chicken tenders
Salt and pepper
2 tablespoons Italian dressing
1 cup chopped celery, large pieces
1 cup carrots, diced
1 cup onions, diced
4 cups chicken broth
2 cups water
Frozen dumplings
1 teaspoon poultry seasoning
1 teaspoon thyme
1 teaspoon oregano
1 teaspoon Cajun seasoning
1 teaspoon garlic powder

Marinate chicken tenders in pepper, salt, garlic powder, and Italian dressing for about an hour. Bake in 350 degree oven for 20 minutes and set aside. (We both think baking the chicken gives it a better flavor than boiling it does!) While the chicken is resting, sauté chopped veggies in oil and garlic in a separate skillet while bringing chicken stock and water to a boil in soup pot. Once the veggies are tender, add to the broth, reduce heat, and simmer while preparing dumplings.

Sure, you can buy frozen dumplings and they're good, but making 'em with your own hands is extra special. Here are Jessica's simple steps to great dumplings: Cut ¾ cup of milk into 1⅔ cups of flour and add a teaspoon each of salt and garlic powder. Mix as little as possible to avoid making your dumplings hard and stringy! Form a ball, roll out, and cut into ⅛-inch strips.

Bring your broth back to a boil and drop the dumplings in one at a time. Pull your chicken into bite-size pieces and return it to the pot. Let it all simmer another thirty minutes or so and step away from the boiler before the crowd stampedes you!

Sassy Sauce for Pork

(SERVES 4)

Sometimes a belle just needs a little something extra to turn the average into the extraordinary. Here's a simple solution that will do the trick, y'all. My Sassy Sauce is just the thing to bring out the best flavor of those everyday pork chops.

    4 nice-size pork chops (bone in)
    ½ pound peppered bacon
    1 cup molasses
    2 tablespoons spicy brown mustard
    1 teaspoon crushed garlic

Preheat oven to 375 degrees. Wrap each pork chop with two slices of peppered bacon and place 'em all in a heavy cast iron skillet. Take a small bowl and combine heavy molasses with spicy brown mustard and crushed garlic. Stir well and pour over chops. Bake for an hour to an hour and a half, or until chops are cooked through.

Plantation Dressing

(SERVES 4)

Go ahead. Get a little fancy every now and then. Not only is my Plantation Dressing delicious, it's also quite pretty at the table presented in a piece of fine china and ladled out with your best sterling. Why serve a ready-made dressing when you can make your salad sing?

1 cup mayonnaise

1 cup buttermilk

1 clove garlic, minced or pressed

½ cup of sliced green onions

1 tablespoon parsley flakes

1 teaspoon tarragon

Salt and pepper to taste

Blend mayonnaise and buttermilk. Add liquid to garlic and green onions in food processor and give it a whirl. Season with a tablespoon of parsley, a teaspoon of tarragon, and salt and pepper to taste. Refrigerate overnight before using.

Easy Cajun Remoulade Sauce

(SERVES 4)

If you have fresh seafood available at your local grocery, you're going to want to keep my simple Remoulade sauce handy. It's twice as nice as store-bought. A few easy steps and you'll be whipping up a seafood feast that would make Paula Deen giggle.

¾ cup olive oil

¼ cup white vinegar

¼ cup Creole mustard

2 tablespoons minced fresh parsley

½ cup finely chopped celery

1 cup finely chopped white onion

Salt and pepper to taste

Dash of All Things Southern hot sauce

Whisk together olive oil and vinegar. Once you've got those two getting along, stir in Creole mustard and add parsley, celery, and finely chopped white onion. Season with salt and pepper and a dash of hot sauce! Refrigerate until cold and serve over your favorite lettuce and/or seafood. YUM!

7

Rein It In, Geraldo

Regional Showdowns with
Side Dishes and Vegetable Recipes
to Iron Out Our Differences

On behalf of my fellow Louisianans, and our many friends in other hard-hit areas of the Southern region, I'd like to have a come to Jesus meeting* with the weather bureaus, and I'm not talking about our local weather people. Oh, no, this is for those of you in the national media who feel compelled to run down here and cling to our light poles. I'm sure other areas of the country have issues with the way you cover their natural disasters, but I'll let them speak for themselves.

Here's the thing. We folks in the Southern states would appreciate y'all reining in the enthusiasm you have for our reoccurring tragedies. My girlfriends and I thought Geraldo might flat-out hyperventilate during Katrina, running around the Big Easy with his little handheld wind meter, trying desperately to report the most dramatic wind gusts! "I've got sixty, sixty-five, now seventy, now seventy-five!" Once, his camera man got carried away and shouted out, "I'll take eighty!" Okay, not really, but still. Farmer Hubby would like to hook Mr. Riviera up with a John Deere cap to corral that wild and wooly hair, but methinks the G-man feels it adds to the drama.

Not to be outdone by Mr. Riviera, I saw a female weatherperson on a competing station—and "competing" would be the key word here as they all try to out-hype the others—who during her live broadcast was handed an update which she eagerly and dramatically began reading aloud while the wind and rain whipped her hair into her mouth. Poor Thing, when she got to the part of the bulletin where it said the hurricane was being downgraded, I thought for sure she was gonna cry right there on camera. Bottom line: You folks are living examples of that old adage "One man's tragedy is another's fortune," and it's wearing a mite thin.

Customer Service H-E-Double L

I'm not trying to be disagreeable here. It's just that I think if anyone deserves to profit from our challenging weather patterns, it should be those of us who live through it. We know a few things about extreme conditions, do we not, fellow Southerners? We spell it h-u-m-i-d-i-t-y. (I can hear the amen corner warming up now.) Summertime in the Deep South can be fraught with danger, and I'm not just talking about heatstroke. Every year, people put themselves at risk of physical injury by saying things like "Hot enough for ya?" I'm just saying, we aren't always in the best of moods when the temp it is a-soaring. I'm reminded of a blistering summer day many years ago.

My little kids and I were vacationing in the customer service department of a local car dealership because our big blue van had died smack in the middle of the road during the height of rush hour traffic. After a rather unpleasant towing experience that involved my babies and I sharing the cab with one very large and smelly, albeit friendly, tow truck driver, we were enjoying the dealership's customer service amenities—a tiny room with a broken air conditioner and a knobless TV fixed on the Weather Channel, all without snacks, toys, or naps. Suddenly, an obnoxious mechanic appeared and interrupted our charming stay. I can still see him propped against the door frame with one hand, while the other hitched his britches up in advance of his big announcement.

"Uh, little lady" [note to male readers, don't call us "little lady"], "Can't find anything wrong with your car . . . took it round the block a few times; 'pears to be working fine, hasn't stopped on me . . ." He trailed off, implying that three hours in customer hell was the best recreational activity I could come up with for me and my babies on this miserably hot August day. I insisted the van had quit. He patronized me some more. I called for the manager and asked for a loaner car. "We could

My daddy was a true Southern gentleman. He worked at a full service gasoline station and was always willing to go above and beyond the call of duty to help anyone he could. One day a lady drove into the station for gasoline and asked if he had a restroom. Daddy was really busy cleaning the windshield and filling the gasoline tank, etc. He thought she had asked if he had a whisk broom, which is why he pointed to the station's air hose and responded, "No, but if you will back it up over here, I'll be glad to blow it out for you."

~Clara Adams,
Monroe, Louisiana

do that," Cocky Mechanic Man's boss said, "but my guy tells me yours is fine."

Well, they had me. It'd been great fun, but the gag was up. I loaded everyone up and drove off. Half a mile up the street our van died again.

With a child on my hip, another by the hand, and sweat running in uncomfortable places, I marched through four lanes of traffic, past the front desk to the service area, hollered at Cocky Mechanic Man, and crooked my finger in the universal signal for "come here before I come there."

Ignoring his questions, I led him outside and pointed wordlessly. His gaze followed my arm to my finger and then to the vehicle, stranded in the middle of a four-lane road. And this is his direct quote: "Well, I'll be, little lady. Did it stop on you?"

I always felt like I should've been rewarded for not sending Cocky Mechanic Man to meet His Maker, and I still say a good lawyer could've gotten me off with justifiable homicide. You know what they say—here in the South we consider "he needed killin'" to be a valid defense . . .

Festival Gator

Of course, being civic minded and all, I recently came up with an idea to help us beat the heat, stimulate the local economy, and have some fun at the same time. (I don't know. They just come to me.)

First, we're gonna need a cute animal like Phil to jump up and give his prediction smack in the middle of June as to whether or not we'll have six more weeks of hot weather. No, not Husband Phil—he's precious—but I'm talking about Phil that groundhog they've got up in Pennsylvania, the one with the less than impressive record of predicting the weather, the one who conveniently speaks *only* to men in tuxes. Are you with me? How hard can this be? If you're thinking, "Of course we'll have six more weeks of hot weather!" you are missing the whole marketing opportunity. Some thirty thousand people will go see that groundhog this year. Can you say tourist dollars?

Now, hold on, folks, we can't just throw up a big tent and have a huge fish fry. That'd work in these parts, but to get the national press corps down here, we're going to need to plan this thing out, and choosing the right weather-predicting animal is one of the most important decisions we'll make. Papa said it'd be fun to use blue runner snakes and have the reporters tap on their open cages. That may be true, but I have reminded Papa that we want *repeat* visitors. Paulette suggested we go with the opossum because it could play dead and we could revive it with special healing mineral water that we could then sell to all the foreigners for an incredibly low price of $19.99. (You would think I could get better help with something this serious.) Myself, I'm leaning toward the black bear. He might get it wrong, but I doubt he'd get called on it.

Unfortunately, at this point my biggest problem is with the festival's steering committee. I got a group of forward-thinking volunteers together at the dock recently to help plan the thing. What with the groundhog party being months away, I thought we should strike while this is, well, hot. Unfortunately, I didn't have time to share half of my good ideas with the board, as the meeting broke up before it got started good! Some folks are saying we may be forced to postpone our inaugural event until next August, and that's only provided we've managed to run Bubba out of town by then. (The boy could've simply suggested we use a polecat. We still wouldn't have gone for it, but after that little show-and-smell exhibit there was no way in Hades I was gonna be able to bring that meeting back to order.)

On the positive side, we did come close to choosing the official "Hot Enough for Ya Weather Predicting Animal"—only it's a reptile. Yeah, after bringing the subject up on my radio show, I got a ton of letters from all five of the people who were excited about my idea and the alligator won hands down.

Rena Dillman from North Carolina was the first one to vote for the gator. Along with her vote, she also provided her own thought-provoking observation about how animals tend to eat more right before the weather changes. And that, y'all, gave me yet another brilliant idea. We're planning the first Hot Enough for Ya Festival for the summer preceding the next presidential election, right? And the election season, if it holds true to form, will be one big pain in the backside, right? Well, if we handle this thing right, we may be able to make it something of a public service. Follow me here.

What if we took three politicians, tied 'em up and placed 'em on the lake bank? If the Festival Gator goes for the Republican, he's predicting six more weeks of hot weather. If he goes for the Democrat, he's predicting an early fall, you know, somewhere around November. If he goes for the Independent, he's saying it's just too hot to bother. Of course, we couldn't actually let him eat the politicians. That wouldn't be fair to the gator.

We're gonna need some good publicity, of course, but I may have that figured out, too. We could always let summer settle in and the humidity start building, and then someone could slide up to one of the local boys and ask, "Hot enough for ya?" I'll have my flip camera ready and shoot his reaction up to YouTube. If we're lucky, he'll go postal and the clip will go viral.

Under the Influence of Slim Whitman

You may have caught that hip reference to the power of the Internet. I do hope so, as it was most certainly intentional. My savvy has not come without great effort. I used to think that going viral meant ignoring your mama's sound advice and taking your runny-nose child out into the unsuspecting public, but I now know that it refers to the phenomenon that happens when someone puts a video, audio, or text column online and it catches "fire" with an audience, spreading faster than good gossip at Vicki's beauty shop by influencing people to send it to their friends, who send it to their friends, and on and on it goes.

By way of illustration, I remember when one particular news piece went viral around these parts. It had to do with the mailman from that old TV show *Cheers*. (I believe the guy's name was Cliff in the sitcom.) Here in the real world he was asking the courts to protect him from his ex-girlfriend. Right, nothing newsworthy there. But here's what caught my attention: He was worried because his ex was, and I'm quoting now, "under the influence of country music." Apparently Cliffie's old girlfriend happened to mention to him that it is fairly common in country western songs for women to set their ex's vehicles on fire, and he decided that this meant she was capable of violence and planning to inflict some.

My girlfriends and I thought he was rushing to judgment on that one. The lady may have been simply making conversation, or she may be a Miranda Lambert fan, but that in itself doesn't mean she's dangerous, now does it? We also took issue with the phrasing "under the influence of country music." Sounds like some kind of controlled substance that's capable of dominating your decisions and forcing you into bad behavior. Please. I've listened to country music all my life and I have never . . . Oh, okay, there was that one time when my sisters and I considered hijacking a car and destroying private property, but it *was* the family car and Papa *had been* playing Slim Whitman through three states and a weeklong vacation. That's what I thought, too.

Besides, I think we should be at least as, if not more, concerned with the influence of some of the other musical genres. Twice now I've seen someone named Lady Gaga perform on TV. I'm sure she's a perfectly nice girl, but the last time I saw her she was wearing a revolving planetary system on her head, standing on the piano bench, and bending over at the waist to peck at the keys. Is this what you want to see at your child's next piano recital? I think not.

And yet it could happen to someone you love. The truth is music absolutely does influence people, but I'm not comfortable with the precedent of it being used to condemn or exonerate the listener in a court of law. And with that, I'd like to offer Cliffie's girlfriend the advice of the late great Mississippi storyteller extraordinaire Jerry Clower. Honey, you find yourself a good country station on your radio, crank it up, and pull the knobs off!

Is There a Target on Our Backsides?

I bring these things up mainly because I feel strongly that we good country music–loving Southerners shouldn't let that type of insinuation go unchecked in the media. It only encourages them, and Lord knows they don't need any encouragement. As it is, we Southerners are about the only group left that's *not* protected by the PC cops. Our accents, our cooking habits, our intelligence—it's all fair game.

As exhibit A, may I remind you of the ridicule all of the talking heads heaped on that adorable little South Carolina beauty queen that got her tongue tied up in front of God and everybody during the Miss Teen USA pageant a couple years back. They were a bit hard on her, don't you think? Okay, so maybe she got a little confused on her interview question. I'm sure it's intimidating for a young girl. Perhaps that's why her answer was a tad confusing, such as, "in the Iraq," but really, people raise your hand

I grew up in the small sawmill town of Fisher, Louisiana. College in Natchitoches and Shreveport was as big as it got. After our marriage, my husband and I rode a train from Chicago to Anaheim as part of our honeymoon. Upon our arrival we went into the depot to get our luggage. The "nice" man asked me, "Do you see your luggage?" I pointed and said, "It's over yonder." He said, "Where?" I repeated, "Over yonder." With a big smile, he said tell me again. When I finally realized he was making fun of my expression I wanted to cry! After that I quit using the expression, unless I was with Southerners who knew where "over yonder" was!

~Jerry Ann Gregory
Efland, North Carolina

if you, as a U.S. American, haven't walked in her high heels without a map.

I'm talking about those painful moments when you hear yourself saying the most inane things at the most inappropriate moments. It's been my experience that, if it's going to happen, it is bound to occur right when you're trying to make a good impression and sound halfway intelligent! At least Miss South Carolina knew a bell would eventually sound to end her distress. I've had moments when I would've paid big money for such a bell.

I'm not saying I didn't get a chuckle out of it (okay, a belly laugh), but at least I'm willing to admit that I can relate to her unfortunate experience. What irritated me to no end was the way all the bloggers cited her Southerness as the reason for her brain fog! Why, she has plenty of bunkmates in the I-can't-believe-I-embarrassed-myself-like-that-on-national-television camp. Two words: Tom Cruise.

Meanwhile a second very newsworthy pageant event got very little media attention. I bet you didn't know that Mrs. Tennessee got bit by a rattlesnake during the same season's Mrs. USA pageant. Yes, ma'am, she did. Mrs. Tennessee took a brief detour to the hospital, got ten vials of antivenom, sucked her stomach in, put some color on, and went right back to the competition like a good little soldier. It's called making the best of a bad situation, and I'd like to point out that it is exactly what young Miss South Carolina did in her post-pageant interviews. The child handled her less than stellar moment in the media's harsh glare with grace and humor. Say what you will, but I believe she made her mama proud.

In Defense of Our Culinary Traditions

Using grace and humor—that's how our mamas taught us to deal with insults. I shall now attempt to employ both to opine on an injustice that happened a couple years ago under our very noses, right here in the heart of the Deep South. The first ever World Grits Eating Championship was held in Shreveport, Louisiana, and the winner, the person who ate the most grits—twenty-one pounds of grits in ten minutes—was a Mohawk-wearing guy from Chicago!

My girlfriends and I were somewhat torn about this. On one hand, none of us can understand how these people call themselves athletes and claim competitive eating is a sport. We think it would almost be funny if it wasn't so nauseating. I know I once watched a few minutes of a hot dog eating contest on ESPN because I couldn't pull my eyes away, and I have not been able to look at a good hot dog the same way since.

On the other hand, there was the whole honor thing. This Yankee did come to our soil and eat more grits, of all things. And, of course, those in the media who loved to ridicule my people practically gloated. Allow me to quote an actual Associated Press headline: "Yankee beats out Southerners eating grits." I feel we should pause for a moment of silence . . .

My Yankee husband once accused me of not being Southern because I didn't cook huge breakfast meals. That is, until the morning after an all night writing binge (spurred on by crazed energy level from a prescription drug error), when I woke him at six a.m. to a Southern spread extraordinaire. I'd made an early morning Wal-Mart run and whipped up everything from bacon and eggs to sausage gravy and stone ground grits. Of course, I gave him the Southern mantra, "And I expect you to eat everything I put on your plate." He's never challenged my Southern credentials again.

~Karen Spears Zacharias
Author of *Will Jesus Buy Me a Double-Wide?*
('Cause I Need More Room for My Plasma TV)

Now, I don't know who the Southerners were who participated, and I'm not prepared to question their heritage (although Paulette did). I feel that our time would be better spent planning our next move. I've spoken to Bubba, and while it took some doing because he has become preoccupied training for a different sort of competition (more on that in a minute), he has agreed to defend our honor with the grits thing. Bubba feels his history of tailgating at the LSU games has given him a head start in the competitive eating world. I hope so. I know confidence goes a long way in any "sport."

The only problem I'm seeing is Aunt Louise. That's Bubba's mama, and she's bound and determined that he "not get up there on stage and disgrace the family with poor table manners." Have y'all seen how those people put the food away? This could be a real handicap. By the way, Bubba said to tell y'all that he's drawing the line on fruitcake. If we have to defend that culinary tradition, someone else is gonna have to step up to the plate, literally. Consider yourself notified.

The grits fiasco serves as an important reminder that people can be quite sensitive about their culinary traditions. That's something I've tried, in vain I might add, to stress to Paulette. The girl's been surfing the Net again. She came by earlier all geared up and clutching an article she'd printed out about Great Britain's eating habits. "This here," she said, as she threw the paper down on my kitchen counter and stabbed it with her index finger, "this is the kind of thing that helps explain why our ancestors booked a one-way cruise. How about a biscuit update from across the pond?"

"Well, I do like to keep up with the culinary news," I said. "Whatcha got?"

"Allow me," Paulette said, launching into her news anchor voice. "A recent survey reveals that half of all Brits have reported being injured by their biscuits." Paulette lowered the paper. "What is that?! Reminds me of that Jerry Clower story about the night the lights went out during supper and someone got his hand forked reaching for the last biscuit."

"It was a pork chop," I corrected her.

Paulette rolled her eyes as if that was totally irrelevant and continued, "Being injured over a cat head biscuit, I get that. Being injured *by* your biscuit, no self-respecting Southerner would ever admit that—not even to the Biscuit Injury Threat Evaluation. Read that right there in the paper. It also said three percent of those folks had poked themselves in the eye with a biscuit and seven percent were bitten by a pet or other wild animal who was trying to get their biscuit." She looked back up at me. "Do they eat in the barn?!"

I saw my opportunity. "Paulette—"

"What?"

"They aren't talking about our kind of biscuit. Their biscuit is more like a hard cookie."

Paulette absorbed that a minute. "Okay," she said, "I still think they sound wimpy, but that's a little different. If I'm not careful, those macadamia nut cookies at the mall can make me hurt myself, too. Hey—speaking of the mall, you wanna ride with me to exchange Jerry Don's shirt?"

Paulette—the girl reminds me of an old quote: "The beauty of keeping an open mind is that there is always a new frontier."

Rock Paper Scissors, a League All Its Own

But, that's enough of Paulette for now. I had promised to tell y'all about Bubba's current obsession. By the way, he's given me permission to discuss this with y'all, but I was warned to be careful about poking too much fun at his new game of choice 'cause there are some passionate players out there. So forgive me if this hits home with you or someone you love, but I just find the whole thing plum fascinating.

It all started a couple years ago out in Las Vegas. Bubba had made a run out there in his 18-wheeler, when he stumbled across the second annual Rock Paper Scissors Tournament. Can you imagine? I didn't realize the game we once played as kids to settle disputes had become a popular adult sport, but Bubba says its big-time! I understand that ESPN was even there filming.

Bubba found the tournament quite accidentally. He had stopped at one of the local truck stops, when someone at the gas station invited him to a throw down, and well, y'all know Bubba; he thought he was gonna see a good brawl. I think he was rather disappointed at first, but the more he saw of the competition the more he got into it. Confession: I, however, had to laugh when he told me about the heavy favorite wearing a red silk boxing gown, à la Rocky Balboa. Bubba said referees counted down the throws, and paramedics stood nearby in case of "wrist or shoulder dislocations." I'm picturing the managers saying something like "Throw the paper, boy. He can't handle ye paper!"

The kicker for Bubba came when a male nurse from Texas won it all and pulled in $50,000 bo-dollars.* That's all it took. Bubba's been throwing down ever since, with anyone and everyone. The boy is in serious training. He goes around wearing these extra-tight shiny compression shorts, drinking orange Gatorade by the gallon, and challenging all comers. Why, the elementary school principal even had to ban him from the schoolyard. The big cheater was over there paddin' his stats.

Official Guide to Speaking All Things Southern

*bo-dollars: an expression Southerners use when they're talking about serious money changing hands

Unfazed, Bubba's trying to sell the Lumber Yard on sponsoring him, said he'd even wear their T-shirt with a logo, "For all your rock, paper, and scissors needs." Far as I know they're still in negotiations, but Bubba's moving forward. He's formed the Redneck Rock, Paper, Scissors League, and he asked me to invite y'all to join him at the boat-landing twice a week to "practice your throws." That's RPS lingo, and Bubba's in it to win it, so if you go, be prepared—the boy's in the zone. Your best bet is to double dog dare him to open with a rock.

Stereotypes, Prototypes, and Real Men

Someone once asked me if I ever worried that by telling bubba stories I was trading in one of the very stereotypes I dislike. It's a fair question, and one I'm not afraid to take on right here. My answer was and remains an unequivocal no. The larger media may paint Bubba as a backward hillbilly and the prototype of every man south of the Mason-Dixon, but real Southerners see the shallowness of that assumption.

For us, "bubbaisms" are endearing simply because they represent one side of the Southern man we know and love. Personally, I tend to use bubba stories to make a larger point: Be it a throw-down or showdown, Bubba is serious about defending what he holds dear. It's one reason why we love him. His stubborn sense of loyalty so characteristic of Southern men allows us, the bubbas' twenty-first-century other halves, to feel cherished, supported, and yes, protected, regardless of whether we choose to tend the home fires or blaze a trail through the deep, dark woods.

Besides, I've just read an article suggesting that the name Bubba could be positioned to gather appeal in regions beyond the South. Let me explain. Naming babies is big business everywhere, right? A rose might be a rose by any other name, but we all know expectant parents invest serious time in choosing just the right moniker, regardless of where they call home. I know my hometown had an official baby boy boom a while back, and name angst was the topic of conversation for months. Thankfully, the young families had all settled on great names for the wee ones by the time they arrived, although some had had a harder time than others. Weeks before her child's birth, one of the expectant moms was still asking folks to write in to her blog with suggestions. If I knew then what I know now, I could've really fixed her up!

See, a scant few weeks after the baby boom, Gary in Missouri sent me an interesting article on naming your wee one. It offered some very unique choices but, get this—it also suggested that you can help ensure the success of your offspring's future career choice by the careful selection of his or her name. For example, the article's suggestions for future chefs included Baker, Basil, Coriander, and Tarragon. Interesting, and I thought Gwyneth Paltrow was just being a silly celebrity when she named that poor child Apple. Apparently, she was shooting for the Food Network from the get-go.

If I might digress a moment, I personally think this sounds a tad controlling. What's gonna happen if little Basil grows up and decides he doesn't want to be a chef? Maybe he wants to be, I don't know, a navy SEAL. His parents aren't gonna have a leg to stand on if he gets a wild hair to change his name to Snorkel or Subway.

But here's what I did think was cool. Right there on the list of potential monikers for future chefs was the name "Bubba." Bubba! It reminded me of another one of my blogging friends, from South Louisiana, who recently birthed a gorgeous baby boy. They named him Jean Yves, although they're affectionately calling him Cornbread. I need to ask Bayou Child if she's mapping out that baby's future. We in the Southern region are glad that y'all are beginning to appreciate the name "Bubba," but if you expectant parents are leaning toward it with Food Network stars in your eyes, I do hope you're looking to raise a Southern Chef. Bubba might need to specialize to make that thing work. You know, Shrump Gumbo, Shrump Creole, Shrump Étoufée . . .

But, back to our discussion on bubbaisms: The main reason we can laugh with Bubba is because we Southerners are so adept at using humor to take the sting out of what others mean as an affront. It's how we turn the tables on our tormentors. Granted, it doesn't always work out like we'd like, but that'll never stop my people and me from trying.

Like many of my fellow Southerners, I'm descended from a long line of fun-loving pranksters whose ranks are peppered by the occasional introvert, forced to endure the more gregarious relatives that have him or her outnumbered. I recall with great fondness the day my mother's no-nonsense mama decided to try her hand at turning the tables on all of the family jokers. We were down at Papaw and Grandmaw Stone's camp on the banks of the Old Mississippi. Grandmaw Stone was a quiet, shy woman, the type of Southern lady who covered her mouth with her hand when she laughed, a pleasingly plump preacher's wife more comfortable serving Papaw's congregation and her large extended family from the shadows than from the stage. Unfortunately for Grandmaw, the meek might inherit the earth— but first they come into the wrong end of a lot of family pranks.

This particular day Grandmaw was looking forward to cleaning up in Papaw's newly designed outdoor shower, a hose hanging from an overhead limb surrounded by a tarp. Even though the men were out fishing and it was just her girls and all us kids around, Grandmaw Stone wasn't about to shower au naturel! She took her shirt off and began "bathing" in her knee-length shorts and her unmentionable. Seconds later one of the aunts called out, "Mama, put your shirt on before you come out; the Meter Man is here."

But Grandmaw was on to 'em. She knew they were pranking. Instead of tripping over herself to find her shirt as they expected, Grandmaw ran out from behind the tarp in her sopping shorts and wet cross-your-heart whitey waving her hands in the air and hollering, "Here I am, here I am!"

To his credit, the Meter Man took the news with a straight face. "Thank you, Mrs. Stone," he responded politely, "but I think I can handle it."

Someone once said a well-brought-up Southerner always identifies people in their yard before they shoot 'em—I reckon it'd be a good practice before you flash 'em, too!

Tips for Those Wanting to Get Along with Southerners

THUS SAITH THE BELLE DOCTRINE . . .

* If thou doesn't start trouble, we will not give thee any.

* Thou shalt leave our music alone.

* If thou doesn't have anything nice to say, thou should stop speaking.

* We can laugh with Bubba but thou shalt not laugh at him.

* If thou are not in our yards, we cannot shoot thee.

Side Dishes and Vegetable Recipes
to Iron Out Our Differences

We'd all do well to look at our cultural differences the way we do side dishes: They add variety to our menus and help us round out our meals. And while I will be the first to admit that I'm a meat-and-potatoes girl at heart, even I recognize that a well-balanced diet includes helpings from all the basic food groups. What follows is a selection of our family favorites. Regardless of whether or not your mama is around to encourage you to eat your veggies (because the woman just never stops, no matter how old you get, now does she?), these scrumptious side dishes will entice you to get your recommended daily allowance. You won't need an excuse not to eat your vegetables when they're cooked Southern style.

Spinach Madeline

(SERVES 5–6)

It should be against the law for anyone to print this recipe, regardless of modifications, without giving a nod to the Baton Rouge Junior Leaguers who first made it famous. This spicy dish has retained a place of honor on the Southern table ever since those Cajun girls debuted it to widespread approval. Velveeta cheese and jalapeños can make anyone a spinach fan!

2 packages frozen chopped spinach

½ cup reserved spinach liquor

4 tablespoons butter

2 tablespoons flour

2 tablespoons chopped onion

3 teaspoons finely chopped fresh jalapeño peppers

1 teaspoon celery salt

1 teaspoon garlic powder

Salt and pepper to taste

1 teaspoon Worcestershire sauce

Dash of hot sauce

6 ounces Kraft Velveeta Mexican cheese, cubed

½ cup evaporated milk

1 teaspoon red pepper

Cook spinach according to package directions. Drain and reserve the spinach liquor (aka the juice).

Melt butter in a heavy saucepan and stir in flour. Once that's blended, add chopped onion and cook down. When onions are tender, add evaporated milk and ½ cup of spinach liquor, stirring constantly to prevent flour from lumping.

Cook until it's smooth and thick, stirring all the while so it doesn't scorch. Add chopped peppers and seasonings. Cube Velveeta cheese so it will melt easier, and add to base. Continue stirring until the cheese melts before adding cooked spinach. The finished product can be poured into a casserole dish and topped with bread crumbs, or served as a nice party dip with toast points. However you offer it, make it the night before and refrigerate it. The flavor will be even better.

Mama's Pinto Beans

(SERVES 4–6)

I think I'd been producing All Things Southern *on the radio and Web for at least five or six years when someone emailed me to ask why there weren't any pinto bean recipes in the archives. As I told that nice lady, I just figured everyone knew how to cook beans. When she assured me that this was not the case, I quickly corrected the omission. I include them here to be doubly sure we're covering the bases.*

> 1 pound dry pinto beans
> 1 teaspoon chili powder
> ½ teaspoon dried oregano
> ½ pound ham hocks (or one large hambone)
> 4 cups water
> 1 onion, chopped
> 1–2 cloves garlic, crushed
> Salt and pepper generously

Soak dry beans overnight in cold water before cooking. Generally, the bad beans will float to the top, and you can pick out the hard and deformed ones. The next morning, drain beans and put in a slow cooker with seasonings, chopped onions, and ham hocks. Cover and cook on high for at least 5–6 hours. Once they're tender, turn 'em down and simmer until time to serve. Warning: Mama taught me to never salt your beans while they're cooking. It'll dry them out. You can salt 'em right before serving if you'd like. (If you don't have a ham hock, try bacon and/or sliced smoked sausage. They're good, too!)

Spicy Black Beans and Rice

(SERVES 4–6)

The purists among us might not call this a true vegetable dish seeing as how it takes black beans and rice and marries 'em with cheese and sour cream. I say that is most unfortunate for the purists' families because this is good eating by anyone's standard. Can I get a witness?

1 cup uncooked rice
1 (10 oz.) can enchilada sauce
1 (14 oz.) can black beans
1½ cups shredded cheddar cheese
¼ cup diced jalapeño
Sour cream
Chopped green onions

Cook rice, cool, and spoon into a greased 9×13 casserole dish. Add enchilada sauce and black beans, cheese and jalapeños. Bake at 375 degrees for 20–25 minutes. Top servings with sour cream and chopped green onions.

Squash and Zucchini Medley

(SERVES 4–6)

Squash and zucchini are very popular vegetables in the Southern garden. By late summer everyone and their mama is trying to pass on the overflow from their overly ambitious gardening plans. Fortunately they can be served raw, stir-fried, grilled, broiled, steamed, boiled, baked, stuffed, tossed in soups, and, my personal favorite—fried! Here's a recipe, however, that bakes 'em to perfection with cheddar cheese and buttery Ritz crackers. By the way, my suggestion for all of us, should we find ourselves with an overabundance of anything, is to find a soup kitchen or a homeless shelter and pay our blessings forward.

3 cups finely sliced squash

2 cups finely sliced zucchini

1 cup each chopped onion and green pepper (I use that handy frozen mix)

2 eggs

¾ cup milk

1 cup sharp cheddar cheese

1 sleeve of buttery crackers (I use Ritz), crushed

½ cup melted butter

Preheat oven to 400 degrees. Place thin circles of sliced squash and zucchini in a skillet with chopped onion and green pepper. Cover with water and cook over medium heat until tender, or about five to seven minutes. Drain and spoon into a greased casserole dish. Combine eggs with milk and add to veggies. In a separate bowl, combine cheese with crushed crackers. Top with remaining cheese and cracker mix. Drizzle with melted butter and cook 25–30 minutes, or until heated through.

Very Veggie French Bread

(SERVES 4–6)

Need another idea for that mountain of zucchini? Cook it down with eggplant and fresh chopped tomatoes, season it well, and layer it on buttered French bread. You'll get a tasty side that pairs especially well with soups and salads.

2 cloves garlic, chopped

⅛ cup olive oil

1 medium eggplant, cubed

1 zucchini, cubed

1 tomato, peeled, seeded, and chopped

2 teaspoons oregano

2 teaspoons basil

Dash of salt

1 loaf French bread

5 teaspoons butter

4 teaspoons garlic powder

Preheat oven to 325 degrees. Sauté chopped garlic in a bit of olive oil. When it begins to brown, add eggplant and zucchini. Fry over medium heat 4–5 minutes, until tender. Add chopped tomato and continue cooking another 2–3 minutes. Season with oregano, basil, and a dash of salt and turn the heat off. Butter both sides of French bread and sprinkle well with garlic powder. Slide bread into the oven and warm for 5 minutes. Spread toasted bread with eggplant mixture and serve in nice large slices.

Shellie's Smashed Tater Balls

(SERVES 4–6)

Let me be clear up front. Food snobs may want to skip this side dish. My Smashed Tater Balls are made with the lowly potato chip. However, while there is absolutely nothing high-brow about these babies, those adventuresome souls who aren't too proud to try 'em will find that what they lack in class, they more than make up for in flavor.

1½ pounds red new potatoes

1 cup crushed sour-cream-and-onion chips (I've tried 'em with
    bar-be-cue chips, too. Fantastic!)

¼ cup grated Parmesan cheese

2 slices bacon, fried, drained, and crumbled (or one 2 ounce
    package of real bacon pieces)

¼ cup finely chopped onion

1 well-beaten egg

Cook and undress new potatoes. (Here's a secret. Don't waste time peeling 'em first. Boil until they're soft, and the skins will slip right off under cold running water.) While the potatoes are cooking, take a pie plate and combine crushed sour cream potato chips with Parmesan cheese. Smash potatoes and combine with bacon pieces and chopped onion. Form potato mixture into small 1-inch balls, dip in well-beaten egg and roll in chips-and-cheese mixture until well coated. Bake on cookie sheet for 8–10 minutes at 400 degrees. Serve as a side dish, or cook and freeze and pop in the oven to warm up for party appetizers.

Sensational Asparagus

(SERVES 2–4)

I took the idea for this asparagus dish from my Sensation Salad recipe. I figured we love Sensation Salad, so one day I tried a similar dressing for my asparagus and found that it was a great fit, too. We eat plenty of asparagus when it's in season because the price can be unreasonable the rest of the year, but the combination of Romano cheese, lemon, and garlic occasionally tempts us to serve those delicious green spears out of season. Challenge the anti-asparagus people in your family with this one and they just may be converts for life.

1 pound asparagus, cleaned, with the woody ends popped off
1 cup grated Romano cheese
¼ cup olive oil
3 teaspoons crushed garlic
1½ tablespoons concentrated lemon juice or the juice of one
    lemon
Pinch of salt and pepper

Preheat oven to 450 degrees. Wash and prepare asparagus by trimming woody ends. Place in a single layer on a baking sheet and sprinkle with Romano cheese. Prepare dressing by combining vegetable oil, crushed garlic, and lemon juice. Drizzle over asparagus. Season with salt and pepper and bake for 12–15 minutes. Serve warm.

South Carolina Fried Cabbage

(SERVES 2–4)

One of my South Carolina porchers sent this recipe in a while back. Mary freely admitted that it probably wasn't the healthiest way to cook cabbage, but it was certainly lip-smacking good. I concur. Mary and I will now illustrate how a Southerner can simultaneously cook a healthy vegetable and whip the health food industry into a frenzy! Come on, it'll be fun.

1 egg
½ cup milk
¾ cup cut-up raw cabbage
Salt and pepper to taste

Whip together egg and milk. Slice and chop cabbage a little larger and rougher than shredded slaw. Soak cabbage well in egg and milk, and drain. Drop by spoonfuls into hot vegetable oil. (Never fry anything in warm grease unless you want it to be soggy.) Fry until golden brown, remove, and season well with salt and pepper.

Company Green Beans

(SERVES 2–4)

These green beans may come out of a can, but they sure know how to dress up and show out for company. A few easy steps will reward you with big flavor. First, onions and peppers offer the dish a sweet base after sautéing in bacon drippings and borrowing a little brown sugar for a caramelized touch. Then, RO*TEL tomatoes and water chestnuts ramp up the volume. But it is undoubtedly the crumbled bacon that takes it over the top.

6 slices bacon

1 cup chopped onion

½ cup chopped bell pepper

2 tablespoons flour

2 tablespoons brown sugar

1 tablespoon Worcestershire sauce

⅛ teaspoon dry mustard

1 can RO*TEL tomatoes with green chilies

1 (16 oz.) can green beans, drained

1 can water chestnuts

Salt and pepper to taste

Preheat oven to 350 degrees. Fry bacon, remove, and drain on paper towels. Sauté onion and bell pepper in drippings. Once they're tender and clear, stir in flour and brown sugar and season with Worcestershire sauce and dry mustard. Add RO*TEL tomatoes, green beans, and water chestnuts, salt and pepper well, and stir until the mixture begins to thicken. Pour into a lightly greased baking dish and top with crumbled bacon. Bake for 20 minutes.

8

Parties, Presents, and a Missing Bubba Perched in a Deer Stand

~~~~

Holiday Survival Tips with Dessert
Recipes for Your Sweeties

Among the many self-appointed duties I've undertaken as The Belle of *All Things Southern* is my commitment to offer holiday assistance and/or color commentary on the calendar's celebratory days. For instance, I once assisted Cupid in rescuing a number of my male readers with a little heads-up about Valentine's Day.

In my efforts to make sure they had the information they needed to avoid a serious relationship setback, I gave them the following advice: "Listen up, guys. We're closing in on the single most romantic day of the year. Your wife's probably been droppin' hints for weeks. That's what all of the big RED X's meant that you saw on the appliance ads in Sunday's paper. It's why she dyed your pancakes with red food coloring, why she's been talking about that new restaurant opening downtown, and why she's been going on and on about that movie she's dying to see. In case your mind wandered, let me fill you in, your Sweet Thang's list of desirable destinations did not include Bubba's Burger Barn, the hunting camp, or the Monster Truck Rally."

Here's another tip I offered back then that I've since felt the need to repeat annually: Dear male people, "I haven't gotten you anything for Valentine's Day, so I hope you haven't gotten me anything" will be an unpopular announcement Valentine's Day morning. Trust me on this. So will "You're not expecting a big deal today, are you?" It's a little rule that transcends time. Call her an eternal optimist, but she's expecting a deal, Romeo, and the bigger the better.

And speaking of bigger and better, I'm reminded of the time I headed off some real trouble. I had read where plastic surgeons were reporting that in recent years men had been purchasing plastic surgery as Valentine Surprises for their sweeties! Well now, I wasted no time in telling my male readers that if they were even considering that move, they should proceed very delicately. If a woman hasn't asked for cosmetic surgery—suggesting it is going to be a romance buster, at best.

Of course, I also told the ladies that it was only fair to let their sweethearts know that they are forever competing with your ghosts of Valentine's Day past. It may not be fair, but it is what it is. Why, I still recall that perfect Valentine's Day when I was nine years old in Mrs. Powell's fourth grade class. That was the year I got not one but two large boxes of chocolates from Jimbo and Herbie. They go by James and Herb now, but if they ever come across this, they'll know who they are. Oh, and to top it off, they pushed each other at recess—over me! It was a great day! Note to my dear husband: No pressure, sweetie . . . Really.

One Valentine's Day, my hubby came home with nada, zilch, nothing. I was not happy. SO, off he went to the Winn Dixie (there aren't too many places to go after 6 p.m. around here in Franklin). When he finally came home, he had duck and sausage gumbo from a friend's freezer, as if that would make up for his behavior. NOT! That meant everyone in the world knew he hadn't done anything. The best thing to come out of the whole situation happened the following year when he took me to a very fine jewelry store. As it turned out, I couldn't make up my mind on which of two beautiful sets I wanted so I got them both!

~Andrea Seyfarth Caffery
Franklin, Louisiana

It's a Wonderful Life, Really!

So, are you ready for the big admission? Wait for it. Holidays aren't always Hallmark card perfect—even for us Southern girls. Not even Christmas. Gasp! It's true. Belles feel the pressure as much, if not more, than the general population. Of course we love the glitz and glamour, and we are obsessively fond of stringing lights as far as the eye can see, but the mounting drama taxes our already busy schedules, too, before culminating in the all too familiar game of musical houses, a game

The mishap occurred during the holidays as I was preparing a huge recipe of chicken tetrazzini to carry to Mom's for a big family gathering. I managed to drop our dog's medicine into the dish! I couldn't locate the small pill and there was no time to start over so I called our vet, who assured me—through his laughter—that it'd be okay. I chose not to tell my loved ones at the time but after the holidays I posted it on Facebook. Of course, it got back to the original partygoers, quickly. Apparently, some of 'em thought it was funny, others not so much.

~Lisa Kiper
Winnsboro, Louisiana

where we Southerners are bent on seeing every family member within traveling distance on Christmas Day.

When my sisters and I were raising small children, our parents did the holiday shuffle each year in a valiant effort to see all of their grandkids on Christmas morning. This provided them with a variety of holiday experiences. My oldest sister, Cyndie, and her family hosted loud Christmas mornings with everyone pinging off the walls. The squealing and hollering began before dawn and then the kids woke up!

Our house was fun, too, if slightly less crazy. Phil and I would get up early to set up the video cam and carefully record our sleepy wee ones entering the fairy tale land of gleaming presents and toys. And then there were the Parkers, my middle sister Rhonda's family. Theirs was a unique Christmas story. Rhonda's three kids were the most somber little partygoers you could ever expect to see. For starters, their parents always had to wake them up on Christmas morning. Rhonda has one picture of their daddy carrying the oldest two into the living room with confused looks on their faces that seem to say, "I still don't know why you woke me up this early. I mean, he's not coming back for this stuff, is he?"

But perhaps the best Parker story comes from the Christmas morning when their somber son Blake was a studious little seven-year-old. The night before, Rhonda and John had joy-fully arranged the unwrapped toys Santa had brought around the room and gone to bed. The next morning, they awoke to find a handmade card from Blake. They were surprised and touched to know that their little boy had stayed up late to make them a Christmas card and leave it beneath the tree.

The two of them opened it with tender hearts. It was an artistic tri-fold design. On the outside were the words "I just want to know one thing." On the inside, beneath the crude childlike drawing of a man and woman unwrapping Christmas presents were the words "Why do you two always open my presents from Santa before I get up?"

Santa Baby, Cry Me Some Tears

Anyone who has ever played the role of Santa is quick to tell you that it often brings that sort of mix to the table, equal parts praise and skepticism, making it, at times, a less than reward-ing experience. I once read a survey that said a third of store Santas report that they've been wet on by little kids. Ninety percent say they get their hair pulled every day. They all com-plain of getting sneezed on and suffering back pain from lifting small children. Wait, I'm not through. They also bemoan being exposed to contagious diseases and getting overheated in their Santa suits.

Oh, please, join me in the traditional Southern expression of sympathy, "Well, bless your heart, Mr. Claus. At least you're getting paid for the pleasure." Honestly, it's been a few years since I've stood in Santa's line with two small children, but I have leftover issues that make it hard for me to conjure up the proper sympathy.

Last Christmas I saw the most realistic Santa I have ever seen in our local mall. He was so authentic with his twinkling eyes and bowl full of jelly I could've cried, and wailed, and clothed myself in sackcloth and ashes and banged my head on the giant-size peppermint cane. Let me be clear. Beloved Hubby and I had the all-time worst run of luck at picking out store Santas. We had a bad habit of waiting so late we couldn't afford to be picky. Thus, we'd find ourselves at the nearest mall, settling for whatever Santa was on call. Our yearly photo cards were inspiring only in a "Good Heavens! Where do they find such dorky Santas?" type of way. We had the Weight Watcher Santa, the preppy Santa, and the "Give me a break. I'm putting myself through college" Santa.

Of course, now that I'm, let's just say "a little older," the part of the Santa survey I can most identify with is getting over-heated in my Santa suit. I'm with you on the hot flashes. One moment I'm freezing, the next second I'm ready to turn the air on and pull the knob off. But at least I know I'm not fit for that mall job. Think about it, Nick old pal. It could be time for a career move.

Santa brought me a full set of encyclopedias as a very small child. I read them cover to cover. The next year he brought me a globe. I remember thinking, what in the world? In the fifth grade he brought me a real Smith-Corona typewriter. None of these things were what I asked for but they were the great-est gifts ever given to me because seeds were planted. I have a feeling God had something to do with it and these gifts revealed God's pur-pose and gifts to me. I do believe the seeds we plant are what help us grow to be an authentic, purpose-ful citizen of this planet. Welcome to my harvest!

~Kathy L. Patrick
Jefferson, Texas
(Founder of the Pulpwood Queens and Timber Guys Book Clubs, the largest "meeting and discussing" book club in the WORLD!)

Should Santa Wash His Mouth Out

I'm not suggesting that anyone retire, it's not my decision to make, but I will say that apparently the Santa grass isn't any greener in other parts of the world. Paulette emailed me the most amusing article last Christmas season, or the saddest. I can't decide. Here's the latest from Down Under, mates, and I'm not even using my Southern storyteller's license. The world's gone so straight running crazy it's not necessary.

A number of Australian stores have put Santa Claus on notice about his rough language. St. Nick should no longer be allowed to say, "Ho, ho, ho!" because "ho" can be construed as a slang term that could offend women shoppers. Paulette said, "Well, if the shoe fits, wear it, honey," but as always, she misses the point.

I challenge you to find a single female, regardless of her chosen profession, who has ever heard Santa's famous greeting and thought he was calling her out! You have to look extra hard for this kind of stupid.

The PC cops think Santa should say "Ha, ha, ha" instead. I say, if it's confrontation we're trying to avoid, we're jumping out of the frying pan and into the fire. Bubba and the boys tend to feel a bit of pressure at Christmastime. If they happen to run into Santa after a long day traipsing around those overcrowded malls looking for just the right present for their Sugar Plums, only to hear the fat man say, "Ha, ha, ha!"—well, it won't be pretty.

I'm not advocating rough language. I was raised to understand there was no excuse for ugly words, not even ignorance. Once, when I was five or six, I told Papa I was ready to join the older kids and take my turn hoeing cotton for him. "I'm a good hoe-er," I said proudly. Papa couldn't shush me fast enough, and I thought Mama was going to faint dead away. They didn't explain. They simply told me not to repeat that proud announcement again, to anyone, ever. It was years before I figured that out.

Let's give Santa a break, friends. There should still be some things that when kids don't know, you don't have to tell 'em.

Sleigh Bells Ring, Are You Stressing?

Surely, no other holiday challenges us to handle the pressure the way Christmas does. Can I have a witness? The trick lies in learning to manage expectations and not letting the celebration handle you instead of the other way around.

We'll start with the obvious. Who do you get what, and where do you get it? Hard, I know. May I make a suggestion? Ask the people on your list for ideas. Ha, ha! Gotcha! Just a little holiday humor there. You do know that method seldom works, right? Most of your potential recipients will say, "Oh, you don't have to get me anything!" This should never be interpreted as "You don't have to get me anything," but rather "Happy Hunting, Sweet Cheeks, I'm too busy with my own list."

Or they might say, "Surprise me." FYI, it's not a good idea to combine the two answers and

One Christmas Day several years ago, my dad got the lovely idea to spare my mom cooking a huge dinner and decided to take us all out to eat. Well, bless him, whatever wasn't closed was backed up to Easter, so we finally had to settle for chicken from the Q Mart! You know, I don't think I've ever had a nicer dinner. He's gone now, but I still smile when I think about that.

~Amanda Pugh
Memphis, Tennessee

surprise 'em by crossing their name off your list. Not that I've ever done that. But recipients be warned, this reluctance to offer suggestions can backfire on you if you're not careful. Not giving the gift giver ideas can leave you vulnerable to what my sisters and I refer to as "the C word," or collectibles. Somewhere around the Fourth of July on, it becomes important in my family to monitor every word that comes out of your mouth. One casual comment like "I thought I saw Elvis at the Hit-n-Git" will get you Elvis souvenirs for the rest of your natural born days, unless you manage to set the holiday hunting club off on a different scent with a subtle line like "I hope no one gets me an Elvis gift this Christmas or next Christmas or any other Christmas, as long as we both shall live, so help me God." Wait—that sounds like a marriage vow, which is sort of a like a collection, if you think about it. You find one person you like, and bingo, you get a group of 'em. Note to my grown and married kids' extended families—I'm not saying this is a bad thing. I love y'all, really!

But I'm digressing into trouble, back to gift-giving. Here's a question for the ladies: Are you still looking for that perfect Christmas gift for your man? He has a watch. Ditto a phone. You know he hasn't used all of last year's cologne, and he doesn't need any more socks, ties, or calendars. Maybe you're thinking about calling it quits and wrapping up all that new camo he bought himself before the season opened. I get it. I know it's not easy Christmas shopping for our men, but ladies, I've just heard about this season's newest thing in male apparel, and I'm begging you, don't do it.

I'm talking about the new body-shaping undergarments for men, very tight undershirts with compression technology that promises to visibly streamline the male torso. They're calling 'em "Spanx for men." Yes . . . man girdles. Now put that Cabela's

I'm the queen of screwball holidays. Our furnace blew up on Christmas Day. When seventeen firemen in three trucks came to the rescue, I ran back in the house to pick my underwear off the floor. Last Easter, my husband and I decided that for our very first Easter together, we'd cook a beautiful and large meal for his family. I got roped into carrying the candle to the altar at church for Easter service. On my way back to the pew, I slipped and busted my [you know what] in front of the entire congregation, and it was televised! In the midst of our post service cooking the oven door fell off, and I had to use my freshly bruised behind to push up against it so the potato au gratin could finish baking!

~Emily DeLoach Gatlin
Tupelo, Mississippi

catalog down, ladies, and pay attention. You're not gonna find 'em in there. I know. The idea of watching your man struggle into a Spanx may seem like poetic justice, but if you'd quit laughing long enough and think about it, you'd agree that seeing your man in a girdle would be disconcerting, distressing, and downright awkward.

Note to Fashion World: Soon as the girls get control of themselves, they may purchase a few of your man girdles for gag gifts, but don't reorder on our account. We all know pigs will fly before your idea catches on with our guys. As the host of *All Things Southern*, I've been told that we Southerners exaggerate our differences—that folks the world over are mostly the same. I beg to differ.

For one thing, to wear a Spanx would require our men to realize they need a Spanx. Pardon my grammar, but it ain't happening. Thanks to our mamas, belles know about suffering for beauty. But our men, well, their idea of suffering for beauty is spending long cold hours in the woods waiting for that trophy buck while dreaming about their Sweet Thang keeping the home fires burning.

You know, that ad did say those man girdles offered temperature control. Nah . . .

Avoiding Bizarre Gift Syndrome

Every year, as the holidays near, I set out to use my work here at *All Things Southern* as a pressure release from the big buildup. A lofty goal, to be sure, and I may or may not succeed in diffusing the pressure for everyone, but this one thing I know: I don't add to it. Never have, never will. You have my word on it.

Case in point, I refuse to give my readers and listeners an update on how many shopping days we have left before Christmas. It's a personal thing. Regardless of how ready or ill-prepared I am, the big countdown always makes me flinch. There have been years when I've twitched more than others. One season stands out in my memory.

It was the week before Christmas, pre–car alarm days. I had two jobs, two teenagers, and one husband back home on the couch recovering from knee surgery, and I was wandering a huge parking lot at midnight with my arms full, sobbing uncontrollably because I couldn't find my car. I remain indebted to the sweet couple who helped me locate it, although I've always wondered why they took down my license plate number as I drove away. Okay, they didn't really do that, but if the shoes were reversed I might have.

The things is, while the last couple of years have found me farther ahead than usual, with no real clue as to how I've managed that, my prior experiences move me to offer any fellow shopping procrastinators a little advice. What you wanna avoid is falling prey to Bizarre Gift Syndrome, a condition causing one out of haste to bestow upon another a gift that's so strange, so unique, it becomes chiseled into the family archives. The other day I overheard a mother-daughter shopping team that can serve as Exhibit A.

Daughter: *"Do you know what you're getting Aunt Susan?"*
Mother: *"Not yet."*
Daughter, *"Okay, but remember, last year you gave her pancake mix."*

Unless Aunt Susan is a serious Aunt Jemima fan, that family has a documented case of BGS.

Last year I asked my readers to tell me about their strangest Christmas presents ever, and I'm still laughing. Leiah in Louisiana reported that her sweet though somewhat crazy grandma once gave her and her siblings six-packs of fruit juice, the six-ounce kind. Leiah remembers her sister getting grape, one of her brothers getting apple, and the other grapefruit. None of her siblings were thrilled with their juice selection, but I thought Leiah's was the hands-down funniest. I told her she should've held hers up, smacked their foreheads, and said, "Don't fuss, guys. You could've had a V8!"

But Leiah's wasn't the only entertaining story to come in about the strange gifts of Christmas past. FYI, teenage girls are not hoping and praying for John Deere snow globes, and at least one ex-wife could be an ex today largely because her man thought she would just love a BB gun. I

Me and Tommie Joe (good Mississippi boy) were engaged back '85 and had no money for presents. Well, I saw this dead raccoon on the side of the road. I watched him for a couple of days and then decided that I would get the hedge clippers and my best girlfriend, Teresa Haney, to go with me to get that coon's tail after the sun went down for his Christmas present. Nobody told us how hard it was to get a tail off of a dead coon, so we had to go back and get her daddy's miter box saw to finally finish the job! Fortunately, another friend of mine knew a taxidermist who helped me pull that bone out of it and tie a ribbon on. By the way, we are still married and Tommy liked it!

~Jennifer Watts-Martin
Nashville, Tennessee

also heard a lot about Christmas gift ruts, what I like to call mandated collections. This is the same thing/different version gift plan, a shopping strategy that works only when both parties are on the same page. One porcher told me his in-laws have given him hunting vests, sweater vests, plaid wood chopper vests, and dressy vests—which would be cool if he liked wearing vests. He doesn't. Here's hoping his tastes change, soon.

Speaking of tastes changing, Papa told us a great story last Thanksgiving. We were talking about tastes changing as they relate to food, and how, as you age, you can grow fond of a dish you never before enjoyed. Papa mentioned that sometimes you can benefit from a little outside help. He told us about the time he skipped his ten-year-old self into the house to see what they were having for supper. He found his mama cooking collard greens, just collard greens. (You may remember from *Suck Your Stomach In and Put Some Color On!* that Papa was one of ten kids and his mama also raised a couple that didn't belong to her. In other words, money was tight.)

Papa turned up his little nose that day and announced, "I hate collard greens. Collard greens are nasty. I ain't eating any stupid collard greens."

Papa said his mama took him outside for a few minutes, and when she brought him back in, he pulled himself up to the table and said, "Pass the collard greens, please." Actually, I think that's a great place to wrap up our discussion on Bizarre Gifts as it brings us all the way back to the value of managing expectations. Regardless of what we find under the tree this Christmas, we'd all do well to remember what our mamas said: "Never look a gift horse in the mouth."

Belle's Rules of Regifting

I understand the experts have agreed that this year's economy is going to be much like last year, if not worse, which means it's shaping up to be another huge year for regifting—you know, passing along a gift first given to you by someone else. This may surprise you, but honestly, I don't think regifting is necessarily synonymous with bad manners. The gift that keeps on giving can be quite thoughtful, if not downright entertaining, especially if all involved have a funny bone. Consider the porcher whose father-in-law once received a jogging suit from her brother and sister-in-law. The next year they found it in his closet, still in the box with the tissue paper and promptly gave it to him again! Poor man was clueless until the family filled him in. The suit has since continued to make a yearly appearance. Leslie says it's in its second decade and it's almost back in style, in a retro kind of way.

Still, because not all regifting stories turn out so well, and some of you are bound to get desperate as the big day closes in, I, Belle of *All Things Southern*, feel compelled to offer four easy guidelines to help make shopping at home as socially acceptable as it is financially rewarding.

Number 4: Pay attention to expiration dates. Items predating

One Valentine's day, years ago, my hubby brought me big, beautiful pink carnations. He's a great husband, but not one to give flowers, so I was giggly and happy about it. The next day, I had to go with him to our local car dealer to co-sign papers on a new truck, the same dealership he had visited the day before to test drive the truck. The salesman presented me with, what else, big, beautiful pink carnations as my "free gift" for purchasing a truck during February. BUSTED! We laugh about it now.

~Janet Hull
Savannah, Georgia

the current season will mark you as a tacky regifter. Say no to pet rocks and lava lamps.

Number 3: Monitor the monograms. Initials really should match unless you're confident you can keep a straight face while trying to sell the recipient on it being an acronym, as in, "I swanee, it stands for Peachy Good Friend! Really!"

Number 2: Don't regift in the same circles. Regifting his family gifts to yours may work, and vice versa, but remember, your mama, her mama, her sister, and her sister's sister know what who got whom ten years ago. It's their job and they're good at it.

And the number 1 and most obvious Rule of Regifting: Don't regift the gifter—which reminds me of another similar Christmas faux pas—reusing crumpled gift bags! My own son, who's apparently allergic to wrapping, has been known to open your gift to him and disappear, only to return with his gift to you in the same bag. You must be very charming to pull this off, and you may very well be. I'll leave you to make that call while we turn our attention to what happens after the big gift exchange.

Maxing and Relaxing with Man Be Looney

Personally, I've always loved the week after Christmas. The mad rush is over, but the New Year hasn't started. It's like a bonus week, you know—like someone hit a great big pause button.

For most of us the pressure is off and it feels good. With the hustle and bustle of the holidays behind us, people the world over are looking forward to relaxing. Rest assured we will not go about this the same way. Exhibit A: I just read about a Chinese man who likes to relax by eating live snakes and washing them down with beer! Man Be Looney, that's not his real name, started this unusual habit ten years ago on a bet, sort of like a double dog dare gone wrong, but he has now, and I quote, "become addicted to eating live snakes." As hard as it is to believe, I find myself in the unlikely and unique position of siding with PETA, who released their most carefully worded and articulate statement to date when they said, "Eating snakes ain't right."

The only thing stranger than eating live snakes is becoming addicted to the practice. I suppose the poor thing has gone through the clinical stages of abuse.

Minimization: "It's just one itty, bitty, snake. Everyone does it."

Rationalization: "It's been a hard day. I deserve to eat a live snake."

And denial: "I don't have a problem. I can quit eating snakes anytime I want."

The good news is that our Chinese friend is 'fessing up to his addiction. That's always the first step in getting help. The bad news is he's apparently passed on a predisposition to this unusual form of relaxation to his son. *Asia Today* writes that Man Be Looney Jr. has already eaten eight live snakes this year alone. Perhaps this was the last straw for Mrs. Looney, who is conspicuously absent in the story. Don't you just know she said something like "I'll be a monkey's uncle if I'm gonna stay around and pick up snakes skins after the two of you!"

I hope Man Be Looney and his son get the help they need. But if they can't beat this thing, I know of a nice dock in Louisiana where they could sit and relax like nobody's business.

No Rest for Jerry Don

To be clear, I said earlier that for *most* of us the pressure is off, because inevitably someone somewhere is always in hot water over their gift-giving, or lack thereof. In my circle, that would generally be Paulette's husband, Jerry Don. I imagine the men on the porch will come to his defense when I tell you that Jerry Don claims he can't win for losing. Paulette says he can't win because he won't try. I'll let you decide.

One year Paulette picked me up to ride to the mall with her and exchange a few gifts. Among them was a heavy plaid electric blanket. She said Jerry Don had presented it to her for Christmas as if it was the Hope Diamond. The girl was fit to be tied.

"When I think about how much time I spent trying to come up with the perfect present for him, and how many hints I left him about my Christmas gift, why, I want to take his arm off and beat him over the head with

Momma and I were clearing the dishes from a wonderful Christmas dinner and I was bemoaning that I'd received from my sweet husband yet another shotgun, fishing pole, and pair of racy panties tucked inside a game bag while she had received a lovely outfit complete with shoes and jewelry. I said, "Daddy always gets you the best gifts. How does that happen?" She said, "Well Darlin' about a week before any gift giving occasion I go shoppin' and buy myself a little something, get it gift wrapped, and give it to Daddy's secretary for him to give to me." I replied, "Oh, Momma where's the romance in that?" And she said, "Where's the romance in sittin' in a deer stand holdin' a shotgun in one hand, wearin' racy panties and drinkin' from a coffee cup that has a woman's breast in the bottom?" Then she winked at me and added, "Darlin' never send a man to do a woman's job."

~Suzanne McLennan
Author of *Praise the Lord and Pass the Biscuits*
Lakeside, Texas

it," she grumbled. "What in the world would lead a man to think his wife wanted an electric blanket for Christmas?"

For the life of me, I couldn't think of a thing. But that's okay. Fortunately, Paulette has been able to retain her wonderful sense of humor about Jerry Don's gift-giving. I know this because Paulette got a bit too quiet on the way to the mall. "Earth to Paulette," I said. "What are you thinking about now?"

"I was just thinking . . . Jerry Don's birthday is coming up. Maybe I'll get him a nice gun."

I was more than happy to change the subject. "That's good. Has he told you what kind of gun he wants?"

"Nah," Paulette said, "he doesn't know I'm gonna shoot him yet." I'm pretty sure she was joking.

Christmas Is Where the Heart Is

Despite the challenges of the Christmas Gift Exchange, it remains true that at Christmas, perhaps more than any other time of the year, our hearts yearn for home. And yet, as illustrated by our next story, sometimes we don't truly appreciate home until we've been away.

Years ago Vicki left her small Louisiana hometown, got a college education, and began working as a surgery nurse for a large hospital in the city. Before long she'd caught the eye of an eligible young doctor. Vicki was flattered. In the course of their early flirting, the doctor asked Vicki if she knew how to cook wild game. "Sure," Vicki replied. "I've got squirrel in the freezer right now." And that's how Vicki found herself cooking squirrel gumbo for the good doctor and a couple of his highfalutin friends. Vicki put on the glitz!

By the time her guests arrived, the table was set with white linens, the candles were lit, the wine was chilling, and the squirrel was simmering—the whole squirrel. Vicki's family prefers to skin their squirrels and freeze the bodies intact. They fall apart in the simmering, don't you know? Well, not every one does . . .

After a polite meet and greet, Vicki began serving the main course. First up was her potential suitor. Vicki ladled a generous helping into his bowl that included the head. The squirrel stared at the good doctor, but the man seemed uncomfortable making eye contact. Before Vicki could say, "Who wants Sweet Tea?" Medicine Man and his friends made a weak excuse and left without touching their meal. Vicki's budding romance was over before it'd begun. Years later, Vicki returned to Louisiana. One day she was telling a family friend about the courtship that wasn't. After shaking his head sadly, the old man offered this helpful commentary: "You know, some folks just don't like the heads." Vicki said that's the moment she knew for sure she was home! I can see that. You see, home is where the heart is precisely because it's where we find people who share our dreams and disappointments regardless of what others might consider a serious lapse in judgment. I hope you can be home this coming Christmas, if only in your hearts.

Holiday Survival Tips

THUS SAITH THE BELLE DOCTRINE . . .

* Thou shalt not give plastic surgery as a gift unless it has been requested.

* Thou shalt not determine thy relative's collectibles.

* Thou shalt adhere to the Rules of Regifting.

* Care should be taken to ensure thou preferred form of relaxation doesn't add extra work for thy loved ones.

* Retaining a sense of humor about the Christmas Gift Exchange can prevent the potential of post-holiday violence.

* Thou shalt not forget to take thy guests' tastes into consideration in the planning of thy holiday menu.

Dessert Recipes for All of
Your Sweeties

A belle knows that she simply must have a certain number of dessert ideas up her sleeve to get her through all of the holiday get-togethers. Occasionally we'll test a brand-new recipe, and sometimes we might try a twist on an old one, but more often than not the desserts we serve during the holiday meals are like the favored carols we sing at Christmas and the familiar stories we tell when we're all gathered around the table. They're tried-and-true family favorites that bring their own comforting memories. Here are some of the repeat performers from my house. I'd be delighted if you would send me some of yours.

Chocolaty Chip Pound Cake

(SERVES 10–12)

Rumor has it that pound cake got its name from the unfortunate fact that it packs on the pounds. There may be some truth to this, but it's never been substantiated. I've heard another theory that seems far more likely. Years ago, recipes were larger than they are now and they often called for a pound of most of the ingredients, like a pound of sugar, a pound of butter, etc. We don't do that anymore, but we still turn out some seriously good pound cakes, like my Chocolaty Chip Pound Cake. It may start with a box but it ends with a bang!

1 yellow cake mix

½ cup sugar

1 (3.9 oz.) package of instant chocolate pudding mix

4 eggs, beaten

¾ cup water

¾ cup vegetable oil

1 cup sour cream

1 cup semisweet chocolate chips

Preheat oven to 325 degrees. Prepare yellow cake mix according to package directions, adding sugar and instant chocolate pudding mix. Whisk together four eggs and stir into the prepared mix. Add liquids and sour cream. Fold in chocolate chips and pour batter into a greased and floured bundt pan. Bake 45–55 minutes, or until you can stick a toothpick in the center and it comes back clean, and enjoy with a scoop of vanilla ice cream or cool whip.

Louisiana Sheet Cake

I think the name may have once started out as Sheath Cake, but somewhere along the way our lazy drawls morphed it's moniker into the Sheet Cake we know and love. Just about every self-respecting Southern cook I know has a Sheet Cake in her repertoire, too. Most of them are what we call six of one and half a dozen of the other. In other words, they have only the slightest of variations. Here's my version:

   2 cups self-rising flour
   2 cups sugar
   1 stick butter
   ½ cup shortening
   4 tablespoons cocoa
   1 cup water
   2 eggs, slightly beaten
   ½ cup buttermilk
   1 teaspoon vanilla

Preheat oven to 350 degrees. Sift together flour and sugar. In a separate mixing bowl, combine butter with shortening, and then cocoa. (We call it "cutting" the butter into the shortening and we often use a fork for the job!) Add water. Stir over medium heat until melted. Add to dry ingredients along with slightly beaten eggs, buttermilk, and vanilla. Mix well and pour into a greased sheet pan. Bake for 15–20 minutes, or until the middle springs back when you touch it.

To prepare icing, add ¼ cup melted butter to ¼ cup cocoa and combine with 1 can sweetened condensed milk. Stir in a pound of confectioners' sugar and 1 cup chopped pecans and spread over the cake while it's still warm.

Darlene's Vanilla Wafer Cake

Here's a golden oldie that's been around awhile. It comes to us through my daughter-in-law, who got it from her mother, who got it from her grandmother-in-law, who got it from . . . I imagine you're getting the picture. Like most golden oldies, this cake lends itself really well to pantry cooking, meaning you can keep the ingredients on hand and whip it up in a hurry. If there isn't a version of this one in your family repertoire, there needs to be!

2 sticks oleo (room temp)

2 cups white sugar

6 eggs

½ cup milk

1 (1 lb.) package vanilla wafers, crushed

1 (14 oz.) package flake coconut

1–2 cups chopped pecans

2 teaspoons vanilla

Preheat oven to 350 degrees. Cream softened oleo together with sugar. Add eggs and milk. Stir in crushed wafers, coconut, and chopped pecans. Add vanilla. Pour into a greased and floured 9×13 cake pan and bake for 45 minutes.

Cuzin Ron's Apple Dumplings

(SERVES 8)

The taste of sliced apples and sugary cinnamon syrup will remind you of your grandmother's apple dumplings. The use of crescent rolls and Mountain Dew just means you'll be in and out of the kitchen faster than your dear old granny could've lit the stove!

- 1 stick butter
- 1 cup sugar
- 1 teaspoon cinnamon
- 2 Granny Smith apples, peeled and cored
- 1 can (8 count) crescent rolls
- 1 (12 oz.) can Mountain Dew

Preheat over to 350 degrees. Melt butter. Add sugar and cinnamon. Divide apple slices evenly among crescent rolls and roll each one up individually. Place in greased casserole dish and pour cinnamon butter over the top. Finish by pouring Mountain Dew on and around the apple dumplings. Bake for 45 minutes and enjoy.

Creamy No-Bake Pumpkin Pie

(SERVES 8)

Should you find that you have a few other things to do around the holidays besides spending long hours coring those pumpkins for fresh pumpkin pie, you're going to really appreciate this one. My Creamy No-Bake Pumpkin Pie asks only that you mix, pour, and chill. How easy is that?

1½ cups regular milk

1 (1 oz.) package instant vanilla pudding mix

1 (15 oz.) can pumpkin

1 teaspoon pumpkin pie spice

1 large carton of Cool Whip

1 (9 inch) pie crust, already baked

Combine milk, pudding mix, and canned pumpkin. Add pumpkin pie spice and 1 cup of cool whip. Beat at a low speed for 1 minute. Pour into prebaked pie crust and top with the remaining Cool Whip. Chill at least 3 hours even if you have to hide it in the back of the fridge. It'll be worth the wait.

Aunt Peggy's Fresh Peach Pie

(SERVES 8)

Aunt Peggy has graciously offered us her Fresh Peach Pie recipe, complete with her suggestions for cutting the calories. I, however, like to make it straight up. It's seriously good eating.

3 large peaches, sliced
Fruit protector, just a sprinkle (I use Bernardin Fruit Fresh)

Custard:

1 cup sugar (or substitute Splenda for baking)
¼ cup cornstarch
2 eggs (or egg substitute)
2 cups milk (fat-free evaporated milk works great)
½ stick oleo
1 teaspoon vanilla
1 (9 or 10 inch) pie shell, prebaked
Fruit Fresh

Sprinkle peach slices with Fruit Fresh and set 'em aside so they stay nice and pretty. To prepare custard, mix sugar and cornstarch. Add beaten eggs and milk. Cook over a medium heat until custard begins to thicken. You can also microwave custard for 8–10 minutes and it'll firm up nicely. Once your pudding thickens, add oleo and vanilla. Pour into prebaked pie shell and arrange sliced peaches on top. They'll sink down into your custard. Finish with whipped topping! Don't hurt yourself, folks—it's that good!

Nutty Caramel Pie

(SERVES 8)

Rich, delicious, nutty, and did I mention rich? The key words here are serving size. Top a small slice of my Nutty Caramel Pie with a dollop of ice cream and you'll be serving some super sweet confection.

- ¼ cup melted butter
- ¾ cup sugar
- 2 eggs, beaten
- 28 caramel candies
- ½ cup water
- ½ teaspoon vanilla
- ½ teaspoon salt
- 1 cup nuts

Preheat oven to 350 degrees. Blend melted butter with sugar and eggs. Melt caramel candies in microwave. (It'll take 30 seconds to a minute, but try 20-second intervals, stirring until they are all melted. You don't want it stiff!) Add melted caramels and water to the first three ingredients. Stir in vanilla, salt, and pecans. Pour into a 9-inch unbaked pie shell and bake for 40–45 minutes. Let it cool before slicing.

Pineapple Chess Bars

(SERVES 16–18)

If you're not familiar with the term "chess bars," just think ooey gooey slices of cake cut into brownie-like servings. Chess bars come in all sorts of flavors. This recipe combines the classic flavor mixture of coconut and pineapple for a wonderfully sweet treat.

3½ cups all-purpose flour, divided

1 cup sweetened flaked coconut

1 cup firmly packed brown sugar

1 teaspoon baking soda

1 cup butter, divided

1 cup sugar

3 large eggs

1 (20 oz.) can crushed pineapple, drained

Garnish: toasted flaked coconut

Preheat oven to 350 degrees. Combine 2½ cups flour with the next three ingredients. Cut in ½ cup butter until the mixture has a crumbly texture. Reserve 1 cup for topping and press the remainder into the bottom of a greased 9×13 baking dish. Bake for 10 minutes. Beat the second half of the butter with sugar until creamy. Add eggs one at a time, gradually beating in the last cup of flour. Stir in drained pineapple. Spread over baked layer and sprinkle with the last of your crumb mixture. Bake another 25–30 minutes, or until a wooden pick inserted in the center comes out clean. Let cool and cut into squares. If desired, garnish with toasted, flaked coconut.

Amy Wiggins' Lemon Streusel Bars

(SERVES 16–18)

If you like lemon icebox pie, you'll love this twist on a favorite old flavor from one of my dearest readers. Amy's Lemon Streusel Bars definitely make a beautiful holiday presentation for a party, but they're every bit as delicious as they are attractive.

Filling:

  1 (14 oz.) can sweetened condensed milk
  2 teaspoons lemon zest
  ½ cup lemon juice

Crust and Streusel:

  ¾ cup softened butter
  1¼ cups packed brown sugar
  2 cups all-purpose flour
  1½ cups rolled oats

Preheat oven to 350 degrees. Combine sweetened condensed milk with lemon zest and lemon juice. Set filling aside. In a larger bowl, combine softened butter with brown sugar until well blended. Add all-purpose flour and rolled oats. Stir until your mixture resembles coarse crumbs. Reserve 2 cups for streusel and press the remaining crumbs into a 9×13 baking pan. Pour the prepared lemon filling over the crust and crumble the remaining streusel on top, patting gently into the filling. Bake 30–35 minutes and cool completely before cutting into squares.

Blueberry Popovers

(SERVES 8)

Popovers are a delightful breakfast treat anytime, but they're especially nice on holiday mornings when the house is brimming with kids, grandkids, or both! Of course, that's also when time's the shortest. No problem. My Blueberry Popovers start with ready-made crescent rolls and cream cheese to help you skip a couple steps so you can offer up that sweet blueberry goodness in record time.

1 can crescent rolls
1 (8 oz.) package cream cheese
½ cup sugar
1 cup blueberries

Preheat oven to 350 degrees. Divide crescent rolls into four rectangles. Combine softened cream cheese with sugar. Spread onto dough and divide blueberries evenly among all four rolls. Take opposite sides of each rectangle and fold it into the middle. (You'll still be able to see the blueberries and the cream cheese mixture, but don't worry, it won't run far!) Bake for 10–11 minutes, or until the crescent rolls are golden brown. Delicious!

9

If All Else Fails, Laugh

~⌒~

Miscellaneous Thoughts from the Belle
of *All Things Southern* with This and That
Recipes to Add to Your Bag of Tricks

For a born and bred storyteller, a lagniappe chapter would have to be on the short list of my most favorite things. Why, having permission to toss in a little something extra as the mood strikes me feels like the ultimate setup. Whatever shall we talk about first?

Chances are you've already figured out that yours truly is an incurable ham with a penchant for wrapping up one story only so I can dive into the next. What may surprise you, however, is to know that as much as I love telling stories, I enjoy hearing them every bit as much, if not more. It's true! One of the things I enjoy the most about traveling and speaking, besides traveling and speaking, is meeting up with y'all at the book table afterward. I love it when y'all tell me your stories after you've heard mine. Please don't tell my publisher, but yours are just as good, and often better. I come home with a load of great stories from every road trip.

When I was eight years old, my family lived in "the projects" in Shreveport, La. Mama and Daddy both worked on Sunday mornings. One day a neighbor in the apartments invited me to go with her to Sunday school at Parkview Baptist Church. She didn't have a car, so we walked. Through that simple invitation, I became a committed churchgoer. At Parkview, I learned many things that guide me still. I haven't seen nor heard from that woman in more than forty years. She has no idea she helped shape me as an author and public speaker—all because she invited a poor little girl to Sunday school. Do whatever you can, whenever you can. You don't have to be rich or famous to have power and influence.

~Judy Christie
Author of the *Gone to Green* series
Shreveport, Louisiana

Of course, sometimes the funny is situational and happens in and around the actual event, like the time my friend Evie and I got lost looking for Crockett Point Baptist Church in Crowville, Louisiana. I hesitate to point fingers, but our trouble may have begun when Evie disregarded the Google directions I'd printed out. Evie decided to go with more of a touchy-feely navigational style, as in "I *feel* like we should turn here." The last left turn Evie "felt" landed us in the boonies. Thankfully, we were able to follow a man home to ask directions, although I still feel bad about scaring him half to death as he chatted on his cell phone in his own carport. Honestly, I thought he knew I was at his car window before I spoke up, but I guess not. The poor thing jumped like he'd heard from heaven. I'm sure the biggest surprise of that religious experience was his next thought: "And He's a she!"

Fortunately we made it to the event on time and with a few minutes to spare. Oh, and I would like the record to show that I didn't intend to out Evie's directional challenges in my opening remarks, but the audience was in such a good humor that I left my preplanned notes even earlier than usual. It is a rare event when I'm able to stay on task and actually tell the stories

I planned to tell from the get-go without letting the competing voices in my head have their say!

Recently, after speaking to a delightful group of teachers in my home state of Louisiana, I found myself telling a lady at my book table how much I'd enjoyed the day and apologizing for my rambling speaking style. "Y'all were a great audience," I said, "which I'm afraid just egged me on. I may have been more scattered than usual, jumping from one story to another the way I did, but I'd have to say, y'all stayed right with me."

"Oh, we're used to it," the nice lady said with a most sincere expression. "We teach Special Ed." As soon as I started laughing, she realized what she had implied. "No offense," she said, red-faced. "None taken," I told her. And there wasn't. I simply took her comment to mean that their experience with those of us who have a harder time concentrating had come in handy. This isn't a prerequisite for my audiences, mind you, but apparently it helps.

You Can Get By with a Little Help from Your Friends

I've even created a special speaking folder stacked with stories I've harvested on the road, like the time I had the great pleasure of sharing a lunch table with a bevy of beauties who were in their eighth and ninth decades. All five of them were still living alone and they all had fantastic attitudes about aging. I'm telling you I did me some listening and learning that day. I especially enjoyed the example of teamwork that two of my lunch mates displayed. Mrs. Ruby introduced herself and her friend, Mrs. Mariana, with a matter-of-fact analysis of their close

> When we asked our parents if we had to go to church, they would say, "No, you don't have to go. You get to." I truly understand that saying now.
>
> ~Allison Horath-Lee
> Ruston, Louisiana

relationship. "We go everywhere together," she told me, "because I can hear but I can't see, and Mariana here, she can see but she can't hear. We make a good team."

Mrs. Ruby went on to illustrate her point by telling me what had happened the previous Sunday. The two dear friends were sitting together in the congregation in their customary pew. Song service was in mid swing. Someone was singing a special, and it was one of Mrs. Ruby's favorites. Unfortunately, she couldn't see who it was singing. Mrs. Ruby squinted as hard as she could but to no avail. She simply couldn't make out who was at the podium. That's when she leaned over to her sighted, albeit hearing impaired, friend. "Mariana," she said, in a loud whisper, "Who's that singing?"

Mrs. Mariana promptly whispered back, "That's the Phillips' boy, Ruby." And then, in the same breath, Mrs. Mariana asked, "What's he singing?"

Now, I thought the story was simply charming as Mrs. Ruby told it, but as it turns out it got even better. Later, a lady who had overheard our lunch conversation informed me that the most precious part of the story was that while Mrs. Ruby and Mrs. Mariana both thought they were whispering, neither of them actually were! You could easily hear them all over the church. And that's why everyone there got to enjoy their Q and A session, even the Phillips' boy who, for the record, is actually the Phillips' girl!

War Stories from the Front Line

Another time I spoke to a group of retired educators. I found them every bit as charming and gracious as the practicing teaching groups I had spoken to previously, but I'll let you in on a little secret. They all tell tales on their students. Think war stories. Granted, they don't name names, and the stories do hearken back a few years, but just in case you ever wondered if your dignified teacher was laughing at you behind your back, trust me on this, the chances are good.

One adorable belle, who seemed to have more stories than time to tell 'em, told about the day she instructed one of her young students, who had missed an important test, to make arrangements to stay after school the following afternoon. "You're going to have to make up a test for me," Mrs. Rozel explained. It occurred to her that perhaps she should've elaborated on that pronouncement when the eager young lady showed up the next day and presented her with a folded piece of paper. Mrs. Rozel opened it to find—you guessed it—the girl's very own made-up test.

I suppose there are a lot of things that need more explanation than you'd expect. Another teacher, Mrs. Delores, was grading a stack of essays once when she came to one with an amusing title. Printed at the top were the words "My S.A." (Yes, you do. Think about it.)

All of their stories were enjoyable, but I remain particularly fond of the one about the grammatically challenged little boy who turned in his test paper with this proud announcement, "Teacher, I ain't made but one mistake, but when I seen I done it, I taken it back!"

Hold the Applause

Perhaps you're beginning to see why I'm so fond of my audiences. On top of entertaining me as much as I could ever hope to entertain them, they also keep me supplied with a fresh source of material. And what with my weekly column deadlines at *All Things Southern*, I am always in need of material. Rare indeed are the times that I'm not appreciative over having an audience, but it does happen. I can think of at least one time in the recent past that I was hoping the curtains were closed . . .

I've often thought I should've been born in the 1800s with Scarlett. But after my recent stay in a beautiful historic hotel, I'm not so sure. Walking into the Victorian foyer felt like stepping into the past. My best friend and I found our second-floor room equally charming, too: yesteryear's appeal with cable TV and central air. All was well, until I matched wits with that authentic claw-footed tub.

My first mistake was getting in the tub before drawing the bathwater. No sooner had I turned it on than it went from lukewarm to cold. Uh-oh! I absolutely had to shampoo my crowning glory. My heart sank right alongside my body temperature when I realized the precious antique spigot stuck out maybe an inch from the tub wall—and pointed straight down. Somehow I was gonna have to get my head under it.

What followed was straight out of *I Love Lucy*, only thankfully, there were no cameras running as I contorted my long frame in every imaginable way, trying to let the cold water trickle over my head. And then it happened.

With my chill bumps sprouting chill bumps and my rarely used abs quivering from the unfamiliar strain—I got the giggles! There was no accounting for it, but there they were, followed by the horrible realization that I hadn't locked the bathroom door. Should my friend misinterpret the sounds coming from the bathroom and feel compelled to check on me, the sight would surely scar her for life. This was a vision I wouldn't wish on my husband, let alone an innocent buddy, but the harder I tried to stop the funnier it became.

Fortunately I made it out of the bath without an audience. With one towel around my soaking head and one around my porcupine body, I dove back under the covers to get my body temp up, only to have my previously beloved BFF chirp merrily that her water had been dangerously hot! Were it not for Mama's pass and repass rule, I think I would've challenged the girl to a predawn duel, weapon of her choice.

Toeing the Line Between Humor and Horse Heads

Actually, I've never polled my mama as to her thoughts on this ancestral style of handling one's differences. It occurs to me that if the matter was serious enough, she might sign off on the idea of a predawn duel, or at least look the other way, but this would only be if it was truly held predawn. Mama would never sanction a public catfight. Girls from good families don't air their dirty laundry in public, don't you know? My sisters and I haven't always abided by this official decree as closely as she would like, but we all know Mama puts a premium on privacy. My parents have both been huge supporters of my work at *All Things Southern*, but there is a limit to the family stories I can tell, and a line I best not cross, lest I find myself in the sort of trouble that befell that female comedian from New York City I once saw in the evening news.

The poor thing was being sued by her mother-in-law for using family material in her routines. Ruh, row! This story was all over the twenty-four-hour news cycle, and then it fell plum off the radar, just as quickly. Who knows? By now they may be one big happy family, they may have settled out of court, or someone may have a horse head in her bed, but I haven't been able to shake it that easily. The future of *All Things Southern* could hinge on this case, and seriously, if you take away my family, who will we laugh at—I mean, what will we discuss?

I'm trying not to be nervous. Like I said, my family does seem to be taking this whole thing with a grain of salt, if you don't count that little threat Mama's been making about doing a rebuttal after my speaking engagements, you know, like the out-of-power party does after the state of the union address? But she's just joking. I think. Still, I wish I had more information on the case and how it turned out. The comic didn't share any of her jokes when she was making the rounds on all the morning shows, so we don't know if she went too far or if her husband's mama just needs a better sense of humor. My own mother-in-law, God rest her soul, had a finely tuned funny bone.

Why, once, I came home to find Mamaw Lucy screaming on my answering machine from her room at the nursing home. I had to come quick, immediately, it was life and death; she needed me now! Lord a mercy, I broke speed limits left and right driving across town and turned into the nursing home parking lot on two wheels! I flew down the hall to her room, burst open the door, and found Mamaw dressed to the nines and knitting quietly. "Really, Shellie," she said, oh so pleasantly. "You need to slow down. Rushing around like you do isn't good for you."

We were never quite sure when Mamaw was pulling one and when Alzheimer's was rearing its ugly head, but one day, I'm gonna write a book just on using humor to deal with that hateful, hateful disease, but rest assured, I'll make sure I have her children's blessing. Laughter's good medicine, but even I know that family should always come first!

It Takes Two to Tangle

The other side of that coin is that sometimes we can all be guilty of taking ourselves too seriously, thereby taking offense where none is intended. In the face of our litigious society, I'd like to suggest that everyone take a healthy dose of self-deprecating humor. While learning to laugh at oneself in harmless situations won't hurt a bit, the skill also comes with an added benefit: It can effectively disarm a more purposeful offense, too. As The Belle of *All Things Southern*, I've had my share of opportunities to learn this lesson.

I'm thinking of the email I once got from someone who wasn't from around here, asking me if we Southerners still ate dirt! After printing her letter on the website with a funny rejoinder, I got an earful from my more loyal readers for not taking her to task. A sample from my inbox read like this note from Luke in the Big Easy:

> *Dear Shellie, I thoroughly enjoy* All Things Southern, *but I've got to ask you something. Surely you don't think Ms. Priss from Boston, the lady who asked the dirt-eating question, was really just curious like she claimed? We all know she was being ugly and rude! Are you really that naive? If you're going to do this, you should stand up for us Southerners more.*

I took the opportunity to remind Luke that I wasn't naive at all; I was just making a conscious choice to take the woman at her word. If she was sincere, I won. And if she wasn't, well, I still won, because I didn't stoop to her level. See how that works? My mama taught me that kind of life skill.

Another time I found an article online where someone had used the spelling d-a-w-g to refer to a Southerner's pronunciation of the three-letter word for canine. It wasn't the first time I'd seen it, of course, and at first glance I was tempted to be offended. "I don't talk like that," I thought to myself, "and no one I know talks like that either." And yet when I took a moment to try and pronounce d-o-g with a short o sound instead of an aw, I had to laugh out loud. Okay, maybe I do say it that way, but if I may use the childish but effective argument that once served me so well when debating my older sisters, "So?!" (Here's a test. If you can say dog and it rhymes with cog, chances are you weren't raised south of the Mason-Dixon.)

The truth is the four-legged friends I have now are dawgs, and the ones I had growing up were dawgs, which being as how we are in the lagniappe chapter, just happens to offer me a perfectly legitimate segue into another story I wanted to tell y'all.

The day I have in mind we kids were working with Papa in the field next to our house. One of our city cousins, known to family as Little Stan, was spending a week of his summer vacation at our house. To my sisters' and my eternal consternation, these kids always thought joining us in the fields was great fun instead of the hard work we knew it to be. Go figure.

Papa was fueling up a piece of equipment late that afternoon when one of our old dogs began lapping up some of the gasoline that had accidentally spilled on the ground. Papa hollered and shooed him out of the dangerous chemical. Well now, that dog took off running like he'd been shot out of a canon! Then, just like that, he stopped on a dime and lay down right there in the field. Little Stan was quick to point this out.

"Look, Uncle Ed!" Stan hollered. "He's just laying there. Whatcha reckon is wrong with him?"

To which Papa replied, "Well, isn't it obvious, son? The poor thing has run slap out of gas."

The moral of that story (should you need one) is that the obvious answer is not always the best one.

Fishing for a Laugh

If you read *Suck Your Stomach In and Put Some Color On!*, you may remember my uncle Stan as the fellow who, in the early years of his marriage, during the more volatile period, was run over twice by his wife, my aunt Marleta. If you can learn to laugh at something like that, folks, you've got something, and they have.

Some forty or more years later, their early battles are all behind 'em and they're more mellow yellow sweethearts than hair-pulling combatants, but they continue to entertain us all with memories from those years, even though Uncle Stan's health isn't so good anymore and Aunt Marleta continues to battle the aftereffects of her countless battles with cancer. Uncle Stan's health issues stem mostly from the time he served in the first Gulf War. Uncle Stan was working for the International Paper Company in Natchez, Mississippi, when his guard unit was called up and he was sent to the Gulf. He was fifty-eight at the time. After the war, Uncle Stan worked a few more years and retired from the Paper Company, but he refused to rest on his laurels. I'm proud to report that he graduated from college several years ago, at sixty-eight years young.

He got his degree in recreational management, with the idea being that he and Aunt Marleta would travel the country, and when and if he chose, he'd take a job at one of the state parks. His thinking was that this would allow him to fish the best lakes and rivers out there. Of course, that was before his health had deteriorated to the point it has now, tying him to his ever present oxygen tank.

Uncle Stan has always loved to fish. Aunt Marleta—not so much; she says Uncle Stan sucked the fun out of it for her years ago. Back then Aunt Marleta was always asking Uncle Stan to take her fishing with him, and he was always finding reasons not to oblige—Uncle Stan was serious about his fishing, and he knew she'd just be hot and miserable. "Leta," he'd say, using his pet name for her, "you know you don't like to sit still, and the fish won't bite if the boat's rocking and reeling."

One day, Uncle Stan finally agreed to take Aunt Marleta fishing. After he gave her a big lecture about being quiet and still, they took off. Sure enough, Aunt Marleta got enough of fishing a long time before her man did. Several times she tried to say something, but each time Uncle Stan would put his hand up. About three hours into their hot little expedition, her legs cramping from being in one place, Aunt Marleta finally shifted her position ever so slightly. Uncle Stan glared at her and huffed. "For heaven's sakes, Leta, I knew it was gonna be like this. Did you come out here to fish—or to dance?" Aunt Marleta's answer said it all:

"I came to fish, Stanley, but I'm willing to fight."

Sometimes it's hard to imagine how those two made it half a century without killing each other, but we're all thankful they worked out their differences. They would be quick to tell you that even in the worst of times, humor helped them cope. It's a life skill that continues to bring dividends for us all. I saw them not too long after their forty-ninth wedding anniversary. Aunt Marleta told me that when they went to bed that night, Uncle

Stan had felt around and groped around for two or three minutes. She said that just about the time he was beginning to get her full attention, he abruptly stopped reaching.

"Why'd you stop?" Aunt Marleta asked him.

"Because," Uncle Stan said, "I found the remote."

We all laughed in the telling of that one, and if I might be so bold, dear reader, I'm guessing you might have a smile playing around your lips, too. Go with it.

Thar's Stories in Them Thar Hills

People always ask me how long I'll be able to tell my Southern stories without running out of material. To which my answer is always that unless my big crazy circle of family and friends all up and die at the same time, I'm good to go. On the rare times when they aren't gifting me with some funny or interesting story, I can usually count on finding material in the news that I can tie into, using a more personal angle.

For instance, not long ago I stumbled upon a most unusual sport that showed potential both as radio material and as a possible source for extra family income. The piece that caught my eye was on a brand-new sport called—wait for it—Extreme Ironing. Yep! You heard it here, folks.

These wrinkle-hating competitors hold obsessive-compulsive contests in remote locations all over the world. They say the sport combines the thrill of extreme outdoor activity with the satisfaction of a well-pressed shirt. No, I did not propose that my family join 'em. They sounded a little shy of center. I did, however, use the concept as a jumping off place for a lively column.

My premise was that we should look into starting our own

sport and consider pitching it to the Home Improvement Channel. It would be called Extreme Vacuuming, and Mama would, of course, be the contestant to beat. That last little surgery she had a while back has slowed her down some, but I felt good about our chances of getting her in tip-top shape. She's a natural. For heaven's sakes, this is the same woman who once vacuumed her attic. Vacuumed her attic! I figured she'd start racking up the wins and Electrolux would cough up big bucks to be her sponsor and we'd be on our way. With a little luck it'd just be a matter of time before you saw my funky bunch on all the major networks—with our stomachs sucked in and our color on, naturally!

That's the sort of stuff that will just fall into a storyteller's lap, if you're looking for it, but you do have to be ready. It helps if those around you get in on the act, and my family and friends are in it to win it. It's gotten to where they'll see something on the news or read something in the paper and immediately call me, text me, or email me about it with this standard note: *This could be a porch chat.* Of course, they do get a little

---

Shortly after returning from our honeymoon, I got food poisoning and began throwing up violently. My husband raced to meet me in the bathroom and attempted to help. Unfortunately, he pulled the toilet seat up just as I leaned down to vomit, hitting me in the mouth with the toilet seat, busting my lip and bruising my mouth! When I couldn't stop throwing up, he took me to the E.R., where the nurses took in my bruised mouth and busted lip and asked him to step out of the room. They proceeded to try and get me to tell them how I "really" got those injuries. They even called in a social worker to encourage me to tell all. Though I continued vomiting through the ordeal, I was still able to overhear their conversation as they left the room. "She says he hit her in the mouth with the toilet seat," one said. "Yeah, right," the others agreed. We still laugh about it today.

~Mary Yetta Alexander
Marshall, Texas

overeager at times, but that comes with the territory—and it reminds me of another story.

Granny Panties and Lessons Learned at the Hospital

A short while ago I had an unforeseen medical emergency that grew into an extended hospital stay. (Translation: A kidney stone tried to kill me.) Throughout my ordeal I heard an oft-repeated refrain from my loved ones that went something like this: "Well, at least she's getting new material." I have two things to say about that: (a) There's more truth there than you may realize; writing and pain are often one and the same; and (b) it is somewhat difficult, however, to capture content when one's being poked and prodded on a regular basis. That being said, however, your loyal Southern correspondent still managed to compose several lessons for y'all gleaned from my oh-so-unexpected hospital stay.

CONCERNING CLOTHING:
It is possible to send your man to Wal-Mart for fresh unmentionables with the correct size and style, along with clear instructions like "no granny panties," and still have him return with undergarments that reach to your bra and are thus capable of doubling as a lightweight Spanx.

CONCERNING SLEEP:
Should you have a reaction to an antibiotic and develop sleep problems, everything will be incredibly funny after you've been awake for thirty-two hours plus, but care should be taken to try

and appear as lucid as possible lest they transfer you to another type of hospital.

CONCERNING DURATION:
When you're being wheeled down the hall for your fourth X-ray in as many days and you pass by a door to the outside world, it may occur to you to make a run for it. If, however, you will take a moment to hit pause, you'll realize that Mr. X-Ray Guy and your ever-present hubby will be able to catch you and your exposed backside quickly. It's better to trust Jesus and the doctors and let nature run its course.

And finally, concerning the big picture, this is one of those times when you will receive such loving concern from family and friends, and people you've never met in person who feel like family and friends, that you will not be able to miss the realization that you are blessed and blessed indeed!

Miscellaneous Thoughts

THUS SAITH THE BELLE DOCTRINE . . .

* Humor is a great Band-Aid, but thou shalt use respect lest it stick to someone's bobo.

* Thou shalt not assume offense is intended if there is another way to take it.

* The obvious answer is not always the best one.

* If thou would look for humor, thou would find it.

* Thou shalt remember and treasure one of life's great gifts: Loved ones shine brightest in the dark.

Lagniappe of Recipes from
The Belle of *All Things Southern*

Legend has it that Mark Twain once referred to lagniappe as "a word worth traveling to New Orleans to get." How perfect is that? Lagniappe is the type of word that just rolls right off your tongue and begs you to find another use for it sooner rather than later. At its origin the word meant something thrown in for good measure, to show the giver's appreciation for one's patronage. Hence, to thank y'all for sharing some time with me between the pages here, I'd like to offer some lagniappe tricks of the Southern trade. What follows is need–to-know info that can save the day in any kitchen.

Basic Roux

Seeing as how she grew up with the phrase "first you make a roux," I suppose it's just natural for a belle to think that everyone in the world knows how to make a basic roux. But just in case you don't know how to whip up that perfect foundation for all your favorite stews and gumbos, I give you Mama's simple instructions.

> 1 cup all-purpose flour
> 1 cup cooking oil

Heat the oil in a heavy skillet over a medium heat. Once it's hot, gradually add flour. Stir constantly to avoid burning. Once mixed, reduce flame and continue to stir until your roux is a pretty dark brown (or as the older women say, right next door to burnt). Be sure and remove your roux from the skillet if you're not going to use it immediately. Otherwise it will continue to cook. When it comes time to add liquid required by your stew or gumbo, turn the heat back up and add room temperature liquid slowly, be it broth or water. Bring to a full rolling boil before reducing heat.

Homemade Tartar Sauce

If you're going to make the effort to cook seafood at home, please don't mar it with store-bought tartar sauce. It really should be illegal. Especially since it's so easy to make a great-tasting one at home! Strangely enough, tartar sauce doesn't have a speck of tartar in it. All you need is a few simple ingredients and you'll be able to create a great tartar sauce with more flavor than those imitation ready-mades could dream of offering.

1 cup mayonnaise
1 teaspoon grated onion
¼ teaspoon horseradish
1 tablespoon minced dill pickle (some prefer sweet pickle)
1 tablespoon lemon juice
Dash of sugar
Dash of white vinegar

Combine, cover, and chill to allow flavors to mingle.

Seafood Cocktail Sauce

At the risk of being redundant, the same rule applies to homemade cocktail sauce. The bottle variety can't compete with the flavor you can create with your own two hands. Here are the basic ingredients. If you like it sassier, go heavier on the horseradish and cayenne. You need not limit cocktail sauce to seafood, either. You'll find it's a tasty dip for veggies, meatballs, chicken tenders, and even bites of cubed cheese.

½ cup chili sauce
½ cup ketchup
2 tablespoons horseradish
¼ teaspoon cayenne
Worcestershire to taste
Hot sauce to taste
Salt to taste

Combine, cover, and chill to allow flavors to mingle.

Sauce When You're Out of Barbecue Sauce

There are plenty of great-tasting barbecue sauces on the store shelves, but what does a belle do when she can't get to the store and she needs barbecue sauce ASAP? She stirs up her own, of course. Keep these staples on hand and the solution will never be more than twenty minutes away.

3 tablespoons brown sugar

½ cup hot water

1½ cups apple cider vinegar

1 tablespoon paprika

1¼ teaspoon cayenne

1 teaspoon salt

1 teaspoon black pepper

Dissolve brown sugar in hot water and stir until completely dissolved. Add remaining ingredients. Stir and cook over low heat for 5–10 minutes.

Louisiana's Party Punch

(SERVES 25–30)

Here in the Deep South we throw wedding showers and baby showers by the dozen, and regardless of what else is on the menu, a good party punch is a must for any belleabration. Here's one of our favorite Louisiana versions. We like to leave the sherbet choice optional, so hostesses can coordinate it with the color theme of the party! It's the belle way.

1 (2 liter) bottle 7UP or Sprite, chilled
1 small ginger ale, chilled
½ gallon sherbet, your choice of flavor

Place sherbet in a punch bowl first. Add liquids slowly, breaking up sherbet with large spoon, and serve!

Holiday Wassail

(SERVES 24)

A Christmas season just doesn't seem right without a cup or two of wassail. This hot, spicy drink is as popular in the South as it is in kitchens around the globe. Here's a recipe for the wassail you'll find simmering in many a belle's kitchen. Of course, if she's really up against the clock and unexpected guests drop in, she may just serve the Cheater's Wassail: apple cider with melted cinnamon candies!

½ gallon apple juice
½ gallon cranberry juice
1 pint orange juice
1 cup brown sugar
2 tablespoons whole allspice
4 tablespoons whole cloves
8 sticks cinnamon

Mix well, float cinnamon in liquid, and simmer 1 hour.

Beth's Coffee Chiller

(SERVES 24)

Several years ago I attended a bridal shower for my nephew Blake and his sweet bride-to-be, Rachel. The hostess served this fabulous coffee chiller, and it was a hit with all. It's a nice fit for all of your fall luncheons and parties.

1 cup instant coffee

½ cup cocoa

1¼ cups sugar

1 cup (boiling) water

2 cups tap water

2 teaspoons vanilla

3 quarts milk

1 pint whipping cream, whipped

½ gallon vanilla ice cream, softened

Combine instant coffee with cocoa and sugar. Add boiling water and stir until the dry ingredients are dissolved. Stir in tap water, vanilla, and milk. Keep coffee mixture refrigerated as guests are arriving. When you're ready to serve, whisk whipping cream and add to the cold coffee. Pour into a pretty punch bowl and top with softened vanilla ice cream. Ladle into pretty cups and absorb the compliments.

Summer's Homemade Orange Sherbet

One of my favorite summer treats from long ago was those orange ice cream push-ups Mama bought at the store. The only problem I had was that one push-up never seemed to go far enough. This recipe fixes that little issue. My Homemade Orange Sherbet tastes just like those push-ups, and you can eat a whole bowl if you'd like. You're just three ingredients and one ice cream freezer away.

2 (32 oz.) bottles orange soft drink
2 cans sweetened condensed milk
1 (20 oz.) can crushed pineapple, drained

Combine ingredients and freeze in homemade ice cream maker, using appliance directions. Enjoy!

After my mom died, my sister and I had to go to the funeral home to give our approval on her appearance. The man in charge asked us how she looked. My sister said she looked great except that her dress was on backwards! Honest mistake. Collar was the same all the way around and should've buttoned down the back. The man, naturally, thought buttons went down the front. Poor fellow, in the room with "the Amazon women" (we're all over six foot!) could've crawled under the table. He began to stammer and apologize. My sister Marcey said, "No big deal. We'll just turn it around." But we couldn't. He had cut it to dress her! He offered to let us bring another dress but we girls agreed it was no big deal. No one would know and who could rest on all those buttons anyway? In the end, Wanda Faye may have gone to Heaven with her dress on backwards, but at least she had her lipstick on!

~Tammi Stutts
Kilbourne, Louisiana